FINANCIAL MARKET RESTRUCTURING IN SELECTED CENTRAL EUROPEAN COUNTRIES

Financial Market Restructuring in Selected Central European Countries

Edited by
KAREN S. VORST
University of Missouri-Kansas City

WILLADEE WEHMEYER
MidAmerica Nazarene University

Routledge
Taylor & Francis Group

LONDON AND NEW YORK

First published 1998 by Ashgate Publishing

Reissued 2018 by Routledge
2 Park Square, Milton Park, Abingdon, Oxon, OX14 4RN
711 Third Avenue, New York, NY 10017, USA

Routledge is an imprint of the Taylor & Francis Group, an informa business

Notice:
Product or corporate names may be trademarks or registered trademarks, and are used only for identification and explanation without intent to infringe.

Publisher's Note
The publisher has gone to great lengths to ensure the quality of this reprint but points out that some imperfections in the original copies may be apparent.

Disclaimer
The publisher has made every effort to trace copyright holders and welcomes correspondence from those they have been unable to contact.

A Library of Congress record exists under LC control number: 98070991

ISBN 13: 978-1-138-31442-9 (hbk)
ISBN 13: 978-0-429-45698-5 (ebk)

Contents

Acknowledgments

This project was funded in part by a grant from Fulbright-Hayes that sponsored our trip to Central Europe in the summer of 1996. We were able to make and confirm commitments from some of the authors at that time. Our universities, the University of Missouri-Kansas City and MidAmerica Nazarene University, also contributed to our support. Additional funding for this project came from a University of Missouri-Kansas City Faculty Research Grant, No. K-2-11458-3000, obtained by Dr. Vorst.

We acknowledge the tremendous efforts and commitment of our authors to this project. Our relationship with each one through the many months of editing has been most rewarding. It has been a privilege to work with this group of professionals.

Finally, we would like to thank our families and friends who have shown the utmost patience, concern and love, especially during the past few months as we brought this project to completion.

Karen Vorst
Willadee Wehmeyer

The Authors

Katalin Botos is Professor Economics on the faculties of the Economic University, Budapest, the Pazmay Peter Catholic University, and JATE University Szeged. She is a former member of Parliament as a delegate of the Hungarian Democratic Forum, President of the State Banking Supervision, and Minister of State responsible for capital markets and banking. Professor Botos has published numerous books and articles. Her latest book is *Lost Illusions: Situation and perspectives of the Hungarian Banking Systems*, published by Economic and Legal Publishing House, Budapest.

Jan Frait graduated from the Faculty of Economics of the Technical University of Ostrava and is currently assistant professor in the Department of Economics at that University. Named "The Young Economist of 1995" by the Czech Economic Society, Frait's research activities focus on the application of balance-of-payments and exchange rate theories in the transition economies. Professor Frait is also affiliated with *Finance a uver*, a leading Czech academic journal, and is a member of the Centre for Euro-Asian Studies at the University of Reading (UK) and its representatives in the Czech Republic.

Eric R. Hake obtained the Ph.D. in economics from the University of Tennessee in 1994 and is currently Instructor in the Department of Economics at Radford University. In conjunction with projects organized by the Civic Education Project at Yale University, Hake has taught in the Department of Economics at the Agricultural University of Nitra, Slovakia and Mendel University, Brno, Czech Republic. Hake has also taught international economics at Webster University in Vienna, Austria. Current research conducted by Dr. Hake focuses on the rise and fall of investment companies in Slovakia and institutional change and economic growth in Poland.

Stanislava Janackova is an engineer and a Candidate of Sciences in the Czech Republic. She has published extensively in well-known professional journals. She is affiliated with the Institute of Economics at the Czech National Bank.

Zora Kominkova is a member of the Institute for Monetary and Financial Studies at the National Bank of Slovakia. After she received the CSc. (Ph.D.) at the Institute of Economics of the Slovak Academy of Sciences, Dr. Kominkova served as Chief of the Department for Macroeconomic Regulation at the Institute and as Chief of the project "Macroeconomic regulation under conditions of transformation of the central planned economy to a market economy." She has also served as editor-in-chief of the Slovak scientific review "Ekonomicky casopis."

Viktoria Muckova received her Doctorate with a specialization in finance at the Faculty of National Economy in 1990. She has been affiliated with the National Bank of Slovakia since 1993. Her research focuses on the relationship between finance, prices, and wages, the labor market, and banking analysis. Dr. Muekova cooperates with universities, research institutes, and central and commercial banks in the Czech Republic, Poland, Hungary, the United Kingdom, Germany, Canada, and the United States.

Zbigniew Polanski obtained his Ph.D. in economics and finance at the Warsaw School of Economics (WSE). Currently a professor and chair of banking at the WSE, Dr. Polanski is also a senior economist in the Research Department at the National Bank of Poland and is associated with Gdansk Institute for Market Economics, an independent think-tank. In the 1990s Dr. Polanski was affiliated with the University of Maryland and Carleton University in Ottawa, Canada. Polanski is the author of *Poland's Money and Financial System in Transition: 1982-1993* (Wydawnictwo Naukowe PWN, 1995) and co-editor and co-author of *The Financial System in Poland in the 1990s* (Wydawnictwo Naukowe PWN, 1997).

Mieczyslaw Pulawski received the Doctor of Economics degree from the Central School of Planning and Statistics in Warsaw, Poland. He is currently chair of the Department of Capital Markets at the Warsaw School of Economics. His research interests include capital markets, futures and options markets, international finance, and financing foreign trade. Professor Pulawski is the author or co-author of five books and more than fifty articles related to economic issues.

Ryszard Rapacki is an internationally recognized economics expert, professor, and researcher who holds Poland's national academic title "Professor of Economics." Rapacki is Head of the Department of

Economics, Collegium of World Economy at the Warsaw School of Economics (WSE). Rapacki has served as consultant to the United Nations Industrial Development Organization (UNIDO) in missions to Zimbabwe, Sudan, Zambia, Uganda, Austria, Germany, Yugoslavia, Albania, and Jamaica. In addition, during the 1990s, he was a visiting Fulbright Professor at Michigan State University and visiting professor at the University of Minnesota. Rapacki has published approximately 90 articles, books, and papers.

Izabela Rutkowska holds her doctorate degree in economics from the Warsaw School of Economics. She has been working as a researcher at the National Bank of Poland, the World Bank and the International Monetary Fund. She has published several papers, both in Polish and in English, on corporate and banking restructuring in Poland and other economies in transition.

Ramji K. Tamarappoo holds a Ph.D. in economics from Clemson University. He is currently affiliated with Clemson Economics Associates, Clemson, South Carolina and has been a member of the Faculty of Economics, VSB-Technical University, Ostrava, Czech Republic. His research interests include the stock return-inflation relationship and managerial behavior in incomplete capital and labor markets.

Erika Voros is a Senior Economic Advisor in the Monetary and Fiscal Research Division of the National Bank of Hungary. Prior to her tenure at the NBH, Voros was affiliated with the Budapest University for Economic Sciences. At the NBH, Voros' research interests turned to the development of the Hungarian money and capital markets.

Karen Vorst is an Associate Professor of Economics of the University of Missouri-Kansas City. She obtained her Ph.D. in economics from Indiana University and specializes in monetary theory, policy, and financial markets.

Robert R. Wagner is a lecturer for Business Administration at the Euro Schools in Gorlitz and Zittau, Germany. Since obtaining the Dipl-Dfm at the University of Dresden, Wagner has been affiliated with the Department of Business Administration at the International Graduate School Zittau (IHI Zittau). The focus of Wagner's current research is the connection between internationalization and environmental protection.

List of Tables and Figures

1 Introduction

KAREN VORST

The events that have taken place in Central and Eastern European (CEE) economies since 1989 have had a tremendous impact on the lives of individuals, on the operations of businesses and on the activities of governments. It is a whole new economic world for most participants who previously had known only the Soviet/Communist system with its central planning and control over the means of production. The economies that embarked upon the journey to a market system have had to make a great number of changes along the way. Governments have had to be willing to relinquish their tight control in many areas, including production quotas, wage rates, the distribution of goods and services, currency convertibility, and ownership of property. Surviving businesses have experienced significant changes in their operations, weeding out the old techniques and struggling to conform to the new standards and technologies. Individuals have witnessed the availability of a wider variety of goods and services, though prices are higher and job security is lower. Countries have embraced a system that is imperfect itself and have tailored it to suit their individual country needs.

All of the transitioning countries have experienced a certain level of turmoil and confusion, clearly an expected result given the tremendous changes that have occurred in their economic systems. Since the initial economic conditions for all of these countries were different, it was expected that the progress achieved in each economy would vary as well. For example, the privatization of state-owned property was a larger issue in Czechoslovakia and Hungary where the state owned over 90% of the means of production, including agriculture, in 1989, while much of the farm land in Poland was already privately owned at that time. On the other hand, as early as 1984, Hungary had passed legislation that gave the management of firms some control over state-owned enterprises, effectively positioning firms for privatization before 1989. Nearly eight years later, the transfer process is still ongoing, with varying degrees of success.

One of the most important links in the transition chain is the development of the financial sector. Instead of being mandated to collect and distribute funds according to a central plan, banks and other financial institutions offer a variety of savings opportunities and provide for an efficient allocation of funds. The establishment of banking and capital markets is at the core of the entire financial market plan and is crucial to the development of the private sector.

This book directs attention to the banking and capital market restructuring that was essential to the progress made in transitioning economies. It focuses on the economic progress of four selected countries: Poland, Hungary, The Czech Republic and The Slovak Republic. Not only does their proximity bring them together, but they have a long, established economic relationship. Trade with each other was promoted through the Council of Mutual Economic Assistance (CMEA) and through trade arrangements in the Central European Free Trade Area (CEFTA). They were the dominant economies in the Visegrad group of countries in Central and Eastern Europe, and they are the countries judged by many economists to be most likely to succeed in the transitioning process. Most of them likely will be among the next group of countries admitted to the European Union. While no longer a separate nation, the former East German economy is also included due to its proximity to these countries and its unique experience in the transition process.

While the book is divided into separate chapters by contributing authors, the chapters are grouped by country. Thus, the next three chapters regard the Polish experience, followed by three chapters on the Hungarian transitioning process, four chapters total on the Czech and Slovak Republics, and finally the chapter on the former East German experience. For each country, the articles include (1) information on the macroeconomic development since 1989, (2) a view of the restructuring process in the banking and financial markets, and (3) an analysis of monetary policy and of the central bank in the restructured system. There is also information regarding privatization issues and stock market development.

Regarding the macroeconomic changes, the papers by Polanski, Frait and Tamarappoo, and Vorst, though also to some extent the papers by Wagner and Kominkova and Muckova, provide an up-to-date analysis of basic economic changes. There is detailed information regarding real GDP growth, inflation, and unemployment. In most cases, there also is data regarding exchange rates, the balance of payments and the government budget.

Economic progress is evaluated most often through an analysis of changes in real Gross Domestic Product, inflation and the unemployment rate. While these data do not tell the whole story and may in fact be biased to some degree, the information we have summarized in Table 1.1 below gives an unrefined baseline of comparison for our selected group of transitioning countries. It is important to stress that the data are greatly influenced by the different initial economic conditions, the progress of legislative changes that were so necessary in setting the ground rules, and the variety of programs and methods used in each country in setting up a market structure.

From Table 1.1, it is clear that all of the countries listed made significant economic progress from 1990. Most countries experienced negative growth rates through 1993, after which they were positive for all. It is important to note that the effect of a series of negative rates is cumulative and that it would take several years of positive rates in order to raise the standard of living of individuals in these countries.

Table 1.1 Basic Economic Data for Selected Countries, 1990-1996

	1990	1991	1992	1993	1994	1995	1996
GDP Real Growth %							
Poland	-11.6	-7.0	2.6	3.8	5.2	7.0	6.1
Hungary	-3.3	-11.3	-3.1	-0.6	2.9	1.5	1.0
Czech Repub.	-0.4	-14.2	-7.1	-0.9	2.7	5.9	4.1
Slovak Repub.	-2.5	-14.6	-6.5	-3.7	4.9	6.8	6.9
Unemployment %							
Poland	6.5	12.2	14.3	16.4	16.0	14.9	13.2
Hungary	0.4	1.9	7.8	13.2	10.4	10.4	10.5
Czech Repub.	1.0	6.6	5.1	3.5	3.2	2.9	3.5
Slovak Repub.	1.5	11.8	10.4	14.4	14.8	13.8	12.4
Inflation %							
Poland	249.3	60.4	44.3	37.6	29.5	21.6	18.5
Hungary	28.9	35.0	23.0	22.5	18.8	28.2	23.6
Czech Repub.	12.3	53.6	11.5	18.2	10.2	9.1	8.8
Slovak Repub.	10.4	61.2	10.0	23.2	13.4	9.9	5.8

Source: Poland: International Economic Report, 1995/96, World Economy Research Institute, Warsaw School of Economics, 1996, p. 29; *Annual Report* of the National Bank of Hungary, 1996; *Annual Report* of the National Bank of Slovakia, 1995; *Annual Report* of the National Bank of the Czech Republic, 1995; and selected papers in this volume.

The negative growth rates and the ongoing struggle for economic expansion is reflected in the unemployment rate as well. The influence of the state as a large employer is still evident in all countries in 1990. As the transition got underway and the state no longer guaranteed employment, the number of people out of work increased. The unemployment rate also is affected greatly by the "speed" of transition. For example, Poland's "shock therapy" approached resulted in relatively higher rates, compared to the Czech Republic's more gradual approach with lower unemployment. It is difficult to say which method works better. The "shock therapy" approach may result in a critical mass of unemployment that eventually could undermine the transition process. Given the consistent commitment of the Polish government to a market system, this has not happened in Poland to any significant degree. On the other hand, the "gradual" approach allows more moderate adjustment without significant unemployment. However, critics of this approach believe that the unemployment problems are simply delayed and that the country eventually will have to face them. Preliminary information for 1997 (not shown on the table) for the Czech Republic indicate slower growth and higher unemployment.

All of the countries listed in Table 1.1 have experienced significant inflation rates during the 1990-1996 time period. As governments relinquished price controls and liberated prices, inflation resulted, especially in 1990 and 1991. It is a continuing problem in each country but progress is being made. While Poland and Hungary continue to experience double-digit rates, the rates in all countries have shown a downward trend.

The papers by Pulawski and Rapacki, Rutkowska, Botos, Hake, Wagner, and Kominkova and Muckova address the major financial market restructuring issues in each of their respective countries. Information is given regarding the changing structure of the banking market, the bad debt problems of banks and their resolution, the number of banks and foreign capital participation. Some of the articles also provide information on capital market development, specifically with regard to stock exchanges, capital mobility and investment funds.

The few banks that existed in these economies before 1989 took their direction from the state. They acted as repositories for savings and extended credit without financial and economic assessment. This lack of efficient allocation of credit led to substantial loan losses, losses that produced problems for each country's banking system and necessitated creative solutions. The bad loan problem and its solution are described for each of the selected countries in this study.

Most banking systems were modeled after the German model of universal banks. The number of banks and branches expanded in each country with the help of (1) the legislative changes that promoted the expansion of the banking system, (2) the re-education of the public with regard to the financial services available, thereby attracting funds into the system, (3) foreign capital that provided assistance to existing banks, and (4) the entry of foreign branch banks. While the number of private banks has increased, consequently decreasing the state's share of ownership, the state has retained at least partial ownership of banks in each of the countries in this study.

Finally, monetary policy issues during the transition are detailed for each country in papers by Polanksi, Voros, Frait and Tamarappoo, Janackova, Wagner, and Kominkova and Muckova. Under the Soviet scheme, a mono-bank system existed that carried out the funding decisions of the government. A few smaller banks existed but were of little importance and had few duties. The 'central bank' regulated the payments system and provided the funds for the government budget. There was no monetary policy.

In the transition process, countries set up a two-tier system headed by a central bank that was designed to be 'independent' of the government and a regulator of banks in the system. The central bank would now devise monetary policy, regulate the money supply and interest rates, and focus on exchange rate stability. It would determine the necessary changes in its policy tools and in banking regulations. These issues, as well as the problems associated with maintaining independent status, are analyzed in the various studies in this volume.

2 Polish Monetary Policy in the 1990s: A Bird's Eye View[1]

ZBIGNIEW POLANSKI

Introduction

At the beginning of the 1990s, the Polish government launched a stabilization program that marked the initiation of new economic policies. One of the most important components of this stabilization package concerned Central Bank monetary management. In 1990 the National Bank of Poland (NBP) began to conduct an anti-inflationary policy that enhanced the development of market mechanisms. Essentially, this policy is still being pursued by the NBP, although it evolved over time mainly as a result of the development of the financial system and the appearance of new economic problems.

This paper provides an overview of monetary policy in Poland in the 1990s. In the next section, a brief account is given of the macroeconomic development in Poland thus far in the 1990s. The third section outlines the main features of monetary policy with respect to price stability, the money supply, interest rates, currency convertibility, and exchange rates. In the fourth section, specific monetary policy issues such as credit expansion, government debt, bank loan problems, and foreign asset flows are discussed. Conclusions regarding important monetary policy decisions are given in the final section.

Macroeconomic Developments Since 1990

As will be shown, the tendencies visible in Tables 2.1-2.3 did not result from central bank policies alone. Table 2.1 shows that the Polish economy

---

[1] This paper is an updated (October, 1997) version of a paper presented at the conference "Monetary Policy in the Transition Period" held on April 25-27, 1996 at Borovets, Bulgaria. The original version was published with other conference proceedings by the Bulgarian National Bank.

witnessed an economic revival, after an initial economic contraction (1990-1991), mainly due to the stabilization program and the disintegration of the Council for Mutual Economic Assistance (COMECON). In 1994 through 1997, Poland's economy was among the fastest growing in Europe.

Table 2.1 Poland's Economic Performance, 1989-1997 [a]

	1989	1990	1991	1992	1993	1994	1995	1996	1997 [b]
GDP	0.2	-11.6	-7.0	2.6	3.8	5.2	7.0	6.1	6.4
Private Consump.	-0.3	-15.3	6.3	2.3	5.2	4.3	3.6	8.7	7.4
Fixed Invest.	-2.1	-10.6	-4.4	2.3	2.9	9.2	16.9	20.6	18.3
Exports	2.6	15.1	-1.7	10.8	3.2	13.1	23.6	12.5	9.2
Imports	4.3	-10.2	29.6	1.7	13.2	11.3	24.3	28.0	17.2
Current Account [c]	--	1.0	-2.6	1.1	-0.7	2.4	4.6	-1.0	-3.5
Unemploy. Rate [d]	--	6.5	12.2	14.3	16.4	16.0	14.9	13.2	10.7

[a] Percent changes from previous year unless indicated otherwise; [b] Forecast by the Gdańsk Institute for Market Economics; [c] Balance as a per cent of GDP; [d] End of year.
Sources: Polish Central Statistical Office, National Bank of Poland and the Gdańsk Institute for Market Economics.

If it were not for the still high unemployment rate, the deterioration of foreign trade and current account balances since 1996, developments in the real economy could be described as a success story. However, our evaluation is not so straight-forward if we take into account the developments in the monetary area.

As can be seen in Table 2.2, the inflation rate in Poland is still high and money supply growth is high, although the latter also results from increases in real money demand.

Poland entered the present decade with very strong inflationary pressures, bordering on hyperinflation. The 1990 program clearly reduced the inflation rate. Despite the continuation of stabilization policies, there are serious problems with reducing inflation below 10 percent. Inflation has been strong for more than twenty years and is thus deeply ingrained into the Polish society. Furthermore, many government actions, like administrative price rises or policies aimed at the protection of the agricultural sector, were additionally fueling inflation.

Table 2.2 Inflation and Money Supply in Poland, 1989-1997 [a]

	1989	1990	1991	1992	1993	1994	1995	1996	1997
Inflation									
-CPI [b]	640.3	249.3	60.4	44.3	37.6	29.5	21.6	18.5	13.2
-GDP									
deflator	298.5	480.1	55.3	38.5	30.5	28.4	28.2	18.5	12.3
Money Supply									
-Total (M2)	527.3	157.9	47.4	57.5	36.0	38.2	34.9	29.4	28.8
-Domestic [c]	190.5	396.3	64.8	57.2	28.8	38.7	50.2	34.4	28.2

[a] Percent changes from previous year; [b] Consumer Price Index. December to December; [c] Total money supply (M2) less foreign currency accounts.
Source: Polish Central Statistical Office and National Bank of Poland.

Table 2.3 Structure of the Money Supply in Poland at the end of 1989 and in 1997 (in percent)

Money Supply	1989	1997
Total Money Supply (M2)	100.0	100.0
Zloty Money Supply	27.5	82.4
Cash in Circulation [a]	10.3	15.5
Zloty deposits of the non-financial sector	17.2	67.0
Households	9.0	45.9
Business	8.2	21.1
Foreign currency deposits of non-financial sector	72.5 [b]	17.6
Households	48.8	14.3
Business	23.7	3.2

Note: Figures may not add to 100.0 due to rounding error. [a] Excluding vault cash.
[b] Using the exchange rate of $1 = 9.500 zl.
Source: National Bank of Poland.

Under these circumstances it is not surprising that the money supply was quickly increasing. However, as demonstrated in Table 2.3, confidence in the Polish currency, despite the above-mentioned problems with the reduction of the inflation rate, has been growing.

In the 1990s we observed a clear shift in the composition of the money supply in Poland. At the end of 1989, foreign currency accounts equaled nearly three-fourths of the money supply; now they account for less than 18 percent. These figures probably best capture the process of growing confidence in the Polish zloty which has resulted mainly from NBP's stabilization policies initiated at the beginning of 1990.

Main Features of the 1990's Monetary Policy

At the cost of some simplification, one can argue that the new NBP policy can be summarized in four main points:
* inflation as the final goal of monetary policy;
* money supply as the intermediate target;
* positive real interest rates; and
* international liberalization and the exchange rate as an important policy instrument.

In all four areas, developments in the 1990s break substantially from previous experiences in Poland.

In January, 1989, at the end of communist rule in Poland, the Act of the NBP was adopted. It stated that "[T]he activity of the NBP is aimed especially at strengthening the Polish currency." Since the fall of 1989, this vague definition of the main mission of the Central Bank has been interpreted by its authorities as an obligation of the NBP to reduce the inflation rate.

Although not without serious problems, the NBP has been achieving this decline in the inflation rate by controlling the money supply. As in the 1980s when the Polish economy displayed very high levels of dollarization, the NBP initially targeted a money supply aggregate that excluded foreign currency-denominated deposits (the so-called 'domestic money supply' aggregate). However, since 1991 the "Total Money Supply," the M2 aggregate, has been the NBP's explicit intermediate target.

From the first half of the 1970s, Poland observed negative real interest rates which at the end of the 1980s reached their lowest values (see Table 2.5 below). Loans granted by the Central Bank to finance the budget deficit had a zero nominal interest rate in the 1980s. Under these circumstances, it is not surprising that the interest rate policy had to be deeply redesigned. This redesign in 1990 has led, however, to many political tensions in subsequent years.

One of the key components of the new policies adopted in Poland at the end of 1989 was the liberalization of foreign exchange restrictions. Consequently, the role of the exchange rate in economic policies in general, and in monetary policy in particular, increased.

In January, 1990, Poland adopted the so-called internal convertibility system, which was effective until 1995. Since June, 1995, Poland officially complies with the rules of Article VIII of the Articles of Agreement of the IMF. In 1996 exchange restrictions were further liberalized according to the suggestions made by the OECD, of which Poland now is a member. It is expected that around the year 2000, Poland will have complete convertibility of the zloty.

Concerning the exchange rate policy, it must be said that it passed through three clearly defined phases: (1) from the beginning of 1990 until mid-October, 1991, the exchange rate was to function as a nominal anchor for inflation, following a policy of a fixed exchange rate;[2] (2) as a result of the strong appreciation of the real exchange rate of the zloty (see Figure 2.1), a pre-announced crawling-peg exchange rate regime was introduced in the autumn of 1991 aimed at stabilizing the real exchange rate; (3) since mid-May, 1995, when the "crawling-band" system was introduced, the zloty has been allowed to fluctuate in a band of ±7 percent around a central rate that is being set by the NBP, subject to the crawling-peg mechanism.

The Evolution of Monetary Policy

As it is well known from economic theory, the money supply in a small, open economy with an administrative (or quasi-administrative) exchange

---

[2] During this phase, two sub-periods can be differentiated: (i) from January, 1990, until mid-May, 1991, during which the zloty was administratively fixed only against the U.S. dollar; (ii) from May, 1991, when the exchange rate regime became based on a basket of five currencies (U.S. dollar, 45%; Deutsche Mark, 35%; British Pound, 10%; French Franc, 5%; Swiss Franc, 5%). The structure of the basket reflected the structure of payments in Polish foreign trade. This basket is still in effect.

rate regime results from domestic and external sources.[3] Domestic credit expansion consist of (i) banks' domestic lending activity (loans granted to the non-financial sector, mainly households and businesses), and (ii) banks' lending to the government (public) sector. External sources consist of net foreign assets (foreign reserves) and result from current and capital account imbalances in the balance of payments accounts.

Table 2.4 uses this framework and shows that four basic periods can be differentiated in the evolution of the sources of the money stock in Poland in the time period under consideration:

- The years, 1990-1991 when the dominating source of the money supply was bank credits granted to the non-financial sector;
- The years, 1992-1994 when a key role was played by the budget deficit;
- The year 1995 when the money supply resulted mostly from increases in foreign reserves;
- The years, 1996-1997 when again the dominating source of the money supply was bank credits granted to the non-financial sector.

Table 2.4 Sources of the Money Supply in Poland, 1990-1997 (in percent)

	1990	1991	1992	1993	1994	1995	1996	1997
Total	100	100	100	100	100	100	100	100
Net foreign assets*	46.0	-2.7	25.9	17.5	32.9	58.7	29.9	41.8
Net indebtedness of the public sector	-12.3	36.9	48.3	47.0	37.3	3.4	12.8	11.8
Credits granted to enterprises and households	66.2	65.8	25.8	35.4	29.9	37.9	57.3	46.4

Notes: "Net balance of other items" omitted. Figures may not add to 100.0 due to rounding error. * Balance of Polish banking system's foreign claims and dues.
Source: National Bank of Poland.

---

[3] See, for example, *Theoretical Aspects of the Design of Fund-Supported Adjustment Programs*, International Monetary Fund, Washington, D C, 1987, chp. 3.

Undoubtedly, the distinction of these four periods is to some extent arbitrary. Some of the factors creating the money supply obviously overlap in some years as was the case, for example, with bank lending to the non-financial sector and to the state budget in 1991 or with the increase in foreign reserves in 1994.

1990-1991: Credit Expansion

As pointed out, the beginning of the new decade coincided with the start of new monetary policy. However, as Table 2.2 demonstrated, in spite of the introduction of stabilization measures, inflation and the money supply continued to grow at very high rates in the 1990-1991 period. The main reason for this is twofold: money supply increases and strong inflation resulted both from credit expansion and the exchange rate policy that led to foreign reserves expansion in 1990. However, in 1990 the state budget enjoyed a surplus, which means that it acted as a factor reducing the expansion of the money supply at that time.

The 1990 stabilization program aimed at restricting credit supply growth. A new interest rate policy was started and reserve requirements were raised to very high levels. In mid-1990, in the rudimentary money market, open market operations based upon money bills issued by the NBP (as T-bills were not available) were introduced as an additional monetary policy tool. These instruments did not reduce credit expansion considerably. Consequently, in the autumn of 1990, credit ceilings (an administrative measure) were explicitly re-imposed by the Central Bank.

Looking at Table 2.5, one could argue that an important factor underlying the strong credit expansion of 1990-1991 was that interest rates in real terms were negative. However, the table presents ex post data while the real interest rate is basically an ex ante concept; that is, it takes into account expected inflation. Although it would be difficult now to prove it empirically, to an observer who witnessed directly the introduction of the stabilization program, it was quite obvious that expected real interest rates for most economic agents were positive in 1990.[4]

---

[4] It should be noted that the rates for the 1989-1995 period in Table 2.5 are annual averages. This is highly misleading because nominal rates were reduced every month in the first half of 1990. In the case of NBP refinancing credit, the interest rate reached 432 percent in January 1990! (This is an annualized simple interest

Table 2.5   National Bank of Poland Basic Interest Rate and Inflation, 1989-1997

	1989	1990	1991	1992	1993	1994	1995	1996	1997
Nominal NBP rate	61.3	103.8	53.9	39.0	35.4	33.7	31.5	22.0	24.5
Real NBP rate -deflated by									
1.Consumer prices*	-78.2	-41.6	-4.0	-3.7	-1.6	+3.2	+8.1	+2.9	+10.0
2.Industrial output prices*	-78.6	-30.4	+13.4	+5.7	-1.2	+4.5	+10.6	+9.7	+12.2

Note: For 1989-1995, NBP basic interest rate is understood as the average annual interest rate on NBP's refinancing credits. For 1996 and 1997, NBP rediscount rate is the end of period rate.
* December to December.
Source: National Bank of Poland and Polish Central Statistical Office.

The main reason for the 1990-1991 credit expansion stemmed from the fact that, despite the banking reform of 1989, most credits, as in socialist times, were supplied by large, state-owned banks to large, state-owned companies. At that time, these agents did not change their behavior substantially. Despite high interest rates, state firms were usually demanding new credits, while banks were usually providing them credit without analyzing the credit-worthiness of their clients in detail. They did this in spite of the fact that the economy was heading into recession.

The second reason for the large increase in the money supply in 1990 is linked to the foreign sector. As we can see in Table 2.1, exports in 1990 sharply increased while imports abruptly declined. This led to a positive foreign trade balance and a surplus in the balance of payments current account. Consequently, foreign reserves unexpectedly increased, becoming an important money supply source.

These abrupt changes in the foreign sector were to a great extent the result of exchange rate policies. As mentioned, in 1990 and in most of 1991, Poland followed a policy of fixed exchange rates. However, before the zloty was fixed, it had been deeply devalued several times. These

rate.) In the second half of 1990 and in 1991, basic interest rates were changed often as well. Only since 1992 have they been modified occasionally.

devaluations are now considered to have been excessive and are blamed for being an important factor contributing to the high 1990 inflation.

Figure 2.1   Zloty's Real Effective Exchange Rate, 1990-1997

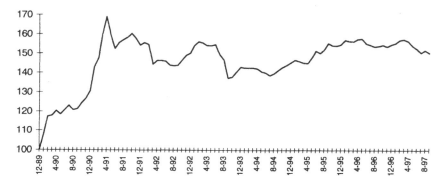

Source: National Bank of Poland.

Since the zloty was fixed in nominal terms for some time and strong inflation persisted, it appreciated considerably in real terms (see Figure 2.1). This happened despite the May, 1991, devaluation. This condition led to a negative trade balance and a deficit in the current account in 1991. Thus, Polish foreign reserves declined that year (see Figure 2.2).

1992-1994: Budget Deficit

In the following three years, the main source of money creation was the budget deficit, which had been basically financed by the banking sector, both from the NBP and commercial banks. The year 1992 was particularly dramatic as the budget deficit reached 6 percent of GDP. In 1993 the budgetary situation improved considerably. In fact, if costs of the public debt are excluded and the so-called primary deficit is calculated, then the Polish state budget would show a positive balance since 1993.

Despite the budgetary improvement, the state budget deficit continued to be the main source of money creation in 1993 and 1994 as shown in Table 2.4. The Polish foreign sector was still quite weak, although in 1994 it demonstrated considerable improvement, particularly as a result of unregistered foreign trade activities.

With regard to credit activities, Table 2.4 shows that credit supply to the non-financial sector, relative to other money supply sources, was very weak during all of the 1992-1994 period, sharply contrasting with the previous period.

Questions concerning the changes in the credit market should be viewed in the context of the incentives shaping commercial bank behavior. Once again, the changes in the credit market should not be attributed to changes in the real interest rates, which have been undoubtedly positive since 1994 (see Table 2.5). The decline in the rate of bank credit supply in 1992 and the following years should be attributed to non-price means by which banks decreased their credit activities.

Table 2.6 State Budget Deficits and Public Debt in Poland, 1989-1997 [a]

Item	1990	1991	1992	1993	1994	1995	1996	1997
Budget deficit								
(-) or surplus (+)	+0.4	-3.8	-6.0	-2.8	-2.7	-2.6	-2.5	-2.3 [b]
Domestic public debt	12.6	16.1	21.1	23.0	24.1	20.6	20.2	20.3 [c]
Sources of financing of domestic public debt (in percent [d])								
1.National Bank of Poland	25.0	29.6	42.3	38.6	35.4	16.7	15.3	20.0
2.Commercial banks	66.7	59.6	54.2	56.3	57.3	63.4	59.5	48.9
3.Non-banking sector [e]	8.3	10.7	3.5	5.2	7.2	19.9	25.2	31.3
Total public debt	89.9	80.6	85.3	86.0	69.9	55.6	49.4	48.7 [c]

[a]As a per cent of GDP unless indicated otherwise; [b]The Gdańsk Institute for Market Economics forecast; [c]Ministry of Finance budgetary assumptions; [d]Figures may not add to 100.0 due to rounding error. For 1997 data as for end of June; [e]Foreign investors on the primary market included.
Source: Ministry of Finance, Polish Central Statistical Office and the Gdańsk Institute for Market Economics.

The dramatic change in Polish banks' behavior was a result of banks behaving very passively in the early 1990s, despite the new macroeconomic policies in place. To a great extent, they behaved in a similar way as in socialist times. As a result, they granted credits which in many cases proved to be bad loans. Additionally at that time, the Council for Mutual Economic Assistance collapsed, leading many firms to bankruptcy and, consequently, to a deepening of the bad loan crisis.

The bad loans crisis peaked in 1992-1993 and was a decisive factor in changing commercial banks' behavior from carelessness to caution. Banks began to ration credit by non-price means in order to avoid the risks inherent in the process of granting credits given the conditions of high uncertainty that characterized the transition economy. As a result of this slowdown in credit activities, the NBP credit ceilings were abolished at the end of 1992.

Table 2.7 Bad Loans in Poland, 1991-1996 (in percent)

Bad Loans	1991*	1991	1992	1993	1994	1995	1996
As share of bank credits granted to enterprises	8.3	16.2	31.4	33.1	30.9	23.5	15.0
As share of banks' assets	-	6.7	10.8	10.2	8.9	6.9	5.0
As share of GDP	1.5	3.8	6.1	6.0	5.1	3.9	2.9

* As of June.
Source: National Bank of Poland and Polish Central Statistical Office.

The change in commercial banks' behavior was stimulated additionally by the fact that the privatization of commercial banks had begun in 1992. On the other hand, budget deficits provided instruments that banks could use as earning assets in their portfolios, thus replacing credits to the business sector. In this context, one should also add that the increasing role of T-bills in bank portfolios has enabled the NBP to conduct open market operations on a regular basis since the beginning of 1993.

In early 1993, a special law on enterprise and bank financial restructuring became effective, introducing new legal solutions that enabled banks on their own to solve the bad loan problems with their corporate clients. This decentralized approach, coupled with stricter banking supervision promoted by the Central Bank, proved to be very successful. As seen in Table 2.7, the volume of bad loans gradually declined from 1994. Against this background of declining economic uncertainty, it is understandable that banks, despite pronounced positive real interest rates on credits, increased their credit activities in 1995 and further in 1996 and in 1997.

1995: Foreign Assets Growth

In 1994, another important phenomenon became apparent. Foreign reserves began to increase quickly, so that in 1995 and in the first months of 1996, they became the key source in the money supply equation. In 1995, Polish gross foreign reserves (NBP reserves) had increased from $6 billion to nearly $15 billion, or two and a half times. At the end of May, 1996, foreign reserves reached $18 billion.

Three factors were responsible for this heavy foreign assets growth:

(1) An unregistered foreign trade surplus. Despite the fact that the officially calculated foreign trade balance was negative, the entire trade balance (the one that includes unregistered trade payments), as well as the balance of payments current account, showed a surplus (see Table 2.1 above). Such developments resulted from efficiency increases, coupled with a squeeze in real wages that followed the early 1990s economic liberalization and that increased the competitiveness of Polish products on the international markets. At the same time, cross-country studies showed that prices in Poland were on average lower than in most Western countries.[5]

Figure 2.2 Polish Gross Official Reserves: 1989-1997

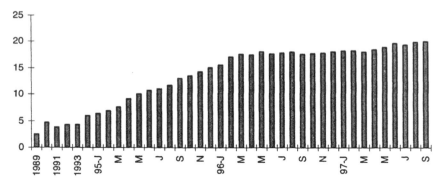

Source: National Bank of Poland.

(2) Short-term (speculative) capital inflows. Due to the co-existence of high positive real interest rates, the pre-announced crawling peg exchange rate regime, Poland's partial opening to international capital markets, and high economic growth, the Polish economy in early 1995, after the Mexican financial crisis, came to be seen by foreign investors as a

---

[5] See for example Kinga Borzym, "Comparison of Exchange Rates of National Currencies with Their Purchasing Power in the EC Countries and in Poland," *Bank i Kredyt*, 1997, No. 3, pp. 4-20.

relatively safe place to make sound investments. This belief was additionally strengthened by the investment rating awarded to Poland by the three leading credit rating agencies in mid-1995.[6]

(3) Long-term capital inflows. In 1995, Poland was also seen as a good place to make foreign direct investments. In the first months of 1996, this process was further stimulated by the privatization of factories with a heavy foreign involvement.

The quick 1995 rise of foreign reserves pushed the NBP to appreciate the zloty several times. The crawling-peg mechanism has been basically retained. As mentioned, the zloty was allowed to fluctuate from mid-May, 1995, and its peg was reduced to 1 percent on a monthly basis in January, 1996 (this rate is still in effect). In mid-1996, the Polish balance of payments current account was close to an equilibrium level.

Concerning the other two sources of the money supply, positive trends were also visible. Bank financing of the public sector deficit decreased considerably in 1995 and the trend is continuing. At the same time, bank credits for the non-financial sector have been picking up gradually.

1996-1997: Credit Expansion Again

In the second half of 1996, the current account balance deficit began to grow quickly. While in 1996 the ratio of the current account deficit to GDP was only 1 percent, it was estimated to be below 3.5 percent in 1997 (see Table 2.1 above). Such developments are seen as potentially dangerous, because they can lead to currency crises similar to those recently witnessed in some South-East Asian countries or in the Czech Republic. Polish foreign reserves, however, continue growing and in mid-October, 1997, NBP's reserves surpassed $21 billion. This means that they are equivalent to nearly 7 months of Polish imports. What is more important, however, is that financial inflows into Poland are mostly direct investments. In 1996, these investments amounted to more than $5 billion, while for the entire 1990-1996 period, they are estimated at above $17 billion.

The foreign trade and current account imbalances result from an excess of domestic demand over domestically-produced goods and services. This

---

[6] According to Standard & Poor's, Poland was graded BB; according to Moody's, Baa3; and according to IBCA, BB+.

excess demand results basically from two sources: (i) budget deficits and (ii) a strong increase in bank credit.

As can be seen from Table 2.8, in 1996 and in 1997, Polish banks very quickly expanded their credit activities. The situation is to some extent comparable to that of the first two years of the decade. However, there are also major differences.

The first difference is that the present expansion takes place in a different (both macroeconomic and institutional) environment. It is accompanied by strong economic growth and a substantially lower, although still high, inflation. In fact, the credit expansion can be partly attributed to the strong growth and to the considerable decline of bad loans (see Table 2.7) resulting in the decline in economic uncertainty. On the institutional side, one should add that by 1997, banking reform made substantial progress and a major portion of banks have been privatized; this should shape the banks' incentives in such a way as to reduce the creation of new bad loans. Another rationale for the heavy credit expansion is that Polish banks, aware of the 1999 opening of Polish financial market to foreign competition, are desperately trying to increase their share of the loan market.[7]

Table 2.8   Credits Granted to Enterprises and Households, 1992-1997*

	1992	1993	1994	1995	1996	1997
1.Total	28.5	33.4	25.2	35.3	42.4	32.4
2.Enterprises	27.0	30.6	23.5	32.4	35.2	28.4
3.Households	67.1	88.0	48.0	68.1	107.8	56.1

* Percent changes from previous year.
Source: National Bank of Poland.

The second major difference from the 1990-1991 credit expansion is a much more pronounced role of credits granted to households (mostly consumer loans) in the second half of the 1990s. In 1996 these credits more than doubled and in 1997 they continued expanding quickly, though at a lower pace. Despite this strong expansion, however, consumer credit in Poland still plays a minor role. At the end of 1997, credits for

---

[7] See *NBP Assumptions of Monetary Policy Guidelines for 1998*, Warsaw, 1997, p. 7.

households accounted to approximately 17 percent of banks' credit portfolios.   Thus, in spite of their lower rates of growth, credits for companies are of crucial importance in generating excess demand.

The National Bank of Poland initiated steps to curb the excess demand as early as December, 1996. It started by raising money market rates via open market operations. In the first half of 1997, reserve requirements were increased twice, so the average rate of obligatory reserves (for all types of deposits) reached 11.7 percent. In early August, 1997, the Bank decided to increase its basic rates by 2 and 2.5 percentage points, leading to high real rates (see Table 2.5). However, all these decisions did not have the expected immediate impact on banks' behavior. Consequently, the NBP undertook an unprecedented action. In mid-September, 1997, the Central Bank began accepting 6- and 9-month deposits (at rates above market rates) directly from the public. The goal of this move was to force banks to increase their deposit rates substantially and, subsequently, their credit rates. The former should contribute to an increase in savings, the latter to the decline in credit expansion. In any case, they should lead to a decline in domestic demand.

Despite these dramatic actions undertaken by the Central Bank, it seems that monetary policy alone will not be able to reduce substantially domestic demand expansion and, consequently, the current account deficit. Obviously, fiscal adjustment (as well as a change in incomes policy) is necessary. The program and personnel composition of the new Polish government created after September, 1997 parliamentary elections seem to suggest that such developments are possible.

Conclusion

With regard to Polish macroeconomic developments in the 1990s, Table 2.2 showed that the declining pattern of inflation was accompanied by substantial money supply increases. We now know how this pattern was generated. What needs to be stressed here is that, despite problems in monetary control, the inflation rate has steadily declined in Poland. Obviously, real money demand for Polish currency increased.   Our analysis suggests that this basically was due to two factors: (1) economic revival that created additional demand for transaction balances, and (2) the NBP's interest rate policy that made zloty-denominated deposits a valuable savings asset (see Table 2.3).

As Poland is preparing itself to join the European Union, the institutional solutions in the area of monetary policy have to be compatible with Western standards, particularly those outlined in the Statute of the European System of Central Banks and of the European Central Bank. On January 1, 1998, a new NBP Act, accompanied by a new Banking Act, became effective. It clearly states the main mission of NBP as to maintain price stability, in a way compatible with the Maastricht Treaty requirements.   In order to solve the problems of accountability and coordination, the NBP adopted a Monetary Policy Board, modeled on the Banque de France.

Poland is also trying to fulfill the macroeconomic convergence criteria as laid out in the Maastricht Treaty. Therefore, fighting inflation has to continue to be a priority for Polish monetary policy. It also implies that the NBP has to remain an autonomous, but accountable, Central Bank.

References

Borzym, Kinga, [1997]. "Comparison of exchange rates of national currencies with their purchasing power in the EC countries and in Poland" (in Polish), *Bank i Kredyt* No. 3, pp. 4-20.

Gdańsk Institute for Market Economics, [1997]. *Quarterly Estimates and Forecasts of GDP for Poland* (in Polish) , Gdańsk-Warsaw.

International Monetary Fund, [1987]. *Theoretical Aspects of the Design of Fund-Supported Adjustment Programs,* Washington, DC.

Information Bulletin, different issues from 1991-1996, National Bank of Poland, Warsaw.

Ministry of Finance [1994-1997]. *Public Debt Quarterly Information* (in Polish), Warsaw, various issues.

NBP Assumptions of Monetary Policy Guidelines for 1998, (in Polish), [1997]. National Bank of Poland, Warsaw.

Statistical Yearbooks and Bulletins (in Polish), different issues from 1991-1997. Polish Central Statistical Office, Warsaw.

3 Privatization and Capital Market Development in Poland

MIECZYSLAW PULAWSKI
RYSZARD RAPACKI

Introduction

Privatization in transition economies often has been conceived (particularly, at the early stages of systemic transformation) as a simple, "one-shot" transfer of ownership rather than a long-run, complex process of social, political, economic, psychological and cultural change. Even under more complete definitions of privatization, it tended to be analyzed as a purely technical (legal) and economic process, with little importance attached to its corresponding behavioral and institutional dimensions [Rapacki and Linz, 1992].

Contrary to the experience of Western countries with well-established market institutions as well as a stable economic and behavioral environment, privatization in former centrally-planned economies was a formidable task, aimed at achieving a much broader and complex set of objectives. On the one hand, privatization in East-Central Europe was designed as a component of a comprehensive systemic transformation package which included stabilization policy, institutional reforms and structural change. The overriding goal of this package was to transform the former command systems into market-driven economies, akin to those prevailing in Western industrialized countries. On the other hand, privatization was to be the core component of the entire package and was expected to become the most powerful vehicle of systemic transformation, including not only direct effects, such as ownership changes and the resulting efficiency gains, but also simultaneously the spillover effects of, for example, enforcing the emergence of principal market institutions and behavioral patterns either non-existent at the outset of the transition or severely distorted as a legacy from the command economy.

At the outset of the transition, the government expected the process of ownership transformation of state-owned enterprises (SOEs) to be fast and smooth.   In its first privatization program published in early 1990, the government spelled out its goal to privatize approximately 50 percent of SOEs in three years, that is, by the end of 1992 [Programme 1990].   This goal was relaxed in September 1990 to be achieved by the end of 1995 [Lewandowski 1995].

The government-conducted, "top-down" privatization was expected to meet multiple objectives, both long-run and short-term [Outline 1989; Jêdrzejczak 1991].   In the long run it was to raise the efficiency of resource allocation in the Polish economy dramatically and to enhance the much-desired institutional and structural changes.   One of the most important dimensions of the former objective was seen in the creation and fast development of the stock exchange, in particular, and of the capital market, in general. Simultaneously, ownership transformations were to contribute to a more equitable distribution of property rights and to create a new middle class, thus providing a new political base for systemic reforms.   In the short- and medium-run, the divestiture of SOEs was expected to eliminate the inflationary overhang inherited from the centrally-planned economy, and hence, through a higher propensity to save, to lessen inflationary pressure.   Also, the proceeds from the sale of state-owned assets as well as increased tax revenues generated by the expanding private sector were to provide a new source of budget revenues and improve the government budget position.

The aim of this contribution is to provide an overview of Poland's privatization record since 1990 and to discuss its role in the emergence and the subsequent development of the capital market in Poland.   The following discussion has been divided into three parts.   In the next section, quantitative results of privatization in Poland to date are presented.   The third section provides an analysis of developments in Polish capital market, with special emphasis on their roots in the privatization process. The final section draws conclusions on the future course of privatization and capital market development prospects.

Privatization Results, 1990-96

Poland, contrary to other former socialist countries (the only exception being Hungary), entered the road to a market economy with a relatively large margin of private enterprise.   Although the Polish private sector started small, employing 600,000 people in non-agricultural activities (i.e.

less than 5% of urban employment) and contributing 3% of GDP in 1980 [Aslund 1985], it grew steadily during the 1980s. By the end of the decade it had contributed in aggregate 19 percent of GDP[1] as compared with 15% in Hungary and only 2-4% in the remaining countries of Central and Eastern Europe [Milanovic 1989, Gelb and Gray 1991, Rapacki and Linz 1992]. The unique feature of Polish economy was its predominantly private agriculture: 75 percent of land was in private hands. The private agricultural sector contributed 10 percent of GDP in 1988 and employed 21 percent of the total work force [Rapacki and Linz 1992].

Non-agricultural private business was concentrated mainly in retail trade, restaurants, repair and other services and generated 8-9 percent of the country's value added in 1989. At the other extreme, industry was almost exclusively state-owned. A similar pattern applied to transport, construction, telecommunications, water and gas and power generation. When the legal framework for the "top-down", government-led privatization was laid down in mid-1990, there were 8872 state-owned enterprises in Poland. Most[1] of them were subject to the privatization program.

The July 1990 privatization law (Act on Privatization of State-Owned Enterprises and their Corporatization) adopted two basic approaches (tracks) to privatization: (1) capital (divestiture or indirect) track and (2) privatization through liquidation (non-divestiture or direct path).[2] Capital privatization was to encompass mainly large SOEs (over 500 employees) in good financial standing. SOEs scheduled for divestiture were first transformed into joint stock companies (so called commercialization) with the State Treasury holding 100 percent of the shares. The shares were subsequently disposed of by public offering or direct sales (auctions or invitations to tender). Privatization through liquidation, designed to embrace mostly medium- and small-scale SOEs in good financial

---

[1] If we include the value added produced in cooperatives which were reclassified in 1990 from the public to the private sector, the share of the latter increases to 29 percent.

[2] Small-scale divestiture, leveraged buyouts, management contracts, asset stripping and fragmentation (splitting) of existing SOEs were also included in the initial program as a means of achieving privatization. In 1991, the Bielecki government, disappointed with the slow pace of ownership changes, introduced some new methods including cluster privatization, mass privatization, express privatization and privatization after restructuring [Mass Privatization 1991, Kwasniewski 1991, Nuti 1991].

condition, did not require legal transformation prior to ownership changes. The liquidation track involved either the direct sale of an SOE's assets to an outside investor, the contribution of liquidated assets to a newly-established company, or the lease of assets to the firm's employees and/or management (M/EBOs). In April 1993, the top-down privatization program was extended to include the so-called Mass Privatization (or National Investment Funds - NIF) scheme.

During the last seven years, the role of the private sector in the Polish economy, as measured by general macroeconomic yardsticks, increased dramatically. By the end of 1996, private firms contributed 60 percent to the GDP and employed 65 percent of the total labor force [GUS 1997]. If 512 NIF portfolio companies (which are majority-owned by NIFs who entered the Warsaw Stock Exchange in June, 1997) are added, these share indices would be revised upwards by 3-4 percentage points.[3] The highest weight of private business, in quantitative terms, was recorded in retail trade and construction, while the lowest was in more capital intensive sectors such as industry and transport (see Table 3.1).

It should be borne in mind that the private sector in Poland is notoriously under-reported by official statistics. The shadow economy could amount, according to different estimates, to 15-25 percent of the GDP. If these unregistered activities and jobs could be included, the urban private sector alone would surely account for over 60% of Poland's GDP and for nearly 70% of urban employment [Johnson and Loveman 1994 and authors' estimates].

It was mostly the "bottom up" (or "grass-root") privatization through the expansion of the existing private business and mass-scale start ups of new private firms that produced the most visible results in transforming the ownership structure of the Polish economy [Rapacki 1995]. During 1989-96 the number of individual private proprietorships (unincorporated firms) recorded a nearly six-fold growth, from 350,000 to over 2 million. By the end of 1996, they employed 2.8 million people (24 percent of the total non-agricultural employment). Worth emphasizing is the relatively large incidence of startups and closures in this category of private business

---

[3] This result is derived from the fact that the NIF companies represent about 8 percent of sales and assets of the relevant corporate sector (mostly industry and construction). Since these sectors' contribution to Poland's value added was at the level of 45-50 %, by multiplying these two figures, we arrive at 3-4 points of the incremental share of the GDP.

which seems to support the idea that entrepreneurialism in Poland has attained a reasonably high level.

Simultaneously, the number of domestic companies has grown from 11,900 to 87,100, while that of joint-ventures with foreign capital equity grew from 400 to over 28,600. Altogether these three categories of private firms employed 5.5 million people by the end of 1995, or 47.5 percent of total non-agricultural manpower in Poland [Poland 1996; Rapacki 1994].

Table 3.1 Share of Private Sector in Output and Employment in Poland, 1989-95

Sector	1989	1990	1991	1992	1993	1994	1995	1996
Macroeconomy								
- Output (GDP)	19[a]	30.9	42.1	47.2	50	53	58	60
- Employment	35[a]	48.9	54.3	56.0	58.9	60.6	62.4	65.1
Industry								
- Output	16.2	18.3	24.6	31.0	35.1	39.4	44.5	51.7
- Employment	29.1	31.2	35.8	37.8	40.7	44.8	49.6	53.4
Construction								
- Output	33.0	41.8	62.6	77.4	84.3	86.2	86.7	87.9
- Employment	37.4	42.1	59.5	71.8	-	79.3	81.9	85.0
Transport								
- Output	11.5	14.2	25.2	33.4	38.7	42.8	-	-
- Employment	14.3	15.2	23.0	25.1	27.5	23.0	-	-
Retail trade								
- Output	59.3	63.7	82.8	86.4	89.0	89.2	92.3	92.9
- Employment	72.7	82.2	88.3	90.5	92.7	94.6	-	-
Foreign trade[b]								
- exports (c)	-	4.9	21.9	38.3	44.0	51.1	56.9	62.7
- imports (c)	-	14.4	49.9	54.5	59.8	65.8	69.7	75.6

[a] 29% output and 44.1% employment if co-operative sector is included. [b]Sales.
Source: Rapacki [1995], GUS [1996b and 1997].

While there was skyrocketing growth in the number and importance of private businesses, the period of 1990-96 witnessed a sharp decline in the volume of economic activity conducted by public firms. In particular, the SOE sector shrank considerably. The number of state-owned enterprises fell by almost 57 percent, from 8,872 in mid-1990 to 3,847 at the end of

1996. The fastest decline in their number took place in agriculture (by over 90 percent) and in industry (by more than 30 percent).

The downward trend in the size and importance of the Polish public sector was largely due to the "top-down" privatization program launched by the government in July 1990. As of the end of 1996, ownership changes embraced 5,592 SOEs, or 63% of their 1990 total number (Table 3.2). Nearly 22% of those subject to privatization (1,227 former SOEs) have been transformed into treasury corporations, as a first step toward their subsequent divestiture through the capital track (including 512 companies covered by the NIF Programme).[4] In 2,711 non-agricultural SOEs, ownership transformations through the liquidation track were initiated, of which 46 percent were subject to privatization procedures and 54 percent were scheduled for actual liquidation due to insolvency [GUS 1997].

Out of a total of 3,938 former non-agricultural SOEs undergoing ownership transformations, 1,963 were actually privatized by the end of 1996 (including 78 cases of debt-to-equity swaps), or 22 percent of the whole group of state-owned enterprises registered at the outset of systemic transition in Poland and 51 percent if compared to their number at the end of 1996. Of the total, 1,715 SOEs were transformed under the liquidation track, while only 170 were divested through the capital route (excluding debt-equity swaps). Among the former category, a much more 'productive' procedure turned out to be privatization through the liquidation of viable SOEs (1,221 privatized firms) than liquidation due to insolvency (494).[5] By December 1995 all former agricultural SOEs were transformed into treasury corporations and 1,206 of them were effectively liquidated [GUS 1996b].

Between August 1990 and December 1996, 1,158 new companies were set up based on the assets of liquidated state-owned enterprises. The overwhelming majority (1,041) were employee-managed companies (M/EBOs). During the last seven years in Poland, there has been a wide stream of spontaneous, informal transformations of state assets. According to some authors, this flow of resources should be ranked among

---

[4] The remaining 78 SOEs scheduled for the NIF Program were transformed into Treasury corporations by June, 1996.

[5] As of mid-1997, the respective figures increased as follows: the total number of SOEs actually privatized amounted to 2,029, of which 1,830 were under the liquidation track and 199 were divested through the capital track (excluding debt-to-equity swaps). [*Statistical Bulletin*, 1997].

the most important engines of the rapid expansion of the private sector [Szomburg 1995, Dabrowski 1996].

A new form of ownership change that developed on a larger scale in 1994 was "debt-to-equity swaps" within the so-called "bank settlement procedures" (i.e., debt rescheduling agreements whereby banks write down a SOE's debts in exchange for equity).[6] At the end of 1994, 97 such settlements had been filed with the Ministry of Ownership Changes, of which 68 stipulated corporatization of the debtor and 60 involved debt-equity swaps (this number increased to 78 by June, 1996). Besides the dealings with banks, this new path of privatization comprised debt-equity conversions between debtor SOEs and other, non-bank creditors. Since some of Poland's largest SOEs were involved in such debt-clearing agreements, they have resulted in a relatively significant reduction of inter-company debt and contributed to the restructuring of state-owned enterprises [Poland 1995].

In December 1994 the long awaited, innovative Mass Privatization (NIF) Programme was launched. Altogether 512 former SOEs have joined the scheme. With a total book value of some 7 billion zloties (US$ 2.8 billion), they represent approximately 8 percent of the corporate sector's sales and productive assets.

The 512 participating companies are majority-owned by 15 National Investment Funds (NIFs), with 33% of shares in each company belonging to a lead NIF and 27% equally spread among the remaining 14 NIFs.[7] The NIFs have been managed by professional, mostly Western fund managers, with a participation of Polish consulting firms and major banks.

Poland's Mass Privatization Program, as compared to similar schemes in other transition economies (e.g. Czech Republic or Russia), displays several salient, novel properties [Rapacki 1996]:

(1) It significantly reduces the pertinent risk for individual investors as it provides all adult citizens, at a nominal fee of $8, with ownership titles to the equity capital of all 15 National Investment Funds instead of direct stakes in participating companies. The distribution of these titles, called

---

[6] For more details on bank settlement procedures and debt-to-equity swaps, see Filipowicz [1994].

[7] The remaining 40 percent of equity are distributed as follows: 15% of the shares are offered free to the portfolio company's employees and 25% are retained by the Treasury (in some circumstances, 15% of shares are offered free to eligible farmers or fishermen collaborating with the company involved; the Treasury then retains 10% of the shares).

universal share certificates, started in November, 1995, and ended one year later. Once NIFs were admitted for the Warsaw Stock Exchange (which took place in June, 1997), each universal share certificate can be exchanged for 15 NIF shares (one in each NIF). In this way Poles will become indirect owners of all portfolio companies (512 or less, depending on individual NIF privatization policies) that are now directly owned by the National Investment Funds.   Simultaneously, this will mark an effective privatization of the NIFs themselves. Between the date of their registration (December, 1994) and their entry on the stock exchange, they have remained, as joint stock companies, the sole property of the State Treasury.   After the public flotation, the Treasury will ultimately retain 15% of the NIFs' shares as a reserve for remuneration of fund managers.

(2) The sequence of steps in the privatization of the National Investment Funds outlined above does not necessarily imply that the same pattern must apply to individual portfolio companies. Depending on the strategy of each NIF, some of them may be divested to private owners or privatized otherwise (e.g. public flotation of individual companies on the Warsaw Stock Exchange) before NIFs themselves become private entities. In fact, several dozens of privatizations of this kind already occurred during 1995-1997 (e.g., three large cement plants were sold to Western investors).

(3) The Polish mass privatization program, contrary to similar schemes in other Eastern and Central European countries, is aimed not only to redistribute the bundle of property rights among the population at large but has been designed with a view also to ensure a genuine, in-depth restructuring of companies involved, to bring in badly needed professional management skills, expertise, technology and capital, and to execute effectively the corporate governance in a competitive environment.

The full implementation of the NIF program would, through different feedback and spillover effects, strongly enhance the already developing trends within the Polish corporate sector toward more advanced forms of market adjustment and competition strategies, particularly for privatized firms.   These trends, well documented in several empirical studies,[8] included such medium-term strategic goals as an increase in the firms' domestic market share, efficiency improvement, and development of new entrepreneurial functions (marketing, financial management, etc.).

---

[8] See, for example, Lissowska [1994], CUP [1993], Markowski [1994], Kotowicz-Jawor [1993] and Rapacki [1994].

Notwithstanding the implementation of the NIF Program, the actual pace of SOE privatization in Poland has been much slower than originally planned. As can be seen from the foregoing statistics, the quantitative goals of the government's "top-down" privatization have not been achieved. Through the end of 1995, only 18% of the initial number of SOEs (as of mid-1990) and 36% of their present number were actually privatized, which falls well short of the targeted 50 percent originally envisaged for the 1990-95 period. Simultaneously, by the end of 1994, as many as 2510 SOEs ownership transformations (i.e. nearly 51% of their total number) had not been initiated whatsoever [Rapacki 1995].

The process of ownership changes slowed down after 1993, after the post-communist coalition came to power. As Table 3.2 clearly demonstrates, the deceleration of the privatization pace has comprised all tracks except for corporatization of SOEs, in particular those aimed at the mass privatization scheme.

Contrary to initial government plans, liquidation rather than the capital track proved the most "productive" method of ownership changes in Poland. The largest group of privatized SOEs was transformed into employee-managed companies (M/EBOs) under lease contracts that authorize the transfer of ownership titles only when 50% of lease fees are effectively paid off. Although M/EBOs have displayed the highest profitability ratios among privatized SOEs, their economic health varied considerably. Most of them were financially sound, but only one fifth enjoyed good development prospects, mainly due to the relative scarcity of resources at their disposal and, in particular, to acute undercapitalization. As a result, most M/EBOs tended to invest little and had to sell off a part of their assets to be able to finance the working capital requirements.

Privatization of state-owned enterprises and assets has become a new source of budget revenues since 1991. Proceeds from SOE divestitures through the capital track as well as from sales, rentals and leases of assets and entire firms tended to grow in a relatively fast pace during the 1991-96 period (Table 3.3). It is interesting to note that this steady growth of budget revenues has taken place despite a parallel slowdown in the pace of privatization in physical terms (number of SOEs transferred to private owners - see Table 3.2), in particular after 1993. This clearly indicates that the average sales price per one privatized SOE must have risen substantially.

The total stream of budget revenues from privatization in 1991-96 amounted to over US $ 4.1 billion. Its growth rate during this period

Table 3.2   Privatization of State-Owned Enterprises, 1990-96

Type of Transformation	1990*	1991	1992	1993	1994	1995	1996
Number of SOEs	8,872	8,228	7,245	5,924	4,955	4,357	3,847
Total subject to privatization	130	1,128	681	653	484	476	386
Transformed into Treas. corporations	58	250	172	156	209	230	152
Scheduled for: privatization							
- individual	58	168	53	137	81	126	74
- mass(NIF program)	-	64	119	19	128	104	78
Privatized through liquidation track	72	878	509	497	275	246	234
- Act on Privatization of SOEs	44	372	246	203	120	113	149
- insolvency	28	506	263	294	155	133	85
- Treas. Agricultural Property Agency	-	-	720	618	307	9	-
Actually privatized (capital track)	6	21	24	45	51	72	29
- public offerings	5	6	1	3	4	3	-
- tenders	-	-	-	-	-	-	2
- trade sales	1	15	23	42	29	22	8
- mixed methods	-	-	-	-	3	2	1
- debt-equity swaps	-	-	-	-	15	45	18
Actually privatized (liquidation), under:	18	256	396	278	262	212	293
- Act of Privatization	15	227	307	184	180	126	182
- Insolvency	3	29	89	94	82	86	111
Through:							
- sales of assets	-	-	-	-	81	56	-
- asset contribution to new company	-	-	-	-	14	23	-
- leasing (MEBO)	-	-	-	-	106	78	-
- mixed forms	-	-	-	-	58	5	-

*Since August 1, 1990.

Sources: GUS [1995]; *Privatization...*[1995]; GUS [1997], OECD [1996].

exceeded inflation levels considerably (both in local currency and in dollar terms). For example, in 1995 total privatization revenues increased in current prices by 65.6% while the GDP deflator increased by 22% [Rapacki 1996].

Table 3.3 Revenues from SOEs' Privatization, 1991-96
(US$ million and %*)

	1991	1992	1993	1994	1995	1996
Total	175.3	355.4	430.1	701.8	1,089.6	1,398.1
Preceding year=100	100.0	182.0	116.0	157.0	129.0	128.0
Divestitures of SOEs	128.7	226.5	242.2	372.6	707.1	733.7
Preceding year=100	100.0	160.0	103.0	148.0	158.0	104.0
Liquidation	31.2	126.0	158.1	142.1	167.5	251.4
Preceding year=100 of which	100.0	238.0	121.0	86.0	98.0	150.0
- leases and rentals	15.4	2.9	96.0	85.4	102.5	-
Divestiture of banks	-	2.9	29.7	187.1	215.0	413.0
Preceding year=100	-	100.0	998.0	604.0	115.0	192.0

* In constant 1995 prices
Source: Report...[1994 and 1995]; CUP [1995]; *Rzeczpospolita* [1995 and 1996]; *Poland* [1997]; own calculations.

Privatization proceeds also displayed a faster pace compared to total budget revenues (in nominal terms). As a result, their share in the latter has shown a steady growth, from 1.5% in 1992, 1.7% in 1993, 2.5% in 1994, 3.2% in 1995 and 3.7% in 1996 [GUS 1996b and 1997]. Nevertheless, their weight as a source of fiscal benefit still remains at quite low levels. As a matter of fact, the prospects of further increases in the medium- and long-run seem about to be exhausted. This may be attributed to the fact that the stock of state assets available for privatization is shrinking and that, except for some specific sectors (e. g. banking, tele-communications and power generation), the most profitable sales opportunities have been exploited already.[9]

---

[9] This does not rule out the possibility of a further, short-run increase in privatization proceeds. In fact, the most recent official estimates indicate that by the end of 1997, budget revenues from SOE privatization may amount to US$ 1,900-2,000 million, or 36-43% above their 1996 level.

Capital Market Development in Poland

Before starting our discussion of the contemporary capital market development, it is worth mentioning that the beginning of orderly securities trading in Poland dates back to 1817 when the Mercantile Exchange was established in Warsaw. In the inter-war period, six stock exchanges were opened in independent Poland and the main exchange was the Stock Exchange in Warsaw. It covered more than 97 percent of the transactions carried out in all exchanges. Securities issued were the subject of primary and secondary trading in securities. For example, in 1939, 140 securities (bonds, stocks and mortgage bonds) were quoted at the Warsaw Stock Exchange.

As soon as the Second World War broke out, the Polish Stock Exchanges suspended their operations and were not reactivated in the Polish People's Republic. The doctrine of central planning applied at that time and abolished trading in securities. Except for two government loans (in 1947 and 1951, though it would be difficult to call them full-fledged securities since they had an obligatory character to some extent), no securities were issued until the mid-eighties. In 1985, the Government Instruction was passed and specified the rules of trading in bonds. However, only state-owned enterprises could issue and purchase bonds and the issue was subject to the approval of the Minister of Finance. Such approvals were granted only three times during the 1985-88 period. In 1988, the Act on Bonds was passed and it clearly constituted an improvement compared to the instruction of 1985. Nevertheless, against the background of a changing economic reality in the late 1980s, the new law proved to be anachronistic. In the second half of the eighties, the issue of shares increased by virtue of the Commercial Code but these securities tended most often to be only "junk papers". New exchanges were established spontaneously but they had nothing in common with that historic, respectable institution, the Warsaw Stock Exchange.

In 1989, Poland's radical reform process began immediately after the fall of the last communist government which was replaced by the Solidarity-led government. Privatization and the creation of a capital market were among the main objectives of the reform package. The legal framework was a vital element in the creation of a capital market. The Act on Public Trading in Securities and Trust Funds was passed by the Polish Parliament on March 22, 1991 after long international consultations and formal discussions. It provided the basis for the main "pillars" of the capital market: the Securities Commission, the Warsaw Stock Exchange, the National Securities Depository, brokerage houses and trust funds.

Public offerings in securities basically proposes the acquisition or transfer of property rights through securities issued in series, via mass media or otherwise, where the proposal for acquisition is addressed to more than 300 people or to an unspecified addressee. Public trading in securities may be conducted exclusively by subjects running a brokerage firm. The leading position in the Polish capital market is held by the Securities Commission. It was founded in 1991 as the central body of the government administration responsible for controlling and supervising capital market development. The Commission consists of a Chairman, two Vice-Chairmen and four members. The members of the Commission are representatives of the Minister of Finance, the Minister of the State Treasury, the President of the National Bank of Poland and the President of the Office for Competition and Consumers' Protection. The Securities Commission is responsible for:

- supervising the compliance with the rules of fair trading and competition in public trading in securities and providing general access to reliable information on the capital market.
- inspiring, organizing and undertaking activities to ensure effective operation of the securities market and protection of investors.
- cooperating with government administration authorities, the National Bank of Poland, institutions and participants of public trading in securities in formulating economic policy to ensure capital market development.
- disseminating knowledge about pertinent rules of the capital market.

The Securities Commission undertakes analyses of prospectuses and information memos being issued, grants permits for admission of securities and companies to public trading, registers securities brokers and advisers in public trading in securities, and grants permits to operate as a brokerage house.

In October, 1997, there were 182 public companies admitted for public trading and 49 entities running a brokerage firm, as well as 10 trust fund companies operating 23 trust funds. There were over 1500 registered securities brokers and nearly 100 individuals registered as advisers in public trading in securities.

The experience of other countries in supervising their capital markets is of particular interest to the Polish Securities Commission. The Commission has been actively cooperating with the International

Organization of Securities Commissions (IOSCO). The Polish Commission was appointed a full member of IOSCO in 1990, even before its formal legal establishment.

In April, 1991, the Warsaw Stock Exchange (WSE) was established (or reopened 52 years after its closure in 1939). The first trading session took place on April 16. The WSE was founded by the State Treasury as a non-profit, joint-stock company. Its shareholders may be banks, entities running a brokerage firm and the State Treasury only. In December, 1996, there were 54 shareholders of the WSE.

Only members of the Warsaw Stock Exchange are entitled to trade on the stock exchange. A member of the WSE must be an entity running a brokerage firm, a shareholder in the Exchange that is allowed to operate on the Exchange if it employs the required number of securities brokers and at the same time is a member of the National Securities Depository.

The trading system at the Warsaw Stock Exchange is order-driven, centralized at a single exchange site and paperless. Only unrestricted securities admitted to public trading may be listed on the WSE. During a trading session a key position may be held by a brokerage house acting as a specialist. Each issuer proposes a specialist firm to the Stock Exchange authorities. The basic duty of the specialist is to establish the security's price at each session. The following securities have been listed on the WSE: stocks, bonds, universal share certificates and subscription rights.

Stocks may be traded in the main market (the value of shares to be admitted should exceed 24 million zloties), in the parallel market (the value of shares to be admitted should amount to at least 12 million zloties) and in the free market (the value of shares to be admitted must exceed 4 million zloties). In 1992, the WSE began listing Treasury bonds also. They can be traded in three ways: (1) they may be traded in the block market, which is essentially geared towards institutional investors; (2) smaller transactions may be conducted on the main market; and (3) inter-bank bond transactions may be carried out off-exchange.

The prices of securities being traded on the Warsaw Stock Exchange are fixed in two ways: through a single price auction or through continuous trading. The specialist determines the single auction price for a given security by comparing limited orders and market orders submitted to the exchange before a session. However, this price will not change during the session and all transactions must be made at this price, including additional transactions after the determination of this price (post-auction trading system). There is a cap on price fluctuations of securities.

Stock prices may change from one session to the next by a maximum of ±10 percent, while the bond prices may change by a maximum of 5 percentage points.

On June 15, 1992, the Warsaw Stock Exchange embarked on a system of continuous trading in bonds (block market). On this market, the opening price is determined according to a single-price quotation system. During the session the price of a Treasury bond changes with the arrival of buying and selling orders, although price fluctuations are limited to a maximum of ±5 percentage points compared to the opening price. The major participants of continuous trading in Treasury bonds are institutional investors, mainly banks.

In July, 1996, the Warsaw Stock Exchange introduced selected equities to continuous trading, in addition to the single-price quotation system. In this case, price fluctuations are confined to ± 5 percent as measured from the opening price.

Also in July, 1996, the trading in universal share certificates began initially in the single-price quotation system and one month later in the continuous trading system. Share certificates were issued by the Ministry of Ownership Transformations (Privatization) within the framework of the Mass Privatization Program. Over 26 million Polish adult citizens purchased the certificates. They were issued in physical form and trading on the WSE started after their dematerialization by the National Securities Depository.

The universal share certificates can be converted into stocks in 15 National Investment Funds, until the end of 1998. Stocks of the 15 National Investment Funds have been listed at the WSE since June 12, 1997. Some of the portfolio companies participating in the National Investment Fund Programme will be traded on the Warsaw Stock Exchange as well.

The quotations of subscription rights are based on the single-price auction system. As of September, 1997, the stocks of 132 companies have been listed on the Exchange, including 106 in the main market, 24 in the parallel market and 2 in the free market. At the same time 56 issues of Treasury bonds have been quoted. The share of bond trading in the overall value of turnover in securities has been small, though it increased rapidly in 1995. This was the first time in the history of the Warsaw Stock Exchange that the value of bond trading exceeded the value of transactions on the stock market (Tables 3.4 and 3.5). This result was due to a simultaneous deep contraction in the latter market and a ten-fold expansion in block (off-session) trading in bonds.

The average market capitalization of the Warsaw Stock Exchange (the main market only) has risen rapidly from 79 million zloties in 1991 to 9,030 million in 1995 and 19,351 million zloties in 1996 (i.e. US$ 7.25 billion) and amounted to 6 percent of Poland's GDP (as of December 1996).[10]

Table 3.4 Major Trends in the Warsaw Stock Exchange, 1991-97*

Indicator	1991	1992	1993	1994	1995	1996	1997
Stock Market							
Main Market							
Number of listed companies at year-end	9	16	21	36	53	66	106
Average capitalization (PLN mn)	79	307	1,962	8,928	9,030	19,351	-
Average capitalization (US$ mn)	75	225	1,084	3,933	3,731	7,247	-
Total turnover (PLN mn)	30	230	7,750	22,640	12,200	25,611	28,954
Parallel Market							
Number of listed companies at year-end	-	-	1	8	12	17	24
Total turnover (PLN mn)	-	-	120	780	1,080	2,460	4,572
Free Market							
Number of Listed Companies	-	-	-	-	-	-	2
Total turnover (PLN mn)	-	-	-	-	-	-	177

* As of September 30, 1997.
Source: The Warsaw Stock Exchange.

In December, 1991, the Warsaw Stock Exchange became an associate member of the International Federation of Stock Exchanges (FIBV) and the Federation of European Stock Exchanges (FESE). In October 1994, it was granted full membership in the FIBV as the first stock exchange from

---

[10] In September, 1997, this ratio increased to 10 percent.

Central and Eastern Europe. Table 3.4 provides basic data illustrating the development trends in the Warsaw Stock Exchange since its establishment.

Table 3.5. Major Trends in the Warsaw Stock Exchange, 1991-97* (Continued)

Indicator	1991	1992	1993	1994	1995	1996	1997
Bond Market							
Single price trading							
Number of listed bond issues at year-end	-	3	8	12	13	14	16
Total turnover (PLN mn)	-	7	115	323	417	1,898	2,368
Continuous trading							
Number of listed bond issues at year-end	-	5	10	20	33	40	40
Total turnover value, double counted (PLN mn)	-	14	185	1,826	3,735	4,007	2,299
Block trades (off-session)							
Total turnover value, double counted (PLN mn)	-	-	256	1,151	15,122	10,313	6,058
Market for Subscription Rights							
Total turnover (PLN mn)	-	-	-	5.4	7	18	21
Market for Universal Share Certificates							
Total turnover (PLN mn)	-	-	-	-	-	3,714	3,774
PLN/US$ exchange rate	1.06	1.36	1.81	2.27	2.42	2.67	-

* As of September 30, 1997.
Source: The Warsaw Stock Exchange.

The trading, clearing and settlement systems of the Warsaw Stock Exchange are fully automated and computerized. Each investor intending to buy or sell securities on the Exchange must hold a securities account and a cash account with a brokerage firm.   Every brokerage house executing transactions on the Exchange must hold a securities account in the National Securities Depository, and a cash account in the clearing bank (currently Bank Slaski).   The process of accounting and data processing for settlement and registration is computerized.   The depository system, based on paperless trading is managed by the National Securities Depository.   All securities of a given issue are deposited in the form of a single global certificate.   The Depository only records changes in accounts of entities running a brokerage firm and banks.   The basic functions of the National Securities Depository are the following:

- keeping and registering securities in public trading,
- holding deposit accounts of the subjects entitled to have securities kept therein,
- registering transactions between entitled subjects,
- controlling the quality of securities issued with the number of securities in circulation,
- issuing deposit receipts, and
  organizing the settlement of transactions.

The National Securities Depository was founded in 1991 as an organizational unit of the Warsaw Stock Exchange and became a separate entity in November, 1994.

Subjects running brokerage firms hold a leading position on the Polish capital market (in an operational sense).   They are allowed by the Securities Commission to offer securities in public trading, to buy or sell securities in their own name for their customers, to acquire securities in their own name for their own account for the purpose of subsequent resale and to manage customers' portfolios of securities.   Currently there are 49 entities running brokerage firms.   The number of investment accounts opened with brokerage houses amounted to over 1 million in September, 1997.

Concluding Remarks

Since the outset of systemic transformation in 1990, the capital market in Poland has become one of the fastest growing among the emerging markets and the most attractive from the perspective of foreign investors in East-Central Europe.   Simultaneously, although not the largest in terms of capitalization, the Polish stock exchange has evolved into the most transparent and has been conceived as the safest and best regulated securities market in the region.

As the foregoing discussion clearly demonstrates, the privatization of state-owned assets has provided a strong basis for the development of the capital market in Poland. The correlation between the fulfillment of the quantitative targets of a "top-down" ownership transformation (i.e. government-led privatization) and the stock market indicators (such as the number of companies listed and capitalization) was not particularly strong after 1993 when the privatization program slowed down. The capital market has expanded at a much faster pace than that of ownership changes.

Despite a further deceleration of "top-down" privatization envisioned for 1997, this year as well as 1998 should mark the beginning of a new stage in the development of the Polish capital market due to three stimuli that will provide a strong impetus for its further expansion. First, in mid-1997, 15 National Investment Funds entered the Warsaw Stock Exchange thus increasing its capitalization by one third (i.e. to 10-11 percent of GDP). Second, a number of initial public offerings (IPOs) of large Polish "crown jewels" were carried out in 1997, including two major state-owned banks (Bank Handlowy and PBK), and the top copper producer (KGHM). Several other IPOs are scheduled for 1998 (Polish Telecommunication Company, the leading bank, PeKaO, and a nationwide press distribution network, Ruch S.A.). Third, according to the most recent government plans, a substantial part of state-owned assets (including minority stakes of the Treasury in privatized firms) is to be geared towards new pension funds (as their initial endowment) that will be set up soon under the new scheme of the pension system reform. Pension funds, together with other institutional investors including insurance companies and the existing trust funds, are expected to bring greater stability to the Polish capital market and to ensure a longer-term perspective in investment decisions.

References

Aslund, Anders [1985]. *Private Enterprise in Eastern Europe.* New York, St. Martin's Press.

CUP [1993]. *Poland 1989-1993. Economic Reform - Structural Transformations* (in Polish). Report by Central Planning Office (CUP), in: *Gospodarka Narodowa,* No. 11, 1993.

Dabrowski, Janusz [1996]. "Effects of Privatization of Polish State-Owned Enterprises" in: R. Rapacki (ed.), *Enterprise Culture in a Transition Economy: Poland 1989-94.* Warsaw: UNDP-Warsaw School of Economics.

Filipowicz, Leszek [1994]. "Privatisation and Enterprise Restructuring in Poland" in: *Trends and Policies in Privatisation.* Vol. II, No. 1, OECD, Centre for Co-operation with Economies in Transition, Paris.

Gelb, Alan H. and Cheryl W. Gray [1991]. *The Transformation of Economies in Central and Eastern Europe: Issues, Progress and Prospects,* Policy and Research Series, No. 17, Washington, D.C.: The World Bank.

GUS [1996]. Central Statistical Office, *Information on Socio-Economic Situation in Poland in 1995,* January 31, Warsaw.

GUS [1996b]. Central Statistical Office, *Concise Statistical Yearbook 1996,* Warsaw.

GUS [1997]. Central Statistical Office, *Concise Statistical Yearbook 1997,* Warsaw.

Jedrzejczak, Grzegorz [1991]. "Privatization and the Private Sector" in: Blazyca and Rapacki (eds.), *Poland into the 1990s. Economy and Society in Transition,* Pinter Publishers, London.

Johnson, Simon and Gary Loveman [1994]. "Private Sector Development in Poland: Shock Therapy and Starting Over", *Comparative Economic Studies,* Vol. XXXVI, No. 4, Winter.

Kotowicz-Jawor, Joanna [1993]. "Capability of Firms to Adjust to the Market Mechanism: Empirical Findings" (in Polish), in: *Development and Transformation* (proceedings from the conference held on December 9, 1993), The Lipinski Foundation for Development Promotion, Warsaw.

Kwasniewski, Jacek [1991]. *Privatization in Poland.* Mimeo, Ministry of Ownership Changes, Warsaw, June.

Lewandowski, Janusz [1995]. "The Overview of the Polish Privatization Process" in: G. Blazyca and J. Dabrowski (eds.), *Monitoring Economic Transition. The Polish Case,* Averbury.

Lissowska, Maria [1994]. "The Evolution of Industrial Enterprises' Behaviour in the 1990s" (in Polish), *Roczniki Kolegium Analiz Ekonomicznych,* No.1, Warsaw School of Economics.

Markowski, Krzysztof [1994]. *Corporate Sector Performance and Investments,* in: Poland [1994].

Mass Privatization - Proposed Program [1991]. The Republic of Poland, Ministry of Ownership Changes, Warsaw, June.

Milanovic, Branko [1989]. *Liberalization and Entrepreneurship: Dynamics of Reform in Socialism and Capitalism,* Armonk, NY: M. E. Sharp, Inc.

Nuti, Mario D. [1991]. "Privatization of Socialist Economies: General Issues and the Polish Case" in: H. Blommestein and M. Marrese (eds.) [1991], *Transformation of Planned Economies. Property Rights Reform and*

Macroeconomic Stability, Centre for Co-operation with European Economies in Transition, OECD, Parus.

OECD [1996]. "Poland" *OECD Economic Surveys 1996-1997* Series, Paris.

Outline Economic Program [1989]. Council of Ministers, Warsaw, October.

Poland. International Economic Report 1994/95 [1995], World Economy Research Institute, Warsaw School of Economics, Warsaw.

Poland. International Economic Report 1995/96 [1996], World Economy Research Institute, Warsaw School of Economics, Warsaw.

Poland. International Economic Report 1996/97 [1997], World Economy Research Institute, Warsaw School of Economics, Warsaw.

Privatization of State-Owned Enterprises, as of 31 December 1994 (in Polish). Central Statistical Office (GUS), Warsaw.

Programme for Ownership Changes in State-Owned Enterprises [1990]. Office of Government Plenipotentiary for Ownership Changes, Mimeo, Warsaw.

Rapacki, Ryszard [1994], "Polish Corporate Sector" in: *Transforming the Polish Economy*, Vol. II. World Economy Research Institute and International Center for Economic Growth (San Francisco), Warsaw.

Rapacki, Ryszard [1995]. "Privatization in Poland: Performance, Problems and Prospects," *Comparative Economic Studies*, Vol. XXXVII, No. 3, Fall.

Rapacki, Ryszard [1996]. "Privatisation and the Public Exchequer in Poland" in: V.V.Ramanadham (ed.), *Privatisation and the Public Exchequer*, Routledge (forthcoming).

Rapacki, Ryszard, and Susan J. Linz [1992]. *Privatization in Transition Economies: Case Study of Poland.* Econometrics and Economic Theory Papers, No. 9011, Department of Economics, Michigan State University.

Report on Ownership Transformations in 1993 [1994]. Ministry of Ownership Changes, Warsaw (in Polish).

Report on Ownership Transformations in 1994 [1995]. Ministry of Ownership Changes, Warsaw (in Polish).

Rzeczpospolita [1995]. July 15.

Rzeczpospolita [1996]. August 21.

Rzeczpospolita [1996b]. September 25.

Statistical Bulletin [1997], No. 8 GUS, Warsaw.

Szomburg, Jan [1995]. "The Political Constraints of Privatization" in: G. Blazyca and J.M.Dabrowski (eds.), *Monitoring Economic Transition, The Polish Case*, Avebury.

4 Banking Institutions in Poland

IZABELA RUTKOWSKA

Structure of the Banking System

After World War II, the Polish economic system was transformed into a centrally planned economy. As a consequence, fixed assets were transferred from private hands to the State, price setting was based on accounting/cost factors, and allocation of resources was determined by central planning authorities. In the financial sector, pre-war banks were eliminated and their functions were transferred to the Central Bank of Poland (NBP).[1] Under this system, the role of banking was reduced to passive allocation of centrally disbursed funds. Moreover, since monetary instruments were not available to it, the NBP had no role in the determination of the money supply. Similarly, the NBP was not involved in the development of banking regulations or in supervision of banking activities. At the end of the 1970s, the Polish banking system consisted of the NBP, which was directly responsible to the Ministry of Finance, and the following satellite, specialized banks:

- Bank Polska Kasa Opieki S.A., concentrating on collecting foreign currency deposits from the population and channeling the funds to the state budget;
- Bank Handlowy S.A., specializing in foreign trade financing; and
- Bank Gospodarki Zywnosciowej, operating as a central coordinator for cooperative banks, specializing in rural finance.
- Powszechna Kasa Oszczednosci (incorporated by the NBP in July, 1975), specializing in collecting domestic currency deposits from households and transferring them into cooperative housing industry and the state budget.

In 1982, attempts to reform the Polish economy brought some important changes to the banking system. First, with the adoption of the Banking

---

[1] In 1938 Poland had a modern (for the time) central bank, 3 large state banks, 27 private banks, 28 finance houses, 19 credit unions, 353 savings associations, 975 local savings associations, and 5597 credit cooperatives.

Act, the NBP gained independence from of the Ministry of Finance and was given a role in developing monetary policy. Second, the new legislation made it possible to create banks as joint-stock companies.[2]

In 1983, additional legislative changes were adopted. These included a redefinition of central planning into a more indicative form; formal independence and self-financing of enterprises, and a greater decision-making role for local governments. Following these changes, it was realized that decentralization of the enterprise sector necessitated decentralization of the credit allocation process. Nevertheless, it was not until 1989 that the Polish banking system was returned to a two-tier framework.

On the basis of a new Banking Act, adopted by Sejm in January, 1989, about 400 branches of the NBP were transformed into nine regional commercial banks. This Act created a legal basis for further changes in the ownership structure of the nine banks. By the end of 1991, all had been converted to joint-stock companies.[3] The National Bank of Poland Act, enacted simultaneously with the new Banking Act, granted the NBP most of the functions of a typical central bank.

While the legislative changes pertinent to the banking sector opened opportunities for genuine reform of the banking system, they coincided with worsening economic conditions. Partial decentralization of the economy, which was not followed by complimentary ownership and political changes, resulted in spontaneous deregulation. State enterprises remained on soft budget constraints and price setting by banks was driven by a policy of low interest rates on credits. Until the stabilization reform of 1990, interest rates on deposits were very low in nominal terms and strongly negative in real terms. High and growing inflation, which at its highest level reached 730 percent per annum (in 1989), and catastrophic shortages in most markets resulted in the dollarization of the economy and erosion of the deposit base in the banking system. The shortage of funds in the banks was compensated by refinancing credit from the NBP, which at the end of 1989 accounted for as much as 62% of total bank credit to the economy. The NBP's refinancing carried lower-than-market interest rates, created disincentives for banks to look for client deposits, and further disturbed the pricing mechanism.

---

[2] In fact, no new bank was created until the end of 1986, when Bank Rozwoju Eksportu S.A. was set up.

[3] At the initial stage, these joint stock companies (S.A.'s) were fully owned by the state.

The political changes in Poland in June, 1989, brought a new approach to the reform of the economy. Beginning in January, 1990, the policy was aimed at fundamental reconstruction of the economy from a command to a market structure. In agreement with the Internal Monetary Fund, reforms undertaken by the Solidarity government, and continued by later coalitions, assumed a restrictive stabilization program. The most important elements of this program were:

- very strict control of the money supply,
- positive real interest rates that would secure growth of savings in the domestic currency,
- an equilibrium exchange rate, which was initially fixed at a rate of PZL 9,500 against the US dollar; this rate was later criticized as too high and considered as one of the main reasons for the very deep recession that followed the stabilization effort, and
- cancellation of subsidies to manufacturing state enterprises and explicit announcement of hard budget constraints for economic units.

The stabilization program was successful in terms of reducing inflation and opening of the Polish economy to international markets. By the end of 1996 Poland's inflation rate had fallen to a relatively moderate 18.5 percent per annum, its currency was fully convertible in terms of the current account transactions, and its budget deficit was 2.5 percent of GDP. More importantly, since 1993, the Polish economy has shown positive growth. In the banking system these positive macroeconomic developments have resulted in an improvement in the rate of saving and the institutional development of banks and banking infrastructure.

The amended Banking Act of 1989 and the liberal approach to licensing opened opportunities for establishing new banks.[4] By the end of 1992 there were 87 new banks (apart from the previously created 9 state banks), of which 84 were Polish-owned. Many of the new banks were private and some were established or co-owned by state enterprises or public institutions. Nevertheless, the capital basis of the new banks was weak and, given the unstable macroeconomic environment, the lack of sufficient capital led to several cases of insolvency. To protect the system from decomposition, the NBP was forced to change its policy toward more

---

[4] The underlying reason for the liberal licensing policy by the NBP and the Ministry of Finance was to demonopolize the banking sector and stimulate competition. To a large extent this policy proved successful since the number and quality of services offered by banks, both private and state, improved significantly.

restrictive screening of the funding basis and professional skills of the newly appointed managerial staff. In line with these changes more adequate prudential regulations were developed and several banks were liquidated or merged with larger partners. By the beginning of 1997, the banking system was comprised of:

- *The National Bank of Poland (NBP).* Since 1989 the NBP has introduced major changes to its functions, including the application and subsequent continual development of indirect instruments for implementing and controlling monetary policy. A regulatory and supervisory body, General Inspectorate of Banking Supervision (GINB), was established within the organizational structure of the NBP in 1990 and currently performs a full range of supervisory functions including on-site and off-site supervision and restructuring of insolvent banks. The GINB is subordinate to the President of the NBP and is physically located in the NBP offices.

- *Specialized banks.* This group includes the largest Polish banks that formerly specialized in servicing separate markets. Currently these banks are being gradually restructured into more universal banking institutions. Their share in the total banking system assets declined from 90.2 percent in December, 1989, to 45.5 percent in December, 1996.

- *Commercial banks.* In 1989, the nine banks in this group were spun off from the former central bank. Since their establishment they have significantly extended their branch networks to overcome initial geographical specialization. The banks now are licensed to provide all types of services assigned to universal banking institutions; several of them have invested in or are partners of insurance companies. Over their relatively short existence, the banks increased their market share from 8.8 percent of the total banking system assets in December 1989 to 30.1 percent in December, 1996.

- *Cooperative banks.* The group of cooperative banks encompasses over 1550 small cooperative banks with a share of total banking system assets of 4.5 percent (as of December, 1996). The tradition of cooperative banking in Poland is very rich and many of these institutions were created long before the central planning era. At present, many of these banks are troubled by bad loan portfolios and insider lending problem. In the period of 1990-1996, there were 40 cooperative banks liquidated or merged with other banks.

- *Private and Foreign banks.* This group is relatively small, compared to its market share, (the 73 reporting to the NBP constituted in December, 1996, about 20.6 percent of the banking sector assets). Many of the private banks were established by state enterprises and gained private status after privatization by their owners or following new equity issues. The banks are small compared to their state-owned competitors and operate on specialized services markets, such as leasing, factoring, etc.

The market entry of foreign banks into the Polish market was handled liberally at the beginning of reforms, but a *de facto* moratorium on new licenses was issued soon after. In 1993, the NBP officially stated its policy of preferring entry of foreign banks through acquisitions of troubled domestic banks in lieu of granting licenses to new entities with foreign capital.[5]

Although the number of banks in Poland increased from 18 at the end of 1989 to 88 in 1996 (active and reporting to the NBP), the share of the 14 largest banks of total banking system assets declined over this time only by 16.7 percent (from 90 to 75 percent). Thus, the core of the Polish banking system remained concentrated in the state or formerly state commercial and specialized banks. Transformation of the system must be continued through transformation and privatization of these banks. The private and semi-private banks funded over the last seven years has remained small and their role of aggravating competition diminished along with the overall stabilization of the system. The small banks, with limited abilities to diversify risks properly, may become dangerous for the system and result in an increased number of bankruptcies. On the other hand, in comparison to foreign financial institutions, especially European and Japanese, even the largest Polish banks are small and lack competitive power. Due to their small volume of assets, undeveloped branch network and the still limited experience of their managerial staff, the banks are not prepared to face foreign competition even on the Polish market. While this is one of the reasons the NBP limited free entry of foreign banks into Polish banking system, such a policy cannot be continued in the long run and Polish authorities continue to aim at consolidation of the banking

---

[5] The Europe Agreements signed by Poland with the European Union foresee a restriction on the market access of foreign banks until 2001.

sector in the near term.[6] A special Law on Consolidation was adopted in June 1996 to allow the State Treasury to group state banks into more efficient bank holding companies.

The final result of the consolidation will depend on many factors with market forces and individual decisions being the most important. As observed earlier, most of Poland's banks and insurance companies have ownership stakes in other financial institutions. The most desirable option, in view of the tendencies observed currently in the most developed banking systems, would be the creation of 4 to 5 large banking groups incorporating smaller banks and life insurance companies.

Complete implementation of the privatization and consolidation plans is constrained by small capacities of the Warsaw Stock Exchange which is already dominated by banks. Another constraint is imposed by the obligation of the state to use privatization receipts for compensation of pensioners. The process will speed up as soon as a program for social security system reform crystallizes. The privatization of banks is supported by the international financial community and financed from a specially created "Bank Privatization Fund".

Banking System Infrastructure

It is important to note that banking systems in developed countries started their existence about 300 years ago and their structures, functions and institutions were shaped gradually in response to requirements created by current events. As a result, the systems, although still in the process of evolution, are well established with mature institutions and a complimentary regulatory framework. In contrast to this, the banking system in Poland, like that in other formerly planned economies, lacks the maturity coming from centuries of experience. Characteristic of this system, most of its components are new or newly rebuilt after 50 years of nonexistence and are in the process of structural adjustment.

The regulatory framework of the banking sector in Poland is comprised of two major legal acts:

*   The National Bank of Poland Act (adopted January 31, 1989). with later amendments, defines the functions, responsibilities and

---

[6] A special Law on Consolidation, adopted in June 1996, allows the State Treasury to group state banks into more efficient bank holding companies.

organization of the central bank and its agencies. On the basis of this Act the NBP carries out banking supervision, issues licenses for banking activities and is authorized to issue implementing regulations and exercise direct control functions. The NBP supervises the lending policy of banks and collects and relays information on the banking system and its overall financial situation and liquidity.

- The Banking Act (adopted January 31, 1989), with later (numerous) amendments, stipulates the procedures for the establishment of banks and their organization, sets prudential requirements and defines responsibilities of the banking supervision. Article 101 of the Banking Act authorizes the President of the NBP to issue recommendations for more detailed procedures regulating operations of banks.

In addition, bank functions are currently regulated by more general legal acts, such as the Civil Code, the Commercial Code (with regard to joint-stock companies), the Law on Cooperatives (regards cooperative banks), the Privatization of State Enterprises Act, and the Law on Consolidation regarding state-owned banks.

Regulations and requirements regarding Polish banks reflect supervisory guidelines prepared by the Basle Committee and prudent practices present in modern banking systems. Western-type loan classification schemes and capital-asset requirements were introduced in Poland in 1992. Full loan loss provisioning became mandatory in 1993, while loan classification must be based on the duration of the payments delay as well as on borrower soundness. The numerous amendments to the Banking Act of 1989 reflect the gradual development of banking supervision on the one hand (the concept, organization and skills), and the strengthening of the banks that are able to meet the supervisory requirements on the other. The Act, in its current version, defines:

- the detailed procedures for dealing with related parties,
- the prudential standards required with respect to liquidity, risk management and capital adequacy (the banks are obliged to maintain an 8 percent capital adequacy),
- the strict provisions regarding opening of accounts and cash deposits above a certain ceiling to counter money laundering.

The legislation sets a limit of 15 percent of a bank's capital on total exposure (loans, guarantees, etc.) to a single or related group of clients. The exposure arising from a single contract cannot exceed 10 percent of capital. Also, a bank's total interest in other economic units cannot be greater than 25 percent of its capital.

The consent of the President of the NBP is required for all changes in bank ownership that lead to a single shareholder acquiring entitlement to over 10%, 20%, 33%, 50%, 66% and 75% of the voting rights at a General Meeting of Shareholders. Any shareholder who has acquired over 5 percent of the voting rights is obliged to notify the relevant bank of this fact.

To protect the system against the negative consequences of bankruptcies, the National Bank of Poland Act grants the President of the NBP numerous instruments for scrupulous screening of the banks. The NBP is empowered to require detailed information from banks on their intentions regarding the scope of activities they perform and to which they are authorized. The NBP is also entitled to demand access to a bank's documentation, accounts, financial reports, plans, etc. For prudential reasons, the President of the NBP may order a bank to increase its mandatory reserves held with the NBP, to increase the number of its shares, to restructure its asset portfolio or to perform a value adjustment of accounts. Pending implementation of the measures required to improve a bank's soundness, the NBP is entitled to suspend a president of the bank in question or any other member of its management whose activity is deemed injurious to the bank or unlawful. If necessary, the NBP may restrict the scope of a bank's operations or order its liquidation. When losses incurred by a bank exceed its capital or when there is danger that such losses may occur, the president of the NBP may place the bank under administration (with the objective of implementing a recovery program) or order a merger or liquidation of the bank.

Prior to the banking system reform in 1989, there was no explicit insurance of deposits in Poland and it was assumed that the state was responsible for the liabilities of the banks. The Banking Act of 1989 introduced the provision that the State Treasury had unlimited liability for claims arising from deposits in banks established before February 10, 1989. In practice, this meant that all the banks, state and private, established after this date were excluded from any deposit insurance scheme. This regulation, however, contradicted the rule of equal opportunities for all banks by granting market advantage to the banks with state guarantee.

Independent deposit insurance was finally introduced at the end of 1994 and is now obligatory for all banking institutions in Poland with the exception of three state banks that retain state-guaranteed coverage of household deposits until 1999. The objectives of the scheme are defined in the Act on Bank Guarantee Fund from December 14, 1994, and the provisions of this Act can be broadened by a decree of the Council of Ministers. The primary objectives of the Fund are:

- monitoring the financial condition of member banks,
- providing financial assistance in the form of loans and guarantees to troubled banks,
- monitoring recovery proceedings and spending of banks under restructuring programs, and
- supervising non-statutory deposit guarantees.

The system of deposit insurance covers all deposits collected by banks and applies to 100 percent of deposits up to 1000 ECU and 90 percent of deposits between 1000 and 4000 ECUs.[7] The amounts over 4000 ECUs are not covered. The scheme is financed by membership fees (in 1996 the fees were established at 0.4 percent of total risk-weighted assets of a bank), internally maintained reserves, incomes from loans and guarantees granted by the Fund, donations from the State Budget, and loans from the NBP. Contributions to the Fund are tax exempt.

In 1995 there were 37 banks in trouble that filed for assistance from the Fund in the form of loans and guarantees. For four insolvent banks, about 90,000 depositors obtained refunds totaling PLN 105 million, of which PLN 86 million were provided by the Fund. Although the upper limit of individual deposits insured by the Fund is low in comparison to other countries, it was estimated that in 1995 about 75 percent of deposits in an average bank were covered by the scheme.

An efficient and reliable payments system is a cornerstone of a well-functioning banking system. Such a system was introduced in Poland only in 1993 when the largest Polish banks, together with the NBP, founded the National Clearing House (known by the Polish abbreviation KIR) in the form of a joint-stock company. Prior to the establishment of the KIR the banks were settling their accounts by using a regular postage system. This procedure worked in a command economy in which the number of enterprises and banks was small and financial transfers rare. Soon after the reforms started, the old clearing system became too slow and inefficient (usually a month was needed to settle accounts between two banks) leading to corruption and the straining of economic relations.

The new clearing system operates through 17 regional branches located in accordance with projected density of banking facilities. The KIR uses a

---

[7] In January, 1998, the upper limit will be increased to 5000 ECUs.

system of courier network (SYBIR) for transporting hard copies of documents and payment instructions, which are the basis and proof of all settlements. A PC-based IT system is used for final settlement of mutual claims. The system is based upon paper documents and services 70 banks with about 1900 branches; it takes up to 3 days to settle claims between all the banks in the system. By the end of 1998, the SYBIR system is expected to be fully replaced by a less expensive and much faster electronic transfer of data (ELIXIR) which allows for settlement in one day. Due to technological reasons, this component of the payment system is currently used only by the 35 largest banks and covers about 28 percent of transactions.

Detailed procedures for the operations of the KIR are laid down in its statute. According to provisions of this document, all banks licensed to conduct banking activities are allowed to participate in the system upon acceptance of its Supervisory Board. The Board issues its decision on the basis of an analysis of the bank's financial status and liquidity. The prime responsibility of the participants is to settle liabilities incurred under the exchange of payment documents through the clearing house, using a current account with the NBP. Failure to do so immediately leads to the banks being excluded from the system.

Moving to a market economy required a completely new attitude toward economic information. Prior to reforms, the information needed for central planning purposes and for the majority of private economic decisions, was not available. The Central Statistical Office (GUS) published aggregated economic information that was more suitable for general macro-structural analysis and comparisons than for micro management. After 1990, new sources of more frequent and adequate information about economic agents developed.

The quality of information in the banking system improved subsequent to accounting reforms (pertaining to both banks and enterprises) that introduced internationally-accepted procedures and standards. The reporting standards in banks was changed in 1991 and at the same time the NBP introduced a new Plan of Accounts. Initially the Plan was designed primarily for the NBP while banks maintained old standards for their own internal management purposes. Banks were able to stop the double accounting when a new Law on Accounting came into effect in January, 1995. This Law introduced standards that were more fitting for both internal and external reporting purposes and were fully compatible with international regulations. On the basis of the NBP pattern, banks prepare their individual charts of accounts. By law, banks (and other public companies) are audited annually by internationally-recognized auditing firms and must make their annual reports available to all interested parties.

Most of the economic information is also available on a commercial basis. Current quotations of exchange rates, interest rates, prices of securities, etc. are published daily by major newspapers. Other institutionalized channels for the dissemination of information about individual economic agents include the following:

- The NBP collects information from commercial banks about individual large debtors with outstanding credits above certain limit, and is obliged to share this information with the banks.
- Since December 1996, it has been required by law to list in court registers all guarantees issued and pledges made on assets; the information about the entries in the registers is paid and can be obtained upon request.
- In 1992 Dun & Bradstreet International established its office in Poland and currently disposes a database containing detailed information about 15,000 companies in Poland; the firm offers information on overdue credits, and is available for domestic and foreign clients.
- Several Polish banks and financial institutions, with support of USAID, founded a rating institution (Central European Center for Rating and Analysis) in 1996 that specializes in providing rating information about firms offering their securities.

All of these developments have had a major impact on the improvement of soundness and stability of the banking system.

Soundness of the System

The nine commercial banks separated from the NBP in 1989 inherited its branch network along with the operating procedures and credit portfolio. The loans inherited by these newly-created banks were granted under the old regime and based upon non-market evaluation criteria. Implementation of the adjustment program of 1990 reestablished badly-needed market relations, but at the same time also exposed the very poor condition of state enterprises, the main borrowers of the state banks.

According to the aggregate data on enterprises, their liquidity started to worsen from the beginning of 1991 when profitability, measured as the ratio of profit before taxes to total costs, dropped rapidly from 29 percent in December, 1990, to 10 percent in January, 1991, and to 3 percent in January, 1992. Negative aggregate net profits appeared for the first time in May, 1991 and in February, 1992, total losses of enterprises (negative net profits) rose to almost 2 percent of their total turnover. At the end of 1991, payment arrears (including tax arrears) began to be the most popular way of maintaining liquidity by enterprises.

The worsening of enterprise finance observed in the aggregate was more directly measured by international auditing firms that were contracted in 1990 to establish the standing of Polish banks. Initially the auditors performed diagnostic reviews for only three spin-off banks and their conclusions were based on detailed analysis of sample borrowers. According to the reviews, at the end of 1989, substandard loans in the three banks amounted to 18 percent of their regular exposure (excluding large loans fully guaranteed by the Ministry of Finance). In 1992 similar reviews were prepared for seven of the nine spin-off banks. According to these reports the loss and doubtful exposure amounted to 38 percent of total loans and guarantees issued by the banks. While most of the substandard loans were inherited from the command economy, it is worth mentioning that the share of substandard loans was also high in the portfolios of the emerging private banks.[8] If data on sample banks were extrapolated to the whole banking system in Poland, the likely level of losses, measured in terms of required provisions, would have reached 7 percent of 1991 GDP or 22 percent of the same year budget revenues, all measured in June 1991 prices.[9]

The crisis in the banking system was caused by (a) a rapidly changing macroeconomic environment, (b) external shocks, and (c) weaknesses in microeconomic management of banks and enterprises.

The macroeconomic circumstances were particularly unfavorable for the development of sound banking practices. The adjustment program, implemented in reaction to hyperinflation and the economic chaos of the 1980s, assumed the liberalization of consumer prices and the withdrawal of subsidies from state enterprises. In the former case, liberalization resulted in rapid price increases and a contraction of real incomes. This was followed by a significant drop in domestic consumption. The

---

[8] S. Kawalec, S. Kikora, P. Rymaszewski, *Polish Program of Bank and Enterprises Restructuring; Design and Implementation, 1991-1994.*

[9] I. Rutkowska, "Banking Distress in Poland," The World Bank, mimeo.

recession was aggravated by the policy of fixed exchange rates which, in spite of relatively high inflation, was maintained at the same level for one and a half years. In the beginning, the overvalued exchange rate strongly favored exporting enterprises (those, however, could not enter foreign markets easily), and discouraged importers of consumer goods as well as investment and supply goods. At the end of 1991, when the exchange rate was undervalued, both exporters and domestic producers lost their competitiveness vis-a-vis foreign firms, adding to a further decline in industrial production (which dropped by 24 percent in 1990 and by 12 percent in 1991).

In the adjustment period, the banks and the enterprises had to face a new monetary policy based on tight control of money outflow. In January, 1990, the NBP's refinancing rate was substantially increased from 7 percent a year to 36 percent a month which allowed it to stabilize in real terms at close to a positive level.[10] The combination of overvalued exchange rates and positive interest rates required Polish banks to earn higher than "normal" income which, in turn, resulted in the growth of interest rates on credits. This caused an immediate contraction of banking credit and a quick buildup of inter-enterprise and tax arrears. The lack of liquidity in the manufacturing sector contributed significantly to a recession and a further worsening of enterprise finance that ultimately was reflected in the banks' assets.

The situation was exacerbated by external shocks coming from an overall reduction in solvent markets in the Central European and former Soviet Union countries. In 1991 the imports that the former Soviet Republics drew from Eastern Europe dropped by 60 percent. For Poland whose export structure was dominated by mainly barter exchange with East Germany and the Soviet Union, the dissolution of these countries was particularly painful. Trade relations with other former COMECON (Council for Mutual Economic Assistance) countries also deteriorated dramatically in 1991. Among the factors affecting this decline were the deepening economic crises in all of these countries, the shortage of goods and currency in almost all of them, the lack of market economy institutions, and their failure to adopt world market norms for business

---

[10] Monthly refinancing rate was set at the following levels: Jan 36%, Feb 20%, Mar 9%, Apr 8%, May 5.5%, June 4%. In July, 1990, the refinancing rate was set at 34% per year.

transactions. These factors strongly affected enterprise finances and their ability to repay debts and to invest.

Table 4.1 Banking System Characteristics in Poland, 1989-1996

Category	1989	1990	1991	1992	1993	1994	1995	1996[a]
Number of Banks Reporting to NBP[a]	18	61	78	82	83	84	86	88
M2/GDP (%)	62	34	32	36	36	37	36	38
Refinancing Credit/Credit to the Economy[b] (%)	62	22	18	14	14	13	11	8
Central Bank Refinancing Rate[c]	104	55	40	38	35	33	29	22

[a] Excluding NBP and cooperative banks. The number does not include banks that obtained licenses but did not start operations and therefore did not report to the NBP.
[b] Credit to the economy is defined as banking system credit to the non-financial sector; it excludes credit to the budgetary sector.
[c] In January 1990, the refinancing rate as set at 36% per month (3900% per year). The rate was gradually lowered to 34% per year in July, 1990 and later increased to 55% in November of the same year. From January 1996, the NBP no longer uses refinancing credit as an instrument; data for 1996 reflecting the rediscounting rate.
Sources: National Bank of Poland various reports; Statistical Yearbook 1996, GUS.

The major weaknesses of the otherwise very complex adjustment program stemmed from a complete lack of a supplementary microeconomic policy. In 1990, when all of the radical macroeconomic reforms were implemented, enterprises had to operate on the basis of minimally modified legal regulations and unchanged ownership structure. Moreover, at the outset of the reform process, state enterprises were characterized by relatively old technology and de-capitalized equipment, hidden unemployment and the associated high costs of social insurance and other benefits, very low levels of operating capital (about 16 percent of current assets on average) which forced them to rely heavily on banking credit, and unskilled management that had never before been faced with the market rules of the open economy. The old, command-type channels of communicating with other economic agents were not replaced by a new informational infrastructure. Many enterprises were engaged in extensive investment projects designed on the basis of non-market criteria and fully financed by banking credit.

State enterprises reacted to the changes in the macroeconomic environment in a number of ways: (1) Extensive exports in 1990 were not followed by reinvestment in assets and technology; the enterprises sold inventory to hard-currency markets below replacement costs, quickly resulting in de-capitalization; (2) After years of shortages, most managers did not anticipate the contraction of domestic and foreign demand; when it came, most of them did not reduce the scope of production and continued to build reserves of final goods in the belief that the macroeconomic changes were temporary; (3) Until mid-1991, there was no employment adjustment; and (4) Following announcements of privatization, there were many examples of intentional mismanagement to lower market value and enable takeover by workers or managers.

The situation in banks was not much different than in the enterprise sector. In 1990, the newly-created banks could be characterized as lacking skills and procedures, being poorly supervised, operating in unstable legal and institutional framework, lacking basic banking infrastructure, and being undercapitalized. The effects of these weaknesses quickly materialized as loans and guarantees to insiders, fraud, mismanagement, and loans to political interests.

In addition, the absence of accrual accounting precluded sound credit and portfolio evaluation. It was quite common among banks to capitalize interest on non-performing loans and thus overstate profits. As a result, most banks paid taxes on uncollectible debt. Furthermore, according to income tax rules that were in effect until the end of 1992, banks could write off provisions for a bad portfolio only when insolvency of the borrowers was confirmed by the courts. Thus, adequate reserves were not built in advance before the crisis appeared on a massive scale.

To meet the performance criteria of the stabilization program, administrative limits on bank credit were imposed. Credit ceilings were tied to the nine commercial banks' total assets as of December, 1989. The lack of coordination between credit activity, banks' own funds and their deposit base hampered the profitable use of their assets. Bank profits declined sharply also because of:

- the shift of households deposits from sight to term deposits, given the shrinking possibilities to increase credits due to credit ceilings;
- growing competition among banks;
- the increased operating costs of banks; the most visible was the growth in rents and personnel expenses (due to competition with private banks for highly-skilled specialists); and

- the limited ability to invest surplus liquidity (the inter-bank market and its instruments were of minor, although growing, importance).

There were also problems specific to the specialized banks. Their rigid organizational and functional structures made them particularly sensitive to shocks coming from the radical changes in the economy. In banks exposed to foreign currency risk, the sharp devaluation of the Polish zloty (by 80 percent in January 1990) caused massive losses. The most exposed banks had to be recapitalized to save them from immediate bankruptcy. In case of the savings bank, PKO BP, the problems were mainly caused by the segmentation of credit and deposit markets. Typical of centrally-planned economies, PKO BP concentrated on household deposits while its credit activity was focused on financing housing at subsidized interest rates. With its large portfolio of fixed, below market yields, PKO BP became insolvent after interest rates were adjusted to market conditions.

The negative effects of macroeconomic and institutional changes were worsened by a moral hazard problem that affected enterprises and banks equally. In economies with a dominance of State ownership, insurance companies were replaced by the State; however the State was not legally obliged to take care of all of its troubled State-owned entities. A lack of rigid criteria for State intervention created room for bargaining about entitlement to financial help, especially on the basis of the unclear responsibility for wrong decisions.

The new banks spun off from the NBP inherited their assets and liabilities without prior assessment of their quality. This created two problems: first, the banks had to deal with bad loans from the outset and second, since responsibility for decisions and their possible negative impact was not clearly assigned, every mistake made by bank managers could be explained away using initial endowment as an excuse. This eroded motivations for prudence and created incentives to bargain for help and subsidies.

Similarly, the incentive for unsound decisions was built into the legal construction of borrowers, mostly state-owned enterprises. The lack of complete property rights at the beginning of 1990s was incompatible with price and exchange rate liberalization. The central planning system was designed to work, at least partly, without clearly defined rights; but the market economy cannot work without them. The Polish experience in this area shows that the question of timing and sequence of reforms and their link to privatization are very important.

The program to deal with the crisis in the banking system prepared by the Polish government focused on the improvement of the qualifications of banks' staff and managers, the recovery of bank and enterprise finances in the long run, and the reduction in the possibility of further moral hazard problems in the economy.

The first objective, improvement of qualifications, was recognized relatively early. However, due to the massive scale of education required, this objective could not be met by regular training and schooling. The approach designed to improve the qualifications of bank personnel was to tie every Polish bank to an established West European bank. The "twinning contracts," signed in April, 1992, envisioned foreign banks cooperating with Polish banks in offering training as well as assistance in credit decisions, technology advice and setting appropriate procedures. The costs of the contracts were to be repaid by the Polish banks after their conclusion. In spite of significant costs incurred, the contracts brought expected positive results and helped to improve efficiency of the Polish banks.

The second objective, improvement of bank and enterprise finances, was addressed in the banking system restructuring program facilitated by a special Law on Financial Restructuring of Enterprises and Banks (LFREB) that became effective in March, 1993. The LFREB had a pre-determined three-year horizon and its scope initially was limited to the nine commercial banks. The main framework of the program was based on the assumption that the financial situation of banks could not be improved in the long run without a radical restructuring of the enterprise sector. The LFREB required that loss and doubtful loans be identified by independent auditors and separated from bank portfolios. Furthermore, each of the participating banks was to create a separate organizational unit staffed with experienced personnel (lawyers, credit mangers and industry specialists) at the management level. The objective of the work-out units was to manage the substandard portfolio and to lead individual debt recovery programs. The LFREB obliged the banks to ensure one of the following actions would be taken before the March, 1994, deadline:

- in feasible cases, loans were recovered in their entirety;
- with financial and conceptual support of creditors, the debtors would regain their creditworthiness, proven by at least a three-month record of servicing the debt;
- conciliation agreements (allowing for debt reduction or rescheduling) with selected debtors and other creditors were reached (or

alternatively, a court arranged an agreement under the Commercial Code and Law on Arrangement Proceedings);

- debtor's bankruptcy was declared by the court; or
- liquidation of a debtor was initiated either under the Law on Privatization or under the Law on State Enterprises.

On the basis of the LFREB, the banks could also sell the loans, swap them into equity stakes, forgive or restructure. Before the conclusion of the portfolio restructuring procedures, they were not allowed to grant any new loans to debtors previously included into the substandard portfolio. It was expected that the implementation of the program would bring new money to enterprises, forcing them simultaneously into radical and permanent changes in their operations.

The banks were encouraged to create loan loss provisions that were later used for estimating the necessary amount of the banks' recapitalization: 100 percent for loss, 50 percent for doubtful and 20 percent for the substandard category of loans. The recapitalization amount was calculated *ex ante* on the basis of the credit portfolio analysis as of December, 1991, and was set at a sufficient level to ensure that the banks upon completion of the program would reach a 12 percent capital adequacy ratio as recommended by the Basle standards. The banks were recapitalized with 15-year redeemable Treasury bonds bearing a close-to-market level interest rate. The bonds in a total amount of approximately US$ 630 million were transferred to the banks in the fiscal year ending December, 1993.

The decentralized approach applied to the restructuring of the banks carried incentive mechanisms aimed at improvement of finances of both the banks and their debtors. The surplus of provisions over actually recovered loans could be included by banks in their extraordinary profits and did not have to be returned to the state budget. In this way, the banks were motivated to recover as much of the assets as possible. On the other hand, since the amount of recapitalization was estimated to cover all the potential losses, the banks could afford to participate in financial restructuring of enterprises that had the potential to become good clients in the future. The program granted the banks responsibility for the choice of the restructuring method, the preparation of individual debt restructuring proposals, their negotiations and implementation.

An important part of the program was the transformation of the participating banks into joint-stock companies (with the State Treasury remaining the sole shareholder) which forced them, even before privatization, to function as profit driven, quasi-private institutions,

Table 4.2 Developments in the Banking System, 1991-1996[a]

	1991	1992	1993	1994	1995	1996
Number of Banks with						
Solvency below 8%[b]	--	--	18	18	13	8
Of Which: Banks with						
solvency ratio below 0%	--	--	13	15	11	7
Non-Performing Loans/						
Total Credit[c]	15.6	30.1	31.2	28.3	21.5	13.4
Profitability						
Costs/Gross Income	--	84.7	99.7	96.5	84.5	80.0
Gross Profit/Total Assets	--	3.8	0.2	0.7	2.9	3.3
Net Profit/Total Assets	--	2.0	(1.3)	(0.2)	1.7	2.2
Structure of Income						
Interest Income	86.2	54.7	50.5	44.8	47.5	48.9
Securities	4.2	9.7	18.4	21.7	28.4	29.5
Fees	2.6	4.8	4.8	4.9	5.0	6.2
Exchange Rate						
Revaluation Gains	6.8	28.2	22.5	14.4	7.1	4.6
Retained Earnings	0.0	1.8	2.7	11.7	10.3	7.5
Other	0.3	0.8	1.1	2.5	1.7	3.3
Structure of Costs						
Interest Expenses	73.3	52.8	52.8	48.3	58.0	57.1
Exchange Rate						
Revaluation Losses	4.4	27.5	18.6	11.0	4.2	3.2
Operating Expenses	10.4	11.3	12.7	15.6	20.2	26.2
Provision for Loan	9.1	5.6	13.2	21.2	13.9	10.0
Losses						
Losses	0.0	0.1	0.1	1.7	0.1	0.0
Other	2.8	2.3	2.4	2.3	3.6	3.5

[a] Includes data on cooperative banks and excludes the NBP; all data are end of year figures, in percent and percent of total. [b]Excluding cooperative banks; [c]Ratio of loss, doubtful and substandard loans to total credits to the non-financial sector. *Sources*: *Statistical Yearbook 1996*, GUS, National Bank of Poland.

controlled by supervisory boards. Members of the Boards were selected by the Ministry of Finance, mostly from among independent professionals in the field of finance, law and others. The objective of the Boards was to represent interests of the Treasury and discipline the banks in order to limit the possibility of moral hazard. Recurrence of this problem in the future was to be avoided through privatization of banks that were provisioned upon successful completion of the portfolio restructuring.

Table 4.3 Balance Sheet Information for the Polish Banking System, 1991-1996*

	1991	1992	1993	1994	1995	1996
Structure of Assets						
Loans to Non-Financial Enterprises	42.8	38.1	36.2	34.3	35.1	32.9
Households	1.6	1.8	2.4	2.7	3.5	5.6
Government	3.2	4.1	2.1	0.7	1.0	1.0
Securities	15.2	15.6	19.9	23.9	27.0	28.3
Structure of Liabilities						
Capital and Reserves	5.4	4.8	5.5	4.5	3.1	4.3
Liabilities to Financial Sector	20.0	12.2	12.4	11.5	11.2	11.9
Non-Financial Sector Deposits in Domestic Currency	30.9	35.3	32.6	35.5	39.6	42.3
Non-Financial Sector Deposits in Foreign Currency	12.7	13.9	17.5	18.2	13.3	11.2

* Includes data on cooperative banks and excludes the NBP; all data are end of year figures, in percent of total. Other assets and other liabilities are omitted.
Sources: *Statistical Yearbook 1996*, GUS, National Bank of Poland.

To prohibit banks for any reason from engaging in moral hazard behavior, a special fund was created (Subsidiary Government Intervention Fund) to address situations that might arise when the sudden liquidation of an enterprise would cause severe negative macroeconomic and social consequences. The Fund was designed to permit the government to support restructuring or cushion liquidation of debtors that were "sensitive" for macroeconomic and political reasons and were unable to reach a conciliation agreement with their creditors. Access to the Fund's support was strictly limited.

The implementation of the restructuring program resulted in a significant improvement of the nine banks' finances. The resolution of the bad debt stock problem allowed the banks to redirect their portfolios into more promising investments. At the end of 1996, substandard loans in the portfolios of the nine banks constituted about 12 percent of their total assets. There were also advanced restructuring efforts initiated in the remaining state banks that are intended to strengthen the banks and enable their privatization by the year 2000.

On several measures, the health and performance of other banks in Poland also improved in 1994-96 period. The burden of non-performing loans in the aggregate fell to 15 percent in the third quarter of 1996. At the same time margins tended to decline, reflecting the development of competition as well as declining costs of provisioning. It is estimated that on average only 2-4 percent of the new credits turned bad in 1994-1996 which undoubtedly reflects the improvement in overall economic conditions but also may be interpreted as a sign of the higher skills and knowledge of bank personnel.

The overall improvement in the operations of banks is reflected in the significantly higher quality of services offered. Evidence points to increasing quality and sophistication of services as well as in the banks' attitude toward their clients. This change is well documented by the developments in the structure of banks' incomes and costs. It is interesting to note the decline in importance of interest on credits and deposits and the increase in operating expenses of banks. This change was caused by the growing activity of banks in the securities market, which in 1996, constituted almost 31 percent of the banks' total incomes. On the cost side a rapid increase in the weight of operating expenses from 6 percent in 1990 to 24 percent in 1996 can be explained by the banks' efforts to improve appeal of their offices, qualifications of personnel (wages, training, etc.), and investments in new technology and products. As banks gain more maturity, these costs should settle at a more stable level.

The structure of banks' assets and liabilities has also changed radically since the beginning of the reforms. The role of refinancing credit declined already in 1990, and since 1992, the share of liabilities to the financial sector in total balance sheet of banks has remained pretty constant. The share of loans to enterprises declined by the end of 1996 by 20.2% in comparison to its year-end 1991 level, as a consequence of banks investing in more secure assets such as government bills and bonds. Also, loans to households displayed a significant increase, particularly in 1996.

The future performance of banks will depend, as in other countries, on the overall macroeconomic situation and on the performance of large debtors. Although after two years of rapid growth, a slowdown in the Polish economy must be expected. The banks seem to be well prepared. Their capital base is relatively secure, while efficiency, measured by the ratio of costs to incomes, improves constantly. Additional measures to protect the system from systemic risks are built up into the existing, however new and inexperienced, banking infrastructure.

Conclusions

One of the issues often discussed in the economic literature regarding the transition from a centrally-planned to a market economy is timing and phasing of reforms. Although the dilemma between a gradual-versus-shock therapy approach has not been finally resolved on theoretical grounds, the empirical evidence shows that shock therapy seems to be more successful in bringing countries to macroeconomic stabilization. To be sustained, the stabilization must be supported, however, by an adequate long-term microeconomic policy aimed at transforming institutions and building a modern real sector. The reforms at this level must be gradual because they affect a whole spectrum of systemic issues such as the adjustment of the legal system, the new division of competencies at all levels of administration and the changes in human knowledge and habits.

This is also confirmed by the recent history of Polish banks, described in this paper. To be sustainable, the banking system reform in Poland had to be supported by significant investments in banking infrastructure and by simultaneous extensive reforms in the enterprise sector. Further, this effort would not be successful without simultaneous investments in human capital. Education of the banking personnel and management was the most important element of the restructuring and adjustment process. It should be mentioned also that an important part of the reforms was changing the business culture and the habits of consumers. The limited knowledge of bank clients about the concept of risk, return, financial instruments and institutions was one of the barriers in the adjustment process.

After seven years of the reforms, all of these problems seem to be well recognized and to a large extent solved, or at least addressed by various government or other programs. As a result, the majority of banks in

Poland now may be considered basically healthy and strong enough to face in a few years the unlimited foreign competition coming along with Poland's joining the European Union. The role of the Polish banks in the future, apart from themselves, will depend upon three important factors:

- the privatization of banks and its coordination with other structural changes in the country;
- further development of the capital market and non-banking financial institutions, resulting from the implementation of social security reform, recently adopted by the Polish Parliament; the newly-created private pension funds will be important competitors for long-term household deposits;
- increasing foreign participation in the Polish financial system bringing new challenges and opportunities.

References

The Financial System in Poland, 1995 [1996]. Mediabank, Warsaw.

Kawalec, S., S. Sikora, P. Rymaszewski [1994]. "Polish Program of Bank and Enterprise Restructuring: Design and Implementation, 1991-1994," paper presented in a session of the Central and Eastern European Privatization Network, Budapest, June.

Monthly Statistical Bulletin [1996]. Warsaw, GUS, December.

Rutkowska, I. [1993]. "Banking Distress in Poland, a Case Study," The World Bank, Washington, DC, August, mimeo.

Statistical Yearbook of Poland, 1996 [1996]. GUS, Warsaw.

Ugolini, P. [1996]. "National Bank of Poland: The Road to Indirect Instruments," IMF Occasional Paper 144, Washington.

Wyczanski, P. and M. Golajewska [1996]. *Polski System Bankowy 1990-1995*, Friedrick Ebert Stiftung, Warsaw.

5 Economic Progress in Hungary[1]

KAREN VORST

Introduction

Like other countries undergoing transformation to a market-based economy, Hungary has undergone significant macroeconomic changes. Changes in its production base and employment structure produced growth rates that were negative for the first several years of the transition. Inflation continues to be a major problem, though the rate of inflation has decreased from a high in 1991 of 35%. The Hungarian Forint is now a convertible currency and its exchange rate with other world currencies has settled down somewhat after several devaluations in the early 1990s. Privatization efforts are continuing, being aided significantly by foreign investors.

This paper discusses these major macroeconomic developments in Hungary since the beginning of 1989. Such a discussion is necessary in order to put the economy and its changes into perspective before reviewing the changes in the banking and capital markets and the role of the National Bank of Hungary and monetary policy, in the following articles. The next section discusses the general macroeconomic changes to inflation, employment, economic growth, net exports, and government debt. The labor market and changes to its structure are detailed in the third section. The fourth section reviews the privatization process and the notable presence of international investors in Hungary, followed by a summary and conclusions.

General Macroeconomic Changes in Hungary

In this section, we first review the connection among economic growth, inflation, and employment changes that occurred in Hungary since 1989.

---

[1] This paper was written with substantial assistance from Judit Barta of GKI Economic Research Co., Budapest, Hungary and from the National Bank of Hungary. Any errors remain my own.

Changes in net exports and in international trade are discussed, together with the developments in the exchange rate of the Hungarian Forint (HUF). Since the transition to a market-based economy has meant substantial changes in government finance, we also discuss government debt and its effects on the economy.

Table 5.1 shows a compilation of general macroeconomic data pertaining to the Hungarian economy during the period, 1990-1995. Real GDP growth from one year to the next (with the preceding year as the base) was negative until 1994 when growth turned positive, although the rates were still fairly low. With 1989 used as the base, the growth rate for the Hungarian economy from 1989 to 1995 was -14.4%, indicating that the economy in 1995 was operating at a level significantly below that of 1989.[2]

These low and negative rates of economic growth resulted from significant decreases in output from industry and agriculture and in decreases in investment and consumption, especially in the 1990-1992 period. The three-year stabilization program implemented in 1990 specified stringent control of demand through appropriate monetary and fiscal policies. The collapse of the CMEA (Council of Mutual Economic Assistance), the opening up of domestic markets, and a world-wide recession constrained output during this period as well. Industry could not recover quickly due to the extraordinary restructuring as a result of the ongoing privatization process, the general shortage of capital and prevailing high interest rates during the early stage of transformation. The Hungarian economy would recover eventually from this initial phase as industries were restructured, policymakers held interest rates down and substantial capital was generated especially through direct foreign investment.

Of particular note in Table 5.1 is the fact that the rate of growth of private consumption was negative or very near zero during this period and that the annual growth rate of agriculture was negative for the entire period also. Private consumption fell for a number of reasons: (1) the level of

---

[2] Estimates show that growth rates for the same period, 1989-1995, for the Czech Republic and the Slovak Republic were -14.8% and -14.6%, respectively. Poland, in 1995, was the first of these countries to show a positive growth rate over 1989. See "Analysis of the Performance of the Hungarian Economy and of the Convergence Criteria Between 1990 and 1995," Part 1, GKI Economic Research Co., mimeograph, and *Poland: International Economic Report, 1995/96*, World Economy Research Institute, Warsaw School of Economics, 1996, p. 37.

output from industry and agriculture fell, resulting in a decline in the number of goods available for consumption; (2) as real wages declined, many goods simply became unaffordable; (3) though unemployment did not begin its steep rise until 1992, lower consumption after 1991 may also be attributed to the higher unemployment rates; (4) household savings increased substantially, despite negative real rates; and (5) household borrowing was not an effective option, either because households were not interested in credit extension, they did not qualify or, more likely, the banks did not provide a significant level of household loans. The fall in the output in the agricultural sector was due primarily to restructuring. As a result of privatization efforts, the number of workers employed in agriculture dropped from 955,000 in 1990 to 348,200 in 1995, by almost two-thirds.

Table 5.1 Hungarian Macroeconomic Data, 1990-96

	1990	1991	1992	1993	1994	1995	1996
GDP (% change from previous year)	-3.3	-11.3	-3.1	-0.6	2.9	1.5	1.0
-Private Consumption	-3.6	-5.6	0.0	1.9	-0.2	-4.5	--
-Agriculture	-4.6	-8.1	-16.6	-7.9	-0.4	-1.0	--
Inflation rate	28.9	35.0	23.0	22.5	18.8	28.2	23.6
Unemployment Rate	0.4	1.9	7.8	13.2	10.4	10.4	10.5
Trade balance (US $ billion)	0.9	-1.2	-0.4	-3.2	-3.6	-2.4	-2.6
Balance of the central budget (HUF billion)	19.2	-94.3	-172.5	-177.6	-277.2	-307.1	-130.4

Sources: CSO, Ministry of Finance, GKI Economic Research and the National Bank of Hungary.

Inflation continues to be a problem for the Hungarian economy. The rate of change of consumer prices began to accelerate in the late 1980s, reaching a high of 35% in 1991. Thereafter, inflation in the 1990s continued to fluctuate between 18% and 28%. While the liberation of prices was an overall goal in the transition and as a result some inflation was expected, approximately 25-30% of the increase in consumer prices during the first part of the 1990s was due in part to administered prices that at times were higher than average.

Prices in the transition period were also expected to increase due to the ongoing structural changes in industry.   Costs were up from the transformation of older, less economical firms to those that was newer in structure and technology.   Industry costs also rose because of   (1) increases in wage costs, though real wages declined, and (2) higher energy and import costs.   These costs were incurred at the same time that government subsidies to firms were cut.   To the extent that these costs could be passed on, they were reflected in higher final goods prices.

An important aspect of any inflationary process is the effect of inflation expectations. With inflation rates consistently between 18% and 35% for the period, one easily could speculate that inflation expectations were a significant part of the inflation process in Hungary.

Inflation control played a dominant role in economic policy.   The Hungarian central bank had the control of inflation as its main goal and it used exchange rates as its main tool of policy.   In order to fight inflation and encourage exports, the central bank and the government supported periodic exchange rate devaluations. The exchange rate of the forint was generally increasing until early 1991 when it underwent a 15% devaluation.   The value of the forint then generally trended downward until the end of 1992, after which time it trended upward until March, 1995, when there was a 9% devaluation. The March, 1995, policy change also included the establishment of a crawling-peg exchange rate system, with periodic, announced devaluations. The forint was devalued monthly thereafter in 1995 by an average of 1.5%, and further devalued in 1996 by 1.2% per month.

Exports were nearly equal to imports from 1990 through 1992. As the exchange rate increased during the 1993-1995 period, imports were substantially above exports. This balance of trade deterioration also was a result of growing domestic demand and generally expansive monetary and fiscal policies. Inflation and devaluation efforts in 1995-1996 contributed to a lower real exchange rate (when measured by producer prices, consumer prices and/or the GDP deflator). Despite these changes, the trade balance for 1996 showed a deficit of USD 2.6 billion. The structure of exports changed slightly in 1996 with 75% of Hungarian goods and services going to advanced countries, compared to 72% in 1995. Exports to former Socialist countries decreased from 22% to 20% during the same time period. The structure of imports remained relatively stable, showing a slight decrease in imports from advanced countries (71% in 1996 from

73% in 1995) and a small increase in imports from developing countries (6% in 1996 from 5% in 1995).[3]

The changes in the unemployment rate were somewhat inconsistent with those in economic growth in the early 1990s. While we will delay a full discussion of the unemployment effects of the transformation on the Hungarian economy until Section 3 below, we note that in 1991 when the rate of growth was significantly negative at -11.3%, the unemployment rate was very low, at 1.9%. This result partially may be attributed to the fact that employment in state-owned industries initially did not significantly decline while output did. Also of note is that from 1992 to 1993, output decreased from -3.1% to -0.6% (a smaller annual rate of decline) while the unemployment rate increased substantially from 7.8% to 13.2%. Though rates of growth since 1994 have been positive, the unemployment rate still hovered around 10%.

The relatively high unemployment rate in the mid-1990s was one of several important factors affecting the government budget. While employment and output dropped, government expenditures on unemployment benefits increased and tax revenues fell, contributing to a government budget deficit as high as HUF -243 billion in 1994. While the proceeds from the privatization process helped somewhat to decrease the deficit, an important factor increasing the deficit was the high interest cost of financing the government budget debt, especially when interest rates trended upward from mid-1993 through the end of 1995. The amount of interest on the government debt increased from HUF 56 billion in 1990 to HUF 477 billion in 1995, or from 2.7% of GDP to 8.7% of GDP, a three-fold increase.[4] The slight decline in interest rates in 1996 meant that interest payments on the debt were somewhat smaller at HUF 445.4 billion, or 6.6% of GDP.[5]

The government deficits have been financed mainly through the National Bank of Hungary, households, the banking sector and institutional investors. The private sector has been willing to fund the government, despite occasional negative rates of return. The average annual nominal yields on Treasury bills, for example, have ranged between 20% and 35% since 1993. By comparison, household deposit rates

---

[3] *Annual Report*, National Bank of Hungary, 1996, p. 48.
[4] "Analysis of the Performance of the Hungarian Economy and of the Convergence Criteria Between 1990 and 1995," Part 1, GKI Economic Research Co., mimeograph, p. 27.
[5] *Annual Report*, National Bank of Hungary, 1996, p. 67.

averaged between 8% and 24% during 1995-1996. The private interest in this financing has to some extent decreased the pressure on the NBH to finance the deficit, which is a vital part of the central bank's stabilization program to fight inflation. With regard to the holding of government debt overall in 1996, institutional investors held 39.4%, the banking sector held 34.9%, households held 16.0%, the NBH held just 7%, while non-residents held 3%.[6]

In the early years of the transition, 1990-1992, there was little perceptible crowding out of private investment. The government budget balance was in surplus in 1990 and then turned down to HUF -172.5 billion in 1992. However, household savings during this time witnessed an increase while private investment demand declined. By 1993, crowding out of private investment became apparent. The household savings rate as a percentage of GDP decreased from a high of 13.9% in 1991 to 5% in 1993, while private investment demand for credit rose.[7] During this time, the banking sector became a main source of credit for the government, while remaining guarded with respect to the extension of business loans. The crowding-out effect was somewhat alleviated after 1993 by foreign credit markets in which interest rates, adjusted for devaluation, were lower than domestic rates, and by increases in the household and corporate savings rate.

The Changing Structure of the Hungarian Labor Market

Any economy that undergoes dramatic changes in its ownership of resources, structure, production facilities and output, will necessarily witness significant changes in its labor market. This section details those changes from the early days of the transition in Hungary through 1996.

Many major industries in Hungary, such as agriculture, forestry, and construction showed signs of declining output as early as 1988. Since unemployment did not rise as a result (there was no official unemployment), productivity levels declined. With the introduction of the market concept of efficient production and the beginning of the change-over of production facilities to more efficient processes, the initial stages of the transition saw production levels fall dramatically. Output from

---

[6] *Ibid.*, p. 72.
[7] *Op. Cit.*, GKI Economic Research Co., p.36.

industry in general dropped 30.5% from 1988 through 1992 before starting an upward trend. For the same time period, output from construction decreased by 26.8% and that from agriculture and forestry decreased by 27.7%. While the output of industry in general turned around in 1993, that of construction and agriculture and forestry continued to decrease for two more years.

As a consequence, employment levels across Hungary were affected dramatically. The average number of full-time employees overall decreased from 4.2 million in 1988 to 2.4 million in 1996, a decrease of almost 43%.[8] For the national economy as a whole, the total number of employees, including full- and part-time employees, decreased from 5.5 million in 1990 to 4.1 million in 1995.[9] As expected, the sectors with the largest declines in output witnessed the greatest decreases in employment. The number of people employed in agriculture and forestry decreased by two-thirds between 1990 and 1995. During the same time period, construction employment dropped by 46%, and employment in transport and telecommunications fell by 24%. However, employment in real estate services (assisting businesses) and in financial services showed moderate gains through 1995.

The state sector, including state administration, social security, education, health and welfare care and a variety of social and personal services initially witnessed little change in the number of its employees. However, total employment in this sector gradually increased during the early-to-mid 1990s, rising in 1995 to almost 1.1 million people, or approximately 27% of the employment in the national economy. Full-time employees in this sector in 1996 amount to approximately 33% of the total of full-time employees. Clearly the relatively large proportion of employees working for the state imposed a substantial burden on the government budget. Yet the government for political and/or social reasons has been unwilling or unable to reduce their payroll. The path to transition taken by Hungary is one of gradualism (as opposed to the 'shock therapy' method used by Poland, for example) and it is expected that the state sector will be reduced only gradually.

Until 1992, the unemployment rate remained under 2% "...reflecting an understandable lack of political will to restructure large firms, harden

---

[8] *Annual Report*, National Bank of Hungary, 1996, p. 198.
[9] *Op. Cit.*, GKI Economic Research Co., pp. 11-12.

budget constraints, and accept the bankruptcy of non-viable concerns."[10] The significant decrease in employment that occurred after 1992 due to significant economic restructuring did not cause substantial social upheaval. A generous unemployment benefit system helped defray the costs of being unemployed and many employees took early retirement. These activities were funded both by the employer and employee, as well as partially through the government budget. The state also funded an active re-training program in an effort to reduce unemployment.

As the output for the economy and the demand for goods and services increased in 1995, the level of unemployment decreased. This reduction also coincided with a tightening of unemployment benefits that was expected to encourage employment. The term of the benefits was gradually reduced from two years to one year and one had to be employed for at least four years in order to receive benefits for one year (if employed for one year, benefits could be received for three months). If one's benefits were exhausted, any additional disbursements were linked to employment. If no employment could be procured and the benefits were exhausted, the individual would no longer be counted as part of the registered unemployed.

Table 5.2   Labor Force Divisions, 1990-1996, Percent of Labor Force

Use of the Labor Force	1990	1991	1992	1993	1994	1995	1996
Persons Employed	84.9	82.4	83.3	69.0	65.9	64.7	63.9
Registered Unemployed	0.4	1.6	6.4	10.5	10.1	8.3	8.0
Economically Active Popn.	85.3	84.0	81.7	79.5	76.0	73.0	71.9
People Working Abroad	0.1	0.2	0.5	0.4	0.4	0.4	0.4
Inactive Population In Working Age	14.6	15.8	17.8	20.1	23.6	26.6	27.7
Of Which: Students	7.5	8.1	8.6	9.0	9.2	9.4	9.7
Pensioners	3.9	4.4	5.4	5.8	5.9	6.2	6.5

Source: *Annual Report* of the National Bank of Hungary, 1996, p. 195.

Counting the registered unemployed may give a distorted view of the actual joblessness in the economy. As indicated in Table 5.2, the percentage of the total labor force that was employed declined from 1990

---

[10] Newbery, David. "The Safety Net During Transformation: Hungary" in *The Emergence of Market Economies in Eastern Europe*, edited by Christopher Clague and Gordon C. Rausser, (Blackwell Publishing Co., Cambridge: 1992): p. 206.

to 1996. As expected in 1993, when the number of employed persons decreased, there was an increase in the registered unemployed. It is worthy of note, however, that as the percentage of employed people declined in 1995 and 1996, the percentage of registered unemployed also declined and the percentage of inactive people in the working age increased. Furthermore, the totals for students, pensioners and the registered unemployed[11] did not make up the total of inactive people in the working age, suggesting some hidden unemployment that may have been as much as 2.7% higher than reported unemployment numbers in 1995 and 3.5% higher in 1996. Early retirement may account for some of the discrepancy with at least part of the rest made up of those individuals whose benefits had run out and who were no longer counted in the total of registered unemployed.

While some unemployment may be attributed to the lack of the economy's ability to expand sufficiently and increase employment, the structural nature of unemployment also has been a significant contributor to this problem. For example, the on-going privatization process inevitably has thrown some individuals out of work across all of the regions in Hungary. This problem is magnified in rural areas and particularly in counties in the north and east that may not have sufficient resources or the connections to international business and information that is so necessary to the revitalization of the economy.

Privatization Issues

Reform communists as early as 1968 began a slow movement away from the strict system of central planning and actively pursued privatization initiatives, unlike the governments of many of its neighbors in Central and Eastern Europe. The Law on Enterprise Councils, passed in 1984, was one of the first pieces of legislation in Hungary that allowed the transfer of some of the functions of state-owned enterprises to enterprise councils that were controlled by the management of the firms.[12] As a result, Hungary

---

[11] There clearly may be some overlap of the data here. For example, students and/or pensioners may be counted as 'inactive' and may be 'registered unemployed'. To the extent that this occurs, the numbers for actual joblessness will be higher than indicated.

[12] Fletcher, C. Edward. *Privatization and the Rebirth of Capital Markets in Hungary*, (McFarland & Co.., North Carolina; 1995): p. 32.

had a head start on other countries in 1989 with regard to privatization since the state's share of value added in commercial and industrial operations was a smaller percentage (65.2%) in 1984 than that of neighboring countries.[13] Still, the state controlled over 90% of the means of production at the beginning of the transition.[14] Hungary's full-scale privatization efforts did not begin until after 1989 and this country, like many others, encountered problems along the way and progress was delayed intermittently.

By 1989, legislation was in place that paved the way for the orderly transfer of state-owned assets to the private sector.[15] So-called 'spontaneous' privatizations occurred quite frequently in Hungary. "Between 1987 and 1990, approximately 150 state-owned companies, representing approximately 8 percent of all such companies, spontaneously privatized themselves," and "[i]n 1990 alone, there were 230 instances of spontaneous privatization..."[16] Such privatizations were usually initiated by the firm's managers, though outsiders could also initiate a privatization project. The key to such deals was to acquire sufficient additional capital for the firm, whether from the managers themselves or from outside sources (not government sources). Foreign capital investors were greatly encouraged to participate. Such arrangements initially resulted in questionable 'sweetheart' deals and negative public reaction slowed the process. This negativism was short-circuited by the establishment in March, 1990, of the State Property Agency (SPA) that would oversee the process and instill integrity into the system by implementing regulations and by approving or vetoing proposals.

While some of the same methods have been used in other countries, one major difference in Hungary's process is that it did not use mass privatization. There were virtually no free transfers of state properties and there was no mass coupon privatization program.

The basic principles behind the privatization program included (1) mandating that the state's assets were to be sold, not given away, (2)

---

[13] By comparison, the state's share of commercial and industrial operations amounted to 97% in Czechoslovakia in 1986 and 81.7% in Poland in 1985. See Fischer (1992), pp. 229-230.

[14] *Op. Cit.,* Fletcher, p. 36.

[15] Three pieces of legislation were important for privatization: The Law on Enterprise Councils in 1984, The Act on Associations in 1988 and the Transformation Law in 1989.

[16] *Op. Cit.,* Fletcher, p. 47 and p. 51, respectively.

establishing 'fair prices' for the firms and the firms' assets, and (3) creating incentives for the purchases by both domestic and foreign investors.

The SPA executed five separate privatization programs between September, 1990 and October, 1991:[17]

- The first program was the so-called sale of the crown jewels, large enterprises that were fairly large and that had reasonable expectations regarding future profits.
- The second program involved the sale of 'shell' companies, companies whose goods assets had been 'stripped' during the Pre-SPA time of spontaneous privatization. This program aimed to sell the remaining assets (effectively liquidating the firm) and to investigate the distribution of the goods assets .
- The third privatization program was specifically designed to privatize the construction industry, an essential industry for rebuilding the economic base for the country.
- Likewise, the wine industry was targeted in the fourth program. Hungarian wines are among the world's best and officials did not want this industry to falter.
- The last program was aimed toward the privatization of small retail shops and restaurants.

By early 1992, other programs were initiated in an effort to speed up the privatization process. These programs included:

- Investor-Initiated Privatization. With notable exclusions,[18] the policy of the SPA was changed so that it was possible for any company to be acquired from the state. Potential owners could be anyone, including present managers and/or employees.
- The Asset Management Program. In this option, potential investors could opt simply to 'manage' state assets, rather than 'own' them.
- Self-Privatization Program. This program was an attempt to decentralize the privatization process after complaints that the SPA had been slowing the process needlessly.
- Privatization Through Liquidation. There were both formal and informal methods of liquidation. The government could formally liquidate a company or, informally, the existing firms could sell their

---

[17] See Fletcher (1995), pp. 54-69 for details of these and the following privatization programs.
[18] *Ibid.*, p. 71.

current assets in order to meet their financial obligations, effectively liquidating it.

- Asset Leasing Program. Various companies could be leased through the SPA by the highest bidder. The hope was that the leaseholder would eventually buy the company.

In addition to these programs, there were other initiatives that attempted to keep the ownership of the assets in Hungarian hands, such as preferential loans to domestic bidders and simply favoring domestic investors over foreign investors for non-price reasons.

Hungary's initial success in privatizing large enterprises involved a total of ten large-scale companies that had been privatized by the end of March, 1991, for a value of nearly $100 million, between 50 and 70 spontaneous privatizations valued at approximately $300 million and outright sales of 41 other firms valued at approximately $200 million.[19] The privatization process continued to move forward. However, the introduction of the 'simplified privatization program' in 1995, which was designed to speed up the privatization process, suggests that the earlier programs were not as successful as expected. In fact, "[m]ore than 50 percent of the proceeds of privatization was collected in the period of 1995-1996."[20] The 1995 program was continued into 1996 and 1997, generating revenues of HUF 5.2 billion in 1996 alone. By the end of 1996, the state still had majority ownership in 245 companies and held a minority share in 262 firms. The assets under direct state management were valued at about HUF 1 trillion in 1996, of which about one-fourth was expected to be privatized in 1997-1998.[21]

One of the difficulties in the privatization process was finding individuals and/or firms that had access to the relatively large amounts of capital that were necessary in order to become the new owners. Individuals with sufficient savings could have come forward, but the knowledge and information they needed for such an undertaking were

---

[19] Thomas, Scott. "Political Economy of Privatization: Poland, Hungary and Czechoslovakia" in *The Emergence of Market Economies in Eastern Europe*, edited by Christopher Clague and Gordon C. Rausser, (Blackwell, Cambridge, MA, 1992): p. 286.

[20] *Annual Report*, National Bank of Hungary, 1996, p. 41.

[21] The numbers in this paragraph were obtained from the *Annual Report*, National Bank of Hungary, 1996, pp. 41-42.

limited.[22]   The pooling of funds was not possible until 1992 and the banking system itself was undergoing significant changes in the early stages of the privatization process and was not a ready source of funds to the private sector. Searching for buyers, the government in the late 1980s encouraged foreign investors to own part or all of the companies that were for sale. Foreign investors initially were very interested in the Hungarian firms that were the most attractive. By 1992, however, the remaining firms owned by the state were losing almost $72.3 million in value every month[23] and were not attractive to investors generally. Foreign investors, in particular, preferred to supply capital for start-up companies and to avoid the problems associated with existing firms. As a result, the foreign direct investment proportion of subscribed capital in new firms was 60.9% in 1992, 70.1% in 1993, 75.6% in 1994, 77.7% in 1995 and 75.6% in 1996.   Overall, the number of firms with some foreign ownership was 5,693 in 1990, increasing to approximately 24,950 in 1995. The share of foreign ownership in such firms increased as well, from 34.2% in 1990 to about 66.3% in 1995.[24]

Summary and Conclusions

In its transition from a command economy to a market system, Hungary faced the macroeconomic problems of inflation and unemployment, the issues regarding government and foreign indebtedness and the privatization of state-owned assets, issues that were typical of other Central and Eastern European countries in transition. Hungary rose to the challenge on all fronts. Significant structural changes occurred, prices were liberalized, government subsidies were curtailed and privatization programs were initiated. It setup the convertibility of the currency and established an exchange rate regime. While much progress has been made, the serious problems of high inflation and high unemployment remain. These, together with the government budget deficit, will need to be addressed more aggressively as Hungary positions itself to join the European Union in the near future.

---

[22] By some estimates, the amount of domestic savings could purchase only about 10% of the state assets in the early 1990s. See Fletcher, pp. 161-162.

[23] *Ibid.,* p. 107.

[24] *Annual Report*, National Bank of Hungary, 1996, p. 194.

References

"Analysis of the Performance of the Hungarian Economy and of the Convergence Criteria Between 1990 and 1995," [1996]. Part 1, GKI Economic Research Co., mimeograph.

Annual Report, National Bank of Hungary [1996].

Fischer, Stanley [1992] "Privatization in East European Transformation," in *The Emergence of Market Economies in Eastern Europe*, edited by Christopher Clague and Gordon C. Rausser, (Blackwell, Cambridge, MA).

Fletcher, C. Edward [1995]. *Privatization and the Rebirth of Capital Markets in Hungary*, (McFarland & Co., North Carolina).

Newbery, David [1992]. "The Safety Net During Transformation: Hungary" in *The Emergence of Market Economies in Eastern Europe*, edited by Christopher Clague and Gordon C. Rausser, (Blackwell Publishing Co., Cambridge), 197-217.

Poland: International Economic Report, 1995/96 [1996]. World Economy Research Institute, Warsaw School of Economics, (Warsaw, Poland).

Thomas, Scott [1992]. "Political Economy of Privatization: Poland, Hungary and Czechoslovakia" in *The Emergence of Market Economies in Eastern Europe*, edited by Christopher Clague and Gordon C. Rausser, (Blackwell, Cambridge, MA), 279-295.

6 The Status and Prospects of the Hungarian Banking System

KATALIN BOTOS

Introduction

Recognition of the failures of the credit allocation mechanism of the centrally-planned Hungarian economy intensified in the early to mid-1980s and led to the establishment of a two-tiered banking system in the second half of the decade. This, along with political changes in 1990, led the way to further developments in the financial sector including the emergence of the Budapest Stock Exchange (BSE) and the Commodities Exchange (CE) in the 1990s. This paper reviews the transition of the Hungarian financial sector and the development of capital markets and exchanges.

Transition in Banking System

The Act on Financial Institutions (AFI), passed in 1991, outlined the main guidelines for the development of the Hungarian banking system. The AFI required that the fundamental norms of international banking regulation be met over a relatively short three-year period of adjustment. Following German and British models, existing banks in Hungary were to become universal banks with broker firms dealing in securities. The AFI also laid out the framework for the establishment of new banks and mandated that state ownership of existing banks be reduced over time.

In 1992, sector banks and individual banks, which were primarily state-owned, were unable to meet either the AFI's requirements or the privatization requirements of the government. Losses in the economy were reflected in the portfolios of banks and these losses could not be covered by income or, in some cases, even by bank capital. However, the loss of capital due to the provisioning requirements did not result in illiquidity (technical insolvency) in the larger banks because these banks experienced relative excess liquidity. This situation continued into 1993 as savings deposited in banks were directed toward inter-bank markets. Nevertheless, it was not possible to privatize banks that included uncovered losses amounting to as much as 20 percent of the portfolio. In 1993, many banks had to be consolidated, despite the government's significant efforts to gain healthy banks in 1992. After lengthy discussions concerning the methods of consolidation, it was concluded that a capital increase would be coupled with an increase in the State's ownership share. Thus, by maximizing ownership shares compared to the management and other owners, the State itself, as a direct owner, began to control the privatization process.

The decision to increase the State's ownership share involved the appearance of a new owner, the Ministry of Finance (MOF), with the government and other institutions in the background. Moreover, it created an almost incomprehensible system of ownership rights. The State Property Agency, the State Holding Company, the National Commission for Technology and Development along with the MOF acted as State owners. The consequences of this complex system of ownership included incomplete coordination of activities and lack of clarity with respect to the principles of asset management. The ultimate result was consolidation of ownership controlled by the MOF and based on contracts. Formally, the MOF, taking on the role of public administrator, entered into contracts with banks and remained the main owner in most cases.[1]

Although the MOF attempted to set up an ownership structure for itself with responsibilities typical of a Board of Directors, the system was flawed. In the early 1990s, there were few banking experts available. This problem was, in turn, exacerbated by the selection of personnel based on loyalty rather than expertise.

The bankruptcies and liquidations of small banks and savings cooperatives in 1992 found the government financially unprepared. However, in 1993 an up-to-date Banking Act was enacted and a deposit insurance system was developed. The National Deposit Insurance Fund (NDIF) benefited from the technical and financial assistance of the State Banking Supervision (SBS) as well as from support from government-provided international experts and consultants.

---

[1] The reality of this arrangement was that one of the departments of the MOF entered into contracts with other departments within the MOF.

In 1993 six new banks were established, reflecting the expansion of the entire banking sector. Joint venture banks (i.e., those owned by foreigners) increased their balance sheet total by almost two-thirds. Moreover, the former high adequacy ratio, which exceeded the required level by 3-4 times, decreased from 30 percent to 24 percent, reflecting the fact that foreign banks established during previous years had begun to experience business expansion. Another obvious sign of change in the banking sector was the beginning of retail banking by joint venture and large banks.

Also in 1993, the State Banking Supervision (SBS) focused on stability in the banking sector and on consolidation. Accepting that risks are included in the investment portfolio and off-balance sheet items of the banks and bringing forward regulatory amendments that would become effective by the end of the year, the government assessed capital requirements of banks on the basis of model calculations. It was decided that external liabilities of all the banks to be consolidated would be covered in the first phase of consolidation and that in the second phase required capital would be raised to 4 percent (May 1993).

Dealing with savings cooperatives represented (and still represents) a large portion of the activities of SBS. Although savings cooperatives are small financial institutions, they are very similar to other banks. Outdated skills and technical equipment, as well as the institutional features of cooperatives themselves, generated even more problems than the ones observed in commercial banks. The government was faced with the decision to liquidate this type of financial institution or to provide assistance for the development of an integrated cooperative network. On the basis of Central European examples, specifically the Raiffeisen Bank Group, the SBS suggested that savings cooperatives should voluntarily clarify their individual relationship with their top bank, Takarekbank, and, with the government's assistance, a protective fund would be created.[2]

The National Savings Cooperatives' Institutions Protection Fund, OTIVA, was established in 1993. Over time, OTIVA has made considerable progress in the area of cooperative thinking and in prevention. The creation of OTIVA, however, did not reduce the institutional and legal responsibility of SBS for the prudent operation of savings cooperatives.

---

[2] Hungarian Savings Cooperative Bank Ltd., a mutual subsidiary bank.

While the previous two years witnessed the integration of savings cooperatives, amendments to the law with respect to bank bankruptcies, and consolidations, 1994 is best characterized as the beginning of privatization. In this year, one of the most important Hungarian banks was privatized and by the end of the year the process of consolidation brought almost all of the banking sector to privatizable status. Unfortunately, since the Hungarian capital market was not developed and the number of domestic investors was relatively low, most of the investors were foreigners. Thus, the ratio of foreign owners in the Hungarian bank market increased above the usual European average.

Although not completed until 1996, a complex revision of the Banking Act was begun in 1994. The Act was modified according to the directives of the European Union and took an initial step toward universality by allowing banks to participate in stock exchange transactions in government securities and close-end issuance. Another important aspect of the Act was the creation of the Hungarian Money and Capital Supervision (HMCS) responsible for the supervision of money and capital markets.

As shown in Table 6.1, by the end of 1995, forty-two financial institutions were in operation in Hungary. Several applications for banking licenses were submitted in 1995 and three new financial institutions with foreign ownership (Deutsche Bank, Rabobank, and Opel Bank, a specialized financial institution) began operations in 1996. Two banks merged with another bank, and two small, state-owned banks were quietly closed, bringing the number of existing banks to 41 in 1996.

Table 6.1 Number of Financial Institutions

	1989	1990	1991	1992	1993	1994	1995
Commercial Banks	22	28	29	30	34	35	34
Specialized Financial Institutions	4	4	6	5	5	7	7
Investments Banks					1	1	1
Banks, Total	26	32	35	35	40	43	42
Savings Cooperatives	260	260	260	257	255	254	248
Credit Cooperatives						4	4
Savings Institutions, Total	260	260	260	257	255	258	252

Source: Annual Report, National Bank of Hungary, 1995-1996.

Structure of the Banking System

With respect to the composition of the banking system in terms of size and majority ownership, large banks with a majority of state ownership lost market share between 1994 and 1995 and small- and medium-size private banks moved in to benefit. The market share of small- and medium-size state-controlled banks remained essentially unchanged while large private banks increased their market share only slightly. The share of savings cooperatives within the banking system did not change significantly between 1994 and 1995.

Medium-size and large banks with foreign ownership had already begun to create competitive pressure and in 1995 this process gained new momentum when corporations showed a preference for foreign borrowing. This allowed the market participants with comparative advantages in foreign currency financing to expand their business activities substantially.

Table 6.2 Number of Banks, By Size and Major Owner

	1989	1990	1991	1992	1993	1994	1995
Large Banks	5	5	6	6	7	7	7
--State Banks	5	5	5	5	5	4	2
--Private Banks	0	0	1	1	2	3	5
Medium-size Banks	4	5	9	8	8	11	12
--State Banks	0	0	0	0	3	3	5
--Private Banks	4	5	9	8	5	8	7
Small Banks	17	22	20	21	25	25	23
--State Banks	3	4	5	5	9	11	9
--Private Banks	14	18	15	16	16	14	14
Total	26	32	35	35	40	43	42
--State Banks	8	9	10	10	17	18	16
--Private Banks	18	23	25	25	23	25	26

Source: Annual Report, National Bank of Hungary, 1995-1996.

The degree of concentration in the banking sector declined in 1996. The combined market share of the largest five banks decreased from 64 percent at the end of 1995 to 60 percent by the end of 1996. In comparison with smaller EU countries, the degree of concentration in the Hungarian banking sector is no longer considered high. The market share of the largest resident bank is below 30 percent (the same as the market share of the largest banks in Finland, Denmark, and the Netherlands) and that of the three largest is 45 percent (compared to more 70 percent in Finland, Denmark, and the Netherlands).

The ownership structure of the banking system changed radically in 1995, as shown in Table 6.2. In contrast with previous years, privatization accelerated with the sale of the majority stake in the Hungarian Foreign Trade Bank in late 1994 and the partial privatization of two additional large banks, OTP and Budapest Bank in 1995. The new owner, APV Rt., acting on behalf of the state, retained 25 percent plus one vote in OTP and sold the remaining shares to foreign institutional investors (23 percent), the Social Security authorities (20 percent), employees (5 percent), and others. Foreign (strategic) investors acquired 64 percent of the shares of Budapest Bank and there was a significant increase in capital in Postabank.

Besides the move to privatize and increase capital, the reduction of registered capital in most of the banks participating in the consolidation program contributed to lowering direct state ownership below 40 percent by the end of 1995 and to increasing the ratio of foreign ownership above 35 percent. Using shareholders' equity rather than registered capital as a basis for comparison, the ratio of shareholders' equity in state-owned banks was approximately 25 percent at the end of 1995.

Table 6.3 Ownership Structure of Banks

	1994		1995	
	Ft bns	%	Ft bns	%
Direct State Ownership	193.3	65.95	86.7	39.44
Social Security Funds	206.0	0.89	8.3	3.78
State Ownership, Total	195.9	66.84	95.0	43.22
Local Authorities	0.6	0.20	2.0	0.91
Other Domestic Ownership	52.3	17.84	44.6	20.29
Domestic Ownership, Total	248.8	84.89	141.6	64.42
Foreign Ownership	44.3	15.11	78.2	35.58
Registered Capital, Total	293.1	100.00	219.8	100.00

Source: Annual Report, National Bank of Hungary, 1995-1996.

The radical structural transformation and the integration of the Hungarian banking sector into the international financial community is evidenced by the fact that by the end of 1995, there were 19 commercial banks and specialized financial institutions among the banks fully held by non-resident financial institutions (i.e., professional investors of financial holdings or groups of companies). Moreover, it should be noted that in four cases, non-resident professional investors have holdings that constitute a majority and controlling position required for actual ownership control (See Table 6.3).

Table 6.4 Balance Sheet Total of Banks, by Size and Controlling Majority

	Balance Sheet Total, Ft. bns.			Distribution %		
	1994	1995	1996	1994	1995	1996
Large Banks	2,234.7	2,518.7	2993.2	71.5	67.3	65.4
Of Which:						
Private Banks	1,494.7	1,805.4	2373.2	7.8	48.3	51.9
State Banks	740.0	713.3	620.0	3.7	19.1	13.6
Medium-Size Banks	494.3	695.2	877.6	5.8	18.6	19.2
Of Which:						
Private Banks	145.8	228.9	384.9	4.7	6.1	8.4
Small Banks	95.3	114.9	100.1	3.0	3.1	2.2
Banking System, Total	2,970.1	3,557.6	4353.7	95.0	95.1	95.2
Cooperative Financial Institutions	156.0	182.4	218.8	5.0	4.9	4.8
Financial System, Total	3,126.1	3,740.0	4574.5	100	100	100

Source: Annual Report, National Bank of Hungary, 1995-1996.

The banking system continued to stabilize in 1995. Capital adequacy and profitability of the majority of participants improved and the liquidity position of the system as a whole strengthened. Nevertheless, writing off losses against registered capital was a major challenge. Banks increased the speed of writing off bad loans and non-profitable investments against existing reserves. Consolidated state-owned banks embarked on internal rationalization projects required by efficient banking operations and several began to reduce staff levels. However, no actual reduction in costs was expected as some of the cost-cutting measures themselves initially created additional expenses.

Due to changes in their liabilities, financial institutions focused more heavily on high quality service in the retail part of their business and in the management of accounts in 1995. In order to offer improved banking access to large corporate customers, several banks, including joint ventures and large banks, installed computer terminals for direct electronic banking. Typically, banks would supply credit to their most active clients, collecting deposits through a widened customer base and opening services to households. With respect to the latter, joint venture banks followed suit by offering a variety of transactions to their retail customers and by giving priority to services tailored to high-income groups. Most banks that were seeking to diversify their liabilities would increase significantly the issuance of bank securities offered to retail customers. Borrowing from foreign sources was another important factor in the expansion of bank liabilities in 1995.

The consolidated balance sheet total of financial institutions increased by 19.6% in 1995. Nevertheless, as shown in Table 6.4, the increase in banking sector operations fell short of real GDP growth. This relationship has not changed since 1991 and may be fundamentally attributed to modifications in corporate borrowing strategies developed as a result of privatization efforts. More funds were raised directly from parent companies and foreign entities and tighter financial discipline was applied as a result of the wave of bankruptcies and liquidations procedures. Savings outside the banking system and government securities issued to finance the budget directly also gained ground. In 1995, some new factors complemented these longer-term developments, including the stronger role of self-financing due to improved corporate earnings and steps taken to restructure balance sheets in order to complete the consolidation process. In 1996, the combined balance sheet total of the financial institutions, including both banking and savings cooperatives, increased faster than real GDP with a real growth rate of 3 percent.[3]

Banking system liabilities with maturities greater than one year increased by 3 percent between 1994 and 1995 while the expansion of shorter-term liabilities increased by 22.2 percent. In 1994 the proportion of liabilities maturing over one year to total liabilities was 22.5 percent. In

---

[3] Deflated by December/December consumer price index. In the period 1991-1995, the share of the balance sheet total of the banking sector in GDP declined continually from 91 percent to 70.5 percent.

1995 this ratio declined to 19.4 percent and it reached 14.9 percent in 1996.

The rise in the own funds of the banking system from HUF 306 billion in 1994 to HUF 356.7 billion in 1995 and HUF 458.2 billion in 1996 was substantially higher than the average increase in liabilities. The growth of income statement profit of HUF 30 billion and in subordinated capital of HUF 18.7 billion was responsible for most of the increase in 1995. The consolidated registered capital of the banking system decreased by 15.3 percent which, coupled with a reduction in operating losses, indicated that several banks increased registered capital while those included in the consolidation program reduced it.

With regard to external funds, the household sector remained the most important source in 1995. Households as ultimate savers continued to increase their share in financing the banking system though most of the savings were short-term, representing 25.41 percent of short-term liabilities in 1994 and 27.1 percent in 1995. This share was essentially unchanged in 1996. Retail deposits with maturities over one year remained practically unchanged in 1995 and 1996, while the volume of deposits fixed for less than one year grew by HUF 218 billion or 27 percent. In this category, most of the increase came from the high growth rate (49 percent) of the stock of foreign currency deposits, which surpassed the rate of devaluation (29.865).

The major element of growth within corporate deposits was the stock of foreign currency deposits. Approximately HUF 76 billion of the total liability expansion of HUF 100.1 billion came from the increase in foreign currency deposits. Representing a minor amount, corporate deposits with maturities in excess of one year increased by 45 percent (HUF 10.9 billion), while deposits fixed for less than one year grew by 17.9 percent during the year.

At HUF 144 billion, foreign funds raised showed the most dynamic growth among the liabilities of the banking system. The high increase was motivated by both foreign funds being less expensive than domestic and the foreign exchange risk becoming easier to calculate. Foreign liabilities with maturities over one year grew by 66 percent, representing 36.4 percent adjusted for devaluation, while those maturing within one year increased by 44.6 percent or 15.0 percent adjusted for devaluation.

Due to improved liquidity positions, banks were able to reduce the stock of short-term refinancing credit on their balance sheets from HUF 45 billion to HUF 9.4 billion. Although the balances of these loans fluctuated widely, the trend was clear. In accordance with the intentions of the central bank, the stock of long-term refinancing credit continued to fall in 1995, which primarily came as a consequence of the central bank canceling the foreign currency deposit swap facility. Thus, the stock of refinancing credit maturing over one year fell by 18 percent or HUF 66 billion. The HUF funds of long-term financing credit decreased further in 1996, from HUF 206.3 billion in 1995 to HUF 146.0 billion.

Developments in lending by financial institutions mirrored those in liabilities in 1995, as the funds allocated for under a year increased at a substantially slower rate of 3.8 percent (HUF 65 billion) than did total assets, while short-term lending showed dynamic growth of 3.6 percent (HUF 413 billion).

Increased participation in the short-term financing of the central budget in 1995 represented the most marked change in the asset side activities of banks, reflected by a rise of HUF 55 billion or 65.7 percent. The explanation for this phenomenon lies partially with the PSBR (public sector borrowing requirements) generating a high level of interest rates in the government securities market. In contrast, the increase in long-term loans extended to the government sector was marginal, reaching about 3.5 percent or HUF 21.9 billion. Thus, a moderate level of growth resulted from the composite effect of these two opposing forces.

Another important change on the asset side of the balance sheet of the banking system was the increase in deposits held at the central bank for less than one year. These grew by 66 percent (HUF 209 billion) in 1995, with foreign currency deposits as the major growth category (HUF 160 billion or 51.6 percent). The long-term assets held at the central bank increased at the much slower rate of 8.5 percent. Repeated increases in reserve requirements and the expansion of liabilities were responsible for approximately HUF 70 billion of the expansion in the settlement accounts of banks.

Bank lending to households continued to decrease in 1995 following the tendency observed in previous years. Insignificant in absolute terms, the loans extended to the retail sector for less than one year fell by 4.3 percent to HUF 17.1 billion, while there was a larger decline of 7.6 percent (HUF 19.5 billion) in loans with maturities in excess of one year. The closing balance of these loans stood at HUF 236 billion at the end of 1995. This tendency strengthened in 1996; household sector loans were reduced to HUF 172 billion from 6.1 percent of all assets in 1995 to 4.0 percent in

1996. This decline was primarily a result of unfavorable terms on construction (housing) loans.

Bank lending to the corporate sector also grew at a substantially slower rate, compared to average lending, of approximately 8-9 percent. This rate included a decrease of approximately 5 percent in loans denominated in forints and a rise in foreign currency loans by 2.5 times. These movements reflected the changes in the structure of bank liabilities. Of similar significance was portfolio cleansing that focused mainly on loans extended in forints during the year. As foreign exchange risk became easier to calculate, enterprises enjoyed more favorable terms in foreign exchange borrowing. Actual corporate sector borrowing was higher in 1995 because enterprises borrowed more funds directly from foreign entities. In 1996 some efforts were made to expand activities in this field; thus, on average, enterprise sector lending grew 28.5 percent while total assets increased by 23.3 percent.

Table 6.5 Qualified Loans of the Banking System

Classification	December 31, 1994		December 31, 1995		December 31, 1996	
	Ft bns	%	Ft bns	%	Ft bns	%
1. Problem Free	1,854.5	78.0	2,129.7	83.4	3,280.6	89.0
2. a) Needing Special Attention	185.5	7.8	186.0	7.3	218.7	5.9
b) Substandard	50.9	2.1	43.5	1.7	36.2	1.0
c) Doubtful	84.8	3.6	61.6	2.4	46.8	1.3
d) Bad	202.9	8.5	133.1	5.2	105.4	2.9
Qualified Loans (a + b + c + d)	524.1	22.0	424.2	16.6	407.1	11.0
Total (1 + 2)	2,378.6	100.0	2,553.9	100.0	3,687.7	100.0
Qualified/Total Loans		22.0		16.6		
(Doubtful + Bad)/ Total Loans		12.1		7.6		4.1
Provisions for Loans	229.1		159.6		132.0	

Source: Annual Report, National Bank of Hungary, 1995-1996.

Total lending by the banking system (claims as well as off-balance sheet contingencies) stood at HUF 2,554 billion on December 31, 1995, representing an increase of 7.4 percent (HUF 175 billion) over the closing balance of 1994. The stock of qualified loans in the banking system dropped from HUF 524 billion at the end of 1994 to HUF 424 billion at the end of 1995. The reduction in the ratio of qualified loans to total lending, from 26.3 percent in 1993 to 16.6 percent in 1995, represented a definite portfolio improvement.

Substandard, doubtful and bad loans included under qualified loans decreased by more than 40 percent between 1994 and 1996 while loans needing special attention increased by some 347.7 percent. Portfolio cleansing was the main factor responsible for the decrease in the stock of qualified loans that led to the selling of HUF 93 billion worth of principle and interest claims. The majority of claims was sold to subsidiaries. Considering also the portfolio cleansing measures in 1994, a total of about HUF 250 billion worth of principal and interest claims has been removed from the assets of financial institutions over the 1994-1996 period.

The ratio of provisions to total qualified loans decreased from 43.7 percent in 1994 to 37.5 percent in 1995. Banks accumulated provisions to cover the loans grouped in the various categories of qualified lending in line with provisions by the SBS that specified a band for the rate of provisions for each category (0-10 percent for those needing special attention, 11-30 percent for substandard, 31-70 percent for doubtful, and 71-100 percent for bad loans). In 1996, the provisions continued to decline and the quality of the portfolio improved. Qualified loans made up only 11 percent of the total loan portfolio, compared to 22 percent in 1994.

After-tax profit in the banking system stood at HUF 36.9 billion at the end of 1995. In contrast to 1994, when thirteen financial institutions reported year-end losses, there were "only" eight loss-making banks in 1995. However, in absolute terms, 1995 losses were more than double those in 1994. In contrast to previous years, the profits of the banking system were increased by (1) higher interest income, and (2) a reduced need to generate reserves. The increase of interest income by 24.1 percent from 1994 to 1995 originated from the expansion of business activities by about 20 percent in the banking system and in the widening of the interest rate margin. However, 1995 brought a turning point in the ratio of interest income to the balance sheet total of different groups of banks. In 1994, state-owned banks recorded a higher ratio, while private banks claimed the same in 1995.

The extremely high proportion of reserves accumulation required by poor portfolios reduced the profitability of the banking system prior to

1995. However, in 1995 reserve accumulation fell to 1.7 percent of the balance sheet total.[4]

The factors reducing profits included (1) lower earnings from other banking operations (commissions, trading in securities and foreign currency, etc.), (2) higher increase in operating costs than in gross operating profits, and (3) deterioration in the balance of other income and expenses, which was primarily due to higher lending losses incurred by selling claims and writing off bad loans.

Expressed in terms of their proportion to the balance sheet total, the income from commissions and the trade of securities and foreign currency declined. Net commission income grew by a mere 7.3 percent, a rate that fell short of both the rate of inflation and the increase in cash flow. Some banks suffered significant exchange rate losses due to the costs of raising funds, and as a result, securities trading created losses across the whole banking system.

The operating costs of the banking system increased at a slightly lower rate (26.1 percent) than inflation. Despite the on-going favorable developments, the increase in operating costs was higher than the rise in the profit of core operations, which led to a slight deterioration of cost efficiency in the banking system.

The banking system continued to cleanse its portfolio, a development that was begun in 1994. In contrast with the positive effect in 1994, these measures had an adverse effect on the results in 1995. Financial institutions released and used a smaller proportion of their reserves than in 1994 and the amount of lending losses charged to the accounts increased. As far as the profitability of the sector in 1996 is concerned, the after-tax profits of the banking sector amounted to HUF 63 billion (preliminary data) in 1996, 61.4 percent higher than in 1995. Four banks closed in 1996 with a loss totaling HUF 1.7 billion. In spite of stagnant interest income, positions improved considerably. Primarily because of the declining level of provisioning, return on equity approached the rate of inflation.

Despite expanding business activity, interest income rose by no more than 3.8 percent. This was to a large extent attributable to the amendment of accounting regulations, as a result of which banks were no longer permitted to charge outstanding overdue interest to income as in earlier years. On the revenue side, changes in the development of interest income were determined by the price competition evolving in the corporate market

---

[4] In 1993 this ratio was about 8 percent.

and on the expenditure side by the intensive fight for household clients in 1996.

Development of Capital Markets and Exchanges

After the closure of the Budapest Stock and Commercial Exchange in 1948, no stock market operated in Hungary until the early 1980s when the first bonds appeared. The market for these bonds developed relatively quickly and this informal "bond market" can be considered the root of the new stock market in Budapest.

Table 6.6 Volume of Trading at the BSE[a]

	1990	1991	1992	1993	1994	1995	1996
Spot Trading at Market Price[b]	6.1	10.1	33.7	185.7	211.2	253.2	1,145.4
Of Which:							
-Shares	6.1	9.8	6.0	18.3	57.1	87.3	490.5
-Govt Bonds	-	0.3	12.4	73.4	53.9	77.2	418.2
-Treas. Bills	-	-	15.1	85.0	81.2	81.1	206.3
-Corp. Bonds	-	0.0	0.0	0.0	0.0	0.0	0.6
-Invest. Units	-	-	0.0	0.1	0.3	3.4	8.9
-Compensation Bonds	-	-	0.2	9.0	18.7	4.2	20.9
Number of Transactions[c]	4.96	14.51	8.57	23.75	73.78	71.24	172.84
Avg. Daily No. Of Transactions	27	58	34	94	293	286	689
Avg. Daily Trading[d]	33.8	40.1	133.6	736.9	838.2	1,017	4,619
Turnover per Contract[d]	1.2	0.7	3.9	7.8	2.9	3.6	6.6
Number of Trading Days	181	252	252	252	252	249	248

[a]From June, 1990 through December, 1996; [b]HUF billions, double counting; [c]in thousands; [d]in HUF millions.
Source: Annual Report, National Bank of Hungary, 1996.

In 1990, the Parliament enacted laws to establish and regulate the Budapest Stock Exchange (BSE). With only one officially-registered offering, Ibusz, the BSE opened its doors on July 21, 1990. The success of trading in Ibusz led to the listing of other shares. By 1996 the number of listings on the Exchange reached forty-five. Along with equity shares, government paper, corporate bonds, investment funds, and compensation coupons are traded on the Exchange while derivative products are traded on both the BSE and the Budapest Commodity Exchange (BCE). These are discussed briefly below.

Almost all of the bonds traded on the BSE are government bonds and Treasury bills. When looking at the government paper market, it is evident that the market's trends are determined by macroeconomic conditions. In 1996, both the general government deficit and the level of public debt relative to GDP declined, savings increased and the rate of inflation and related expectations abated. Additionally, the reduction in the interest rate can be linked to the improvement in the country's risk rating. Also, in 1996, important institutional and market structural changes aimed at enhancing efficiency took place in the government paper market. Secondary market liquidity grew as a result of standardization of securities and a decrease in the number of papers in circulation. Moreover, auction became a regular method of issuing bonds. This was in line with the international tendencies replacing the less efficient technique of using consortia with auctions. In 1996 a primary dealer system in government paper was introduced. The main reason for setting up this system was the need to decentralize the secondary market which had previously been concentrated primarily in the hands of the NBH. This institutional change also aimed to improve efficiency and market transparency.

Corporate bonds, which may be placed between equity shares and government paper in terms of riskiness, were not traded substantially on the BSE until the mid-1990s and still represent only a small part of bond trading on the exchange. The low level of corporate bond trading can be attributed to lack of public confidence resulting from recent bankruptcies of firms that issued such bonds.

In 1991, the Act of Investment Funds was created by the Parliament. The idea behind the Act was to make it possible to collect the small private investor's money into funds that could efficiently invest their money. The law defined two types of funds, stock and real estate. While the law authorized open-end funds in real estate, those that are currently active are closed-end. At present, stock funds are the most popular. The total value of institutional investment in funds reached HUF 360 billion in 1996.

Introduced to the stock market in 1991, the compensation coupon is a Hungarian specialty. The compensation coupon continues to be considered a "temporary security" since they were offered only once and are expected to drop out of trading eventually. Thus far, however, there are no signs of their disappearance. Because of the coupon-to-equity swaps, both the turnover and the price of the compensation coupon has increased considerably.

Table 6.7 Stock Exchange Capitalization at the BSE*

	1990	1991	1992	1993	1994	1995	1996
Shares	16.4	38.2	47.2	81.7	181.5	327.8	852.5
Govt. Bonds	-	15.3	82.3	241.7	392.9	454.0	703.4
Corporate Bonds	-	0.1	0.1	0.3	1.8	1.7	1.3
Treasury Bills	-	-	54.4	74.0	239.6	376.3	697.2
Investment Units	-	-	1.9	5.5	19.3	42.8	43.6
Compensation Coupons	-	-	16.0	53.8	48.7	18.7	95.0
Total	16.4	53.6	201.9	457.0	883.8	1,221.3	2.392.9

* December, 1990, to December, 1996; double counting.
Source: Annual Report, National Bank of Hungary, 1996.

In 1995, trading of derivative products, including foreign exchange futures, Treasury bill futures, BUBOR (an interbank interest rate index) and BUX (the index of the BSE) futures, began on the BSE. A specialty of the Hungarian capital market, the foreign exchange futures started not on the BSE but on the Budapest Commodity Exchange (BCE). The BCE opened its market for foreign exchange futures by offering USD and DEM contracts in 1993. Contracts of 90-day interbank deposit rates and the JPY (Japanese Yen) contract were added as new money market instruments in 1994, and ECU contracts have been available since November 1995. (ECU futures became leaders on both futures exchanges in early 1996 because European "money" makes up 70 percent of the official basket of foreign currencies to which the forint is pegged.) The range of products traded in the financial sector of the BCE increased further in 1996 including futures in Italian lire, Pound sterling, and Swiss francs. Since the Fall of 1996, futures trading has also been possible in the BUBOR.

The futures market's turnover on the BSE lagged substantially behind that of the spot market. The turnover on the spot market amounted to HUF 572.72 billion, while that of the futures market was HUF 194.92 billion. The BUX is the most popular and its share of the market is 26.73 percent. Its participants are mainly small investors, adventurers who expect high yields, and domestic and foreign investors with larger portfolios. Presumably with the new legal requirements, the distribution of investors and, therefore, the characteristics of the market will change. Trading in options is not standardized yet, so trading is quite difficult and the liquidity of the market is very weak. The foreign currencies futures were administered mostly through the futures forex section of the BCE out of the two Hungarian exchanges. Turnover realized on the BCE was 7.5 times the foreign currency turnover of the BSE. It can be expected, since there are signs in the legislature to do so, that the two exchanges will be merged in the future and that improved efficiency will result.

Trading in securities is shared by the BSE and the OTC markets at a rate of 51 percent to 49 percent. Ninety-eight percent of shares, 47 percent of government bonds, and 29 percent of Treasury bill are traded on the BSE.[5] In the past seven years, the stock exchange has improved immensely; however, the same cannot be said of the OTC market. It has no trading system, the connections are bilateral, there are no guarantees of fulfillment, activity of traders is almost chaotic, and the information flow is very poor. Because of these problems, there is a need to reform the OTC system and companies have been directed toward the stock exchange.

When the distribution of trading at the BSE is examined by the type of security, figures show a strengthening in the stock market. In 1995, shares accounted for 34 percent of trading and their proportion rose to 43 percent in 1996. The stock exchange capitalization of shares rose by 160 percent. Reasons for this include the unexceptional increase in stock market prices and the increases in the number of shares listed on the BSE.[6]

The best indicator of the growth in prices is the BUX index that rose by 170.4 percent (133.5 percent in terms of USD). Similar growth rates were registered only at the stock exchanges of St. Petersburg and Caracas. The BUX rose not only in nominal but also in real terms, as measured in 1996 dollars. A large portion of the rise in prices in 1996 countered the price

---

[5] In Hungary, the development of the securities market was concentrated on the stock exchange.

[6] In 1996, there were six introductions to and three withdrawals from the BSE.

increases of the past few years, which remained short of the rate of inflation and the rate of the value loss of the forint against the dollar. Price increases sped up particularly toward the end of the year. This rising trend in 1996 was not specific to Hungary. The CESI index representing all of the Central European stock markets (Czech Republic, Poland, Hungary, Slovakia, and Slovenia) grew by 54.3 percent. However, the Hungarian stock exchange index substantially exceeded the Central European average.

One of the reasons for the increase in share prices was the successful management on the part of companies listed on the stock exchange. Their profits improved during 1996. In addition to world market tendencies and the profits of the companies listed on the BSE, the Hungarian investments of foreigners also must be mentioned as the primary reason for the rising tendency of the BUX. International institutional investors tend to develop their investment policies for longer periods, taking into account the comparison of macroeconomic positions of the different countries and change in their credit ratings. Therefore, an improvement in credit ratings almost automatically results in an increase in the demand for the stock exchange papers of the given country. International competitiveness of the Hungarian market has been improved by the fact that KELER, the central depository, was rated an "acknowledged depository" according to US laws, so the risk rating of securities deposited with KELER improved further for foreign investors. Public offerings also contributed to the rise in prices at the BSE. Issuers priced and allocated their shares in the course of introductions to the stock exchange such that the market reached an equilibrium at a higher price over the long-term only.

Conclusions

This study has described the parallel evolution of the Hungarian banking and capital markets. After the political changes initiated in 1990, efforts were made to reestablish the stock exchange in Budapest and to create a modern legislative framework for the two-tier banking system that had begun to function in 1987. In retrospect, we can say that regulations, in harmony with international standards, attempted to introduce all of the directives of international organizations, including the EU. As a result of the continuous improvement of the Hungarian banking laws and capital market regulations, on January 1, 1997, there was a new act implemented on credit institutions and their financial undertakings and a new securities exchange law. A joint supervision of both areas controls the institutions and their operations in the Hungarian market.

Because of the lack of capital, professional skills, and management, not to mention the collapse of the COMECON, banks were in great need of consolidation and restructuring. It was one of the most important economic policy programs in the 1990s and it had widespread effects on the whole economy. Restructuring of the banking sector has enabled industry privatization. While privatization did not lead immediately to listing of shares on the BSE, beginning in 1995 trading in shares accelerated and by 1996 reached record levels.

References

Annual Report, [1993, 1994, 1995]. State Banking Supervision.

Annual Report, [1995, 1996]. National Bank of Hungary.

Annual Report, [1993]. South American Reserve Bank.

Botos, Katalin, [1996]. Elveszett Illúziók (Lost Illusions), Közgazdasági és Jogi Kiadó, Budapest, p. 285.

Balassa, Ákos, [1996]. "Restructuring and Recent Situation of the Hungarian Banking Sector," NBH Workshop Studies 4, p.103.

The Director's Book - The Role of a National Bank Director, [1987]. Office of the Comptroller of the Currency.

7 The Hungarian Monetary System

ERIKA VOROS

Introduction

The transition from a centrally-planned to a market-oriented economy requires fundamental changes in the financial systems. The main features of this process are the recovery of the role of money in the economic system and the creation of a two-tier banking system with a central bank as the monetary authority and a network of commercial banks. The two-tier system is a precondition for an independent monetary policy that would replace the previous regime of public financing in which the central bank accommodated the borrowing requirements of the government budget. This paper describes the metamorphosis of the National Bank of Hungary (NBH) and of monetary policy in the transition period.

After a brief introduction of the National Bank of Hungary, section two describes the institutional changes that took place including the growing independence of the central bank and briefly outlines the decision-making process. Section three explains the changes in the system of monetary targeting and instruments reflecting the financial development of the Hungarian economy since 1987. The clear commitment toward a market economy, the liberalization of markets and the improved economic performance in Hungary created a quickly developing financial system with obvious market-oriented characteristics and behavior. These changes made Hungary one of the most popular destinations of capital flows in Central and Eastern Europe. Section four outlines the importance of the convertibility of the Hungarian Forint while Section five contains a summary.

The Organization of the National Bank of Hungary

The National Bank of Hungary was established in 1924 as the first Hungarian central bank. It was the legal Hungarian successor of the former Austrian-Hungarian Bank.   After 1948 a strongly centralized banking system was developed.   By the end of the seventies,[1] the Hungarian financial system was based upon four banks and a network of savings cooperatives. As a consequence of the economic reforms of 1968, some small banks and joint venture banks began operations in the eighties, but they had no important effect on the financial system.   The two-tier banking system was reestablished in 1987, when the contradictions between a decentralized (and increasingly market-oriented) corporate sector and the strongly centralized (and underdeveloped) banking system became obvious and insupportable.   Some departments of the NBH, especially those dealing with corporate financing were separated into three new banks[2] on January 1, 1987.   Two previously existing banking institutions received commercial bank charters as well.   Appendix 1 outlines the main responsibilities of the NBH according to Act LX of 1991 (the Central Bank Act) on the NBH and its various amendments.

Legal Framework and Central Bank Independence

The NBH is a joint-stock company with its shares owned by the State. The State is represented by the Minister of Finance. The organization of the NBH includes the General Meeting, the Central Bank Council, the Board of Directors and the Supervisory Commission.

The latest amendment to Act LX of 1991 on the National Bank of Hungary came into force on January 1, 1997. This amendment redefined the relationship between the central bank and the government in order to strengthen the independence of the NBH. The Amendment to the Act prohibits direct financing of the government by the central bank. Government can only have an overdraft facility on its current account with the NBH.   The amount of this overdraft must not exceed 2% of the planned revenues of the central government. It may exist continuously at most for 15 days and must be reduced to zero by the end of the year. This Amendment, coupled with the Act CXXIV of 1996 on the budget of 1997 solved the problem of public debt items included in the NBH's balance

---

[1] The four banks were the NBH as the central bank, the National Savings Bank for retail banking, the Hungarian Foreign Trade Bank and the General Banking and Trust Co. Ltd. Besides these, there were a few specialized financial institutions.

[2] These were Budapest Bank, National Commercial and Credit Bank and Hungarian Credit Bank.

sheet.[3] Moreover, the Amendment to the Central Bank Act (a) altered the profit and loss accounting of the NBH, (b) adjusted the Act to accommodate recent changes regarding financial intermediation and legislation and (c) adjusted the rules of appointments and incompatibility.

Regarding the institutional independence of the central bank, the amendment included new regulations on the Central Bank Council, the appointment of deputy presidents and addressed the incompatibility regarding the Council and staff of the NBH. Formerly, any change in the monetary instruments was the responsibility of the Central Bank Council. The new amendment gives responsibility to the Council for only the significant changes set by the annual Monetary Policy Guidelines. According to the former system, the President of the NBH and at most five Deputy Presidents were appointed by the President of the Republic upon the nomination of the Prime Minister. The term of office of Deputy Presidents was three years and that of the President was 6 years. With the new amendment, the Deputy Presidents are nominated by the President of the NBH. After being accepted by the Prime Minister, the candidate is appointed by the President of the Republic. The Deputy Presidents are all appointed for six years. They participate in strategic decision making, are leaders of the Bank and are responsible for the activity of the departments subordinate to them.

It is important to note that all the operational monetary policy decisions are the exclusive responsibility of the President of the Bank in instances when it is not against the Monetary Policy Guidelines accepted by the Central Bank Council. Coupled with other changes, this amendment strengthened the independence of the National Bank of Hungary and that of monetary policy.

---

[3] Before 1991, the foreign exchange debt of the government was held among the liabilities of the NBH. The central bank borrowed from abroad in foreign exchange, then credited the whole amount to the government in HUF and took the risk of official HUF devaluation. The balance sheet of the NBH contained this devaluation loss as an unspecified-duration, interest-free debt of the government to the NBH. The government had started to securitize this debt stock in 1993 gradually, but official devaluations increased the stock further. The Act on Budget of 1997 replaced this debt stock with an equal amount of foreign-exchange-dominated loans with the same maturities and interest rates as that of the NBH's net foreign exchange debt. The short position of the NBH was closed and the central bank retained the facility to raise foreign debt for reserve management purposes.

Development in the financial sector in the last five years made it necessary to alter the regulations applied to financial institutions. The Hungarian regulations moved toward the standards of the EU and focused on the capital adequacy requirements. This was (and will be) accompanied by the establishment of new institutions, the merger of some established institutions and the changes in the role of the NBH in regulation. The amendment incorporated these changes.

The issue of the independence of central banks worldwide came into the foreground at the second half of the eighties and the beginning of the nineties when the reduction of inflation was given a primary role in the system of monetary targets. In one of the important papers on this topic, K. Rogoff[4] explained that in the question of credibility and/or flexibility of monetary policy, economic welfare could be improved by delegating monetary policy to the central bank, since the central bank has a greater inflation-aversion than society as a whole. This is only one aspect of independence, however. The institution itself and its monetary policy should be independent. In fact, institutional independence should be required even if central banks are obliged to support economic policy of the government by law. In addition, the personal independence of the top executives is required, which usually can be attained through a longer-than-legislative term of office, when it is not possible to terminate the tenure of those individuals except for serious professional reasons. Finally, autonomy in the selection of monetary instruments must exist. This is closely linked to the functions of a central bank as the issuer of money and as the monetary authority. The independence of a central bank in this respect means the exemption from non-central banking activities, too (for example, primary financing of the government). In each of these areas, the NBH reached a relatively high degree of independence by 1997.

Between 1987 and 1991, the NBH worked under the supervision of the Council of Ministers. Its main task was to implement money and credit policy settled by the Council of Ministers but there were important developments compared to the past:

- The volume of direct financing of the budget deficit was determined now by the Parliament.
- The NBH enjoyed a relatively high degree of independence in elaborating and implementing monetary policy by law (weak economic

---

[4] K. Rogoff, [1985].

performance and the difficulties of transition made it strongly limited in practice).

- The normative regulation was preferred instead of the former individual treatment of banks and enterprises.

Since 1991, personal independence is partly provided by a six-year term for the office of the president and by the dominant role of the President of the Republic in the appointment. The President of the NBH is obliged to report on the activity of the NBH to the Parliament instead of to the Government.

Regarding the conduct of monetary policy and the selection of instruments, the situation is quite complicated. From a legal standpoint, independence is almost perfect and the remaining constraints are being reduced. However, one particular restriction on independence was the financing of the government. While such financing was strongly limited by the Central Bank Act of 1991, the large government deficit made the restrictions partly untenable. The NBH was allowed to withdraw in March 1995 from financing the government by purchasing government securities at the primary issues. Legislative changes on the central bank at the beginning of 1997, as indicated earlier, created a final solution to this problem.

With regard to exchange rate policy, the Central Bank Act says: "The order of determining and/or influencing the exchange rate is approved by the Government in agreement with the NBH". [5] As far as necessary and possible, the NBH must maintain and influence this exchange rate with its interventions. This regulation is important because of the central role of the exchange rate in monetary policy. In the former exchange rate regime, called "fixed, but adjustable," this regulation was a de facto constraint on exchange rate policy even if the Government accepted proposals of the monetary authority. Since the beginning of the crawling peg system, as a consequence of the characteristics of this system, the NBH has had a decisive role regarding exchange rate policy and the budgetary policy has to be in line with this system, as an indispensable prerequisite for maintenance of this regime.

Apart from the existing legal constraints, the most important restrictions on perfect autonomy come from the fact that the central bank

---

[5] Act LX of 1991 on the National Bank of Hungary (which had been amended by The Acts of LXIX of 1991, LXX of 1992, CXI of 1993, IV of 1994, CV of 1995 and CXXIX of 1996).

is required to support the general economic policy. This support has been the main source of "classical conflicts" between central banks and ministries of finance in many countries, about which there is much written. Central banks in Eastern Europe are under direct constraint of the quickly developing and strongly market-oriented financial system (and private economy in general), while governments partly want to maintain some elements of the former centralization. This conflict enhances the responsibility of the central bank during transition. The liberalization steps toward a market-oriented economy create new methods and instruments of monetary policy, provide a wide range of information for policy purposes and create a need for regulation. At the same time, they reduce the efficiency of monetary policy due to the loss of direct intervention.

The transition changed the functions of the central bank. The National Bank of Hungary separated non-central banking tasks and obligations into institutions that are adequate for the tasks. For example, the NBH disposed of its quasi-fiscal activities. Since the beginning of the transition, the NBH has transferred corporate financing and the commercial trade of foreign exchange to commercial banks. The issue of government papers has become the responsibility of the Treasury. In another step toward central bank independence, the sub-standard public debt items included in the central bank balance sheet were converted into market-rate bearing instruments in 1997.

The Monetary Policy Decision-Making Process

The NBH provides annual monetary policy guidelines for the upcoming year. The guidelines cover the present and future tendencies of economic and monetary developments and estimate the essential figures for next year's monetary policy from these developments. The figures and expected trends determine the necessary changes in the monetary instruments and/or monetary targeting that are explained in the guidelines. In the monetary policy guidelines for 1997, however, the NBH focused on the longer run and derived the targets and instruments from the long-term requirements of price stability, the final target. The guidelines are prepared by the Monetary Policy Department but they are widely discussed inside the bank and approved by the Central Bank Council. The NBH reconciles its intentions with those of commercial banks. It also consults with the Ministry of Finance on the guidelines and on the annual budgetary estimates from the point of view of implementation. The Government then establishes its position with regard to the guidelines of monetary policy before they are presented to the Parliament. This mutual reconciliation serves to establish the consistency of the economic policy, though the central bank is not obliged to alter the monetary policy guidelines if other authorities reject it or parts of it.

The highest monetary policy body of the NBH is the Central Bank Council. The members of the Central Bank Council are well-known experts on the economy and have well-established backgrounds. The Central Bank Council holds meetings at least once in every quarter or whenever the monetary/economic situation requires additional attention. It decides (1) the annual monetary policy guidelines, (2) the essential modifications of the policy instruments (including the exchange rate), and (3) other monetary questions as necessary. The Council makes its decisions by simple majority of the votes cast.

The operative monetary policy and reserve management decisions are made at the regular meetings of the Monetary Committee, the Banking Committee and the Assets and Liabilities Committee (ALCO). The Monetary Committee regularly surveys the monetary situation, notes the deviations from the monetary policy guidelines and makes operative monetary policy decisions, especially about monetary instruments. The President of the NBH is allowed to refer any questions to the Committees. The Banking Committee discusses legal questions of the banking system, the operation of the banking sector in order to avoid liquidity crises, the establishment, abolishment or changes in chartered activities of single banks, etc. The ALCO decides questions regarding foreign exchange reserve management, external debt management, etc.

The Board of Directors is the consultant group to the President and supports the President in implementing policy. Its main responsibilities include the discussions about the economic policy of the government, monetary concerns of the budget, monetary policy guidelines, the system of foreign exchange management, and questions of the payment system and those of the banking system.

Monetary Policy and Instruments

Many changes have occurred concerning monetary instruments. After the initial attempts to create the new financial system, there was a rapid change of direct instruments (based on quantity limits) into indirect (price-type) instruments until 1993. Since then, there has been an improvement in indirect instruments and in their application. At the same time, the NBH strove to limit the interventions on the shorter end of the money market in order to avoid disturbances in the yield curve due to policy changes.

Changes in monetary policy as reflected in monetary policy targeting and central bank behavior were not so clear. Hungary had experienced an unsuccessful attempt to stimulate economic growth when the two-tier banking system began to work. The lack of economic growth resulted in the deterioration of the current account and a further increase in foreign debt. The current account and the level of foreign debt both play a central role in the Hungarian economy due to the high degree of openness of the economy and due to the requirements of managing an extremely high level of foreign debt since the seventies. Consequently, these issues had absolute priority in real economic and financial stabilization after 1987.

As a result of this orientation and the dominant role that the government budget had in the economic transition (new taxes, e.g. VAT and consumption tax, liberalization, etc.), the inflation rate increased between 1987 and 1991. Due to the high inflation and the requirements of the Central Bank Act, the NBH attempted double targeting after 1991. The final objective of monetary policy was to reduce inflation *and* to balance the current account, though the emphasis on each varied (e.g., 1992-1993: inflation; 1994: external equilibrium). The new target system, introduced parallel to the adjustment package of 1995, included inflation as a final target, the nominal exchange rate as an intermediate target and interest rates (differentials) as an operational target. The inflationary development of 1995 clearly reflected the contradiction between an inflation target and an exchange rate target in a fixed-type exchange rate system. The current account deficit decreased significantly and the annual inflation rate went up again to 28%.

A detailed account of monetary policy issues for the entire transition period follows. Three distinct subperiods are discussed: 1987-1991, 1992-March, 1995, and March, 1995-1997. These subperiods were separated by the most important changes in the monetary policy framework. Table 7.1 at the end of this article gives a general overview of the whole transition period from a monetary policy viewpoint. It shows the three subperiods, summarizes the main features of each and indicates the changes in the target and instrument structure of monetary policy in Hungary between 1987 and 1997.

First Period: 1987- 1991

During this period, monetary policy was affected by foreign stabilization efforts, growing inflation and the progressively increasing effect of the government on the financial market. The NBH conducted a restrictive monetary policy in order to provide the financing of the budgetary deficit and keep inflation under control. The policy was designed to reduce liquidity in the enterprise sector through different channels of the transmission mechanism, while protecting household savings. As a result, the growth of M2[6] declined and the velocity of M2 accelerated. The increase in domestic credit was less than the growth of nominal GDP.

The structure of domestic credits shifted toward credits of the government, while the growth of corporate financing was slowed. The access of enterprises to credits was unbalanced. The big state-owned enterprises had good access, while others did not. There was a remarkable growth of forced inter-enterprise credits that subsequently began to decline in 1992 due to the Act on Bankruptcy. It is worth mentioning that due to the economic shock in 1990-91, not only the credit ability of firms but also the demand for corporate loans decreased significantly during this period. As a result, the crowding out effect of the budget was not tangible.

The proportion of household credit to total domestic credit fell significantly as a result of the prepayment of housing loans[7] and very high credit interest rates. After two years of "shopping tourism,"[8] household savings went up quickly and many preferred to hold their savings in foreign exchange deposits. This way of safeguarding the purchasing power of savings remained until the beginning of 1996. Commercial banks began to borrow from abroad in 1990-91, thereby shifting the structure of Hungarian foreign debt from the public sector (Government

---

[6] M2 = money + quasi money, according to the terms of IMF. M2 includes cash in circulation + deposits in HUF and foreign exchange. It excludes securities issued by commercial banks.

[7] The Government imposed an interest rate tax on the former housing loans with extremely low interest rates in 1989 and allowed these loans to be paid back early.

[8] After liberalization of passport regulation, Hungarian people went to Austria and Germany to buy durable goods that were in short supply in Hungary.

and the NBH) to the private sector (commercial banks and, somewhat later, enterprises).

Monetary policy was successful in stabilizing the external financial situation. The current account was in surplus in 1990, net foreign debt decreased and the maturity structure of gross foreign debt became more favorable. However, inflation went up from 8.6% in 1987 to 35% in 1991. Monetary policy was forced to adjust to fiscal policy which led to a growth in the financing of the budget deficit by the NBH.

The NBH had an active role in the implementation of economic policy and the establishment of the new financial system. It carried out a wide range of direct interventions and instrument changes in order to restrict domestic demand for money and goods. The main instrument of monetary restriction during this period was the radical reduction of normative refinancing quotas[9] of commercial banks. At the beginning, in the case of short-term refinancing, quotas amounted to 80% of the balance sheets of commercial banks. This percentage fell to 5% by 1991. While such measures did not affect government spending and enterprises without credit links, they were disadvantageous to enterprises with credit facilities. The NBH partially had to offset the disadvantages of this radical change. At first the liquidity crises was handled through individual agreements with banks; later, a few new credit instruments were introduced.

Refinancing rates were increased by the NBH several times during the period. Contrary to the restrictive efforts, some preferences remained regarding agriculture, privatization, small enterprises, convertible exports, etc. The export pre-financing credits (introduced in 1988) and HUF credits against foreign exchange deposits became main forms of short-term refinancing by 1991. The NBH had a "channel" role with regard to long-term refinancing credits. It borrowed long-term sources from international financial organizations (World Bank) and foreign states (Japan, Germany, Italy, etc.) in foreign exchange and channeled it into commercial banks in HUF. Due to the lack of long-term savings in Hungary, these credits were almost the sole source of investment funds.

However, the high rates and normative quotas did not limit the use of refinancing credits. Refinancing credits were subject to liquidity requirements, but not to reserve requirements (that were introduced in

---

[9] These quotas were associated with an automatic refinancing credit up to a given percentage of a bank's equity and capital.

1987) as were deposits. As a result, refinancing credits were the cheapest form of access to central bank money.

In 1988 reserve requirements mandated daily maintenance with different ratios for different types of liabilities of commercial banks. Household deposits, refinancing credits, and external liabilities were excluded. The ratio was set at 15% in March 1988, raised to 18% in September 1989, and decreased to 15% in November 1990. By this time, household deposits were subjected to reserve requirements and these requirements became one of the most important instruments in 1991. Regulation became standard for all commercial banks, the ratio was increased by 1% (to 16%), and the forward operations (with securities as collateral) came under reserve obligation. Requirements on foreign exchange liabilities had to be done in HUF. These measures were taken in order to finance the budget deficit without the inflationary effects of issuing central bank money.

The NBH did not pay interest on mandatory reserves between January 1, 1989 and September 15, 1991. After that, the NBH began to pay interest on reserves in order to avoid a deterioration of profitability of commercial banks and a resulting widening of the interest rate margin. For reserves on foreign exchange deposits, the rate was 34.8%; and for reserves on HUF deposits, it was 15.4%. Both rates went down by the end of the year (to 32.2% and 11.0%, respectively). Inflation was 35% and it began to decline by the middle of the year.

The system of daily liquidity requirements was introduced in 1991. Commercial banks were obliged to hold 5% of their balance sheet in liquid assets (cash or liquid T-bills).

Though the scope of open market operations was limited, remarkable progress was made in this area. The interbank money market, the market for government securities and the system of repurchase agreements were established during this period, though the market for government securities was negligible. Open market operations were based upon certificates of deposits issued by the NBH.

Short-term T-bills were introduced in March 1988, and central bank certificates of deposit (with maturity of one to three years) appeared this year as well. The first auction of T-bills was held by the NBH in December, 1988. T-bills were well received due to their liquidity and relatively high yield. The small amount of bills issued made the scope of monetary policy very limited. Due to the lack of a secondary market, the NBH began to issue repurchase agreements on its own certificates of deposits at market interest rate in 1989. The secondary market for T-bills began to operate in 1990 when discount T-bills were introduced. They could be bought solely by legal entities (banks, enterprises and government institutions).

In 1991, there were five types of government paper on the market. New T-bills were introduced with a progressively growing interest rate depending on the date when it was to be repurchased by the government. There were 30-day and 90-day discount T-bills. The first government bonds were issued on December 1 with three-year maturities. Three-month liquidity T-bills were issued solely to financial institutions and a special type of 90-day discount T-bill was issued to resident commercial banks.

With regard to interest rate policy, this period witnessed a shift from direct regulation of interest rates to indirect regulation via different central bank rates. Interest rates had an upward tendency during the period due to increasing inflation and the growing competition for savings between commercial banks (and enterprises) and the government.

In the early years of the transition, the refinancing rates and the administrative interest rate ceilings of household deposits dominated interest rate policy. Parallel to the decline of refinancing credits, the role of refinancing rates decreased, too. The deposit rate ceilings were abandoned gradually. In 1990, the central bank prime rate was introduced. The two components of this rate were the average cost of foreign funds of the NBH and the change of the real effective exchange rate of the Hungarian Forint. This rate usually was lower than the market rate. The interest rate on current deposits of commercial banks with the NBH, the longer-than-one-year refinancing credit rates and the rate on government loans with the NBH were linked to this prime rate which provides financing of preferred loans at rates cheaper than the market rate.

By the end of this period, inflation began to decline but interest rates remained at their high level, reflecting high inflationary expectations, the dominance of deficit financing constraints and the impact of tight monetary policy on money market rates. The NBH tried to decrease market rates by reducing central bank rates, but this attempt had an impact only on the yields on discount T-bills.

The exchange rate policy of the NBH was strongly limited by stabilization constraints and the dominant role of Government in elaboration and implementation of exchange rate policy. The NBH was allowed to revaluate the nominal exchange rate by ± 1% until 1989 and up to ± 5% after 1989. Otherwise, the revaluation of the exchange rate was the common responsibility of the government and the NBH.

The exchange rate of the Hungarian Forint was pegged to a weighted basket of nine currencies until November, 1991. The weights were set annually according to the currency composition of Hungary's convertible foreign trade. The basket was changed in order to reduce the share of the US dollar in December, 1991. The basket of 50% US$ and 50% ECU helped to avoid excessive fluctuations of the HUF due to changes in the US$ against major currencies. Altering the basket served as a basis of the interbank foreign exchange market in 1992. The NBH altered the system of quotation of exchange rates (daily basis, introduction of value-date bookkeeping for HUF transactions, etc.). Buying and selling rates were set in a range of ± 0.25% around the middle rate of each currency.

The exchange rate policy aimed to cut inflation and to increase efficiency and international competitiveness of the Hungarian economy. Given these (sometimes abhorrent) goals, the exchange rate of the HUF was devalued in real effective terms in 1988-89. The correction of the exchange rate was made subsequently, when expectations (speculation against the HUF) forced it. In 1990, when the current account had a small amount of surplus, the NBH conducted a neutral exchange rate policy in real effective terms. The exchange rate policy was altered again in 1991, when the East-European market collapsed and inflation went up further. The nominal exchange rate was devalued two times during 1991, but the Forint appreciated by more than 11 percent in real terms. The real appreciation was allowed in order to cut inflation and the role of real appreciation remained important in subsequent years.

Second Period: 1992 - March 1995

The system of indirect instruments was retained in this second period. The existing direct instruments were terminated gradually and the use of indirect instruments became decisive after 1992. The most important development occurred in open market operations when the central bank's certificates of deposits were substituted by government securities. The interbank foreign exchange market began operations in 1992 and direct (re)financing by the central bank was replaced by forward operations after 1992. When setting the target for monetary policy, the NBH hesitated between inflation and external equilibrium as ultimate goals. An inflationary target was set in order to cut inflation in 1992-93 but when the current account ran a large deficit in 1994, the current account became the target.   The stock of foreign direct investment grew rapidly but the increasing deficit in the balance of payments overwhelmed it in 1993 and 1994. As a result, the stock both of gross and net foreign debt went up.

At the beginning of the period, monetary policymakers tried to reduce interest rates through aggressive action.   After this attempt failed, policymakers announced a flexible policy that would follow, instead of determine, money market development. Commercial banks had relatively easy access to central bank money through different channels of short-term refinancing.   Policymakers delayed the closing of these channels which resulted in a slight increase in indirect financing of the government deficit by commercial banks and finally by the NBH. The method was simple and profitable for commercial banks: they entered into forward deals with the NBH (repurchase agreements in 1993 and medium-term foreign exchange swaps in 1994) at the central bank prime rate. Then they bought discount T-bills with the highest yield in the market. The two preconditions of these deals were (1) the lagged reaction of monetary policy and (2) the extremely high and growing deficit of the budget.   The financing requirements of the budget were the main characteristics of the money and capital markets and contributed to high interest rates. The stock of credits to enterprises included in the banking survey[10] increased slowly[11], the stock of household credit declined and the weight of the government in the total domestic credit stock went up significantly.   In other words, the crowding out effect of the budget was working.

The role of refinancing credits in monetary regulation was negligible during this period. The stock of short-term credits was low due to former restrictions.   As a result, monetary policy was not able to use them for further tightening of liquidity. The main forms of short-term refinancing were credit lines to rediscount bills of exchange, discounting of export documents and factoring of receivables.   Export pre-financing was abandoned in March, 1993. The demand for long-term refinancing credits was low due to the slack in investment activity and the limited scope for using them.   The NBH partly mediated external funds to the corporate

---

[10] The Banking Survey is the consolidated balance sheet of the banking system as a whole including the NBH as well.

[11] It is important to note that enterprises can avoid the banking sector and borrow from abroad directly and that the proportion of off-balance sheet items is growing. These items probably contain a relatively large amount of funds to enterprises.

sector and partly assisted exports, privatization and economic restructuring.

Reserve requirements traditionally are introduced in order to protect deposits against bankruptcies. In recent approaches, obligatory reserves are indirect taxes imposed on commercial banks and they serve to provide a stable demand for central bank money. The system of reserve requirements has not been able to support this stable demand function in Hungary yet because of frequent changes in regulation. Restrictive monetary policy during the first period was accompanied by an increase in reserve rates, a broadening of the range of liabilities subjected to requirements and a cut in interest rates on obligatory reserves. Bank losses and the unfavorable international comparison regarding reserve rates[12] resulted in an easing of reserve requirements during the second period. Monetary policy did not neutralize the entire amount of excess liquidity in the money market in order to cut high interest rates, inflationary expectations and inflation itself.

A reserve ratio of 10 percent was introduced for investment banks in 1992. Foreign exchange deposits of commercial banks were excluded from reserve obligations in the same year. The ratio was decreased to 14% on January 1, 1993, and a further reduction of liabilities subjected to reserve requirements was made. Interest, contribution debts and foreign exchange funds from abroad were excluded in 1993. Interest on required reserves was decreased radically. The most important step regarding obligatory reserves was an alteration of the maintenance period. The system of daily maintenance was replaced by a fortnightly average maintenance period. The reserve ratio was decreased and the interest rate on reserves was raised significantly in 1994.

Daily liquidity requirements were introduced in 1991 in order to reveal liquidity problems of banks. While each bank could meet these requirements, there still were bankruptcies in 1992. As a consequence of this, liquidity requirements were raised from 5% to 10% in 1992. Supplementary liquidity reserve requirements of 10% were imposed on net illiquid assets in 1993 and abolished in 1994.

In 1992, the Hungarian money market was characterized by large excess liquidity coming from capital inflow and an increased demand for money. Inflation fell from 35% to 23%, but the decline in nominal interest

---

[12] Among developed countries, Italy was the only country that had higher rates than Hungarian reserve rates.

rates was delayed due to inflationary expectations. As a result, deposits carried high real interest rates. Household savings jumped and savings by the corporate sector exceeded its credits. Discount T-bills with maturities of 180 and 360 days were issued in 1992 but the stock of government securities held by the NBH was low. The average yield on 90-day T-bills at auction reflected the short-term money market rates and the yield of this paper became the indicator rate of the Hungarian money market. The issuance of certificates of deposit of the NBH, the collateral in repurchase agreements, was abandoned. The maturity of interbank deals was shortened to 1-7 days. Under these circumstances, open market operations had limited scope.

The interbank foreign exchange market began operations on July 1, 1992. Participants were commercial banks licensed for foreign exchange transactions and the NBH. The official exchange rate was quoted daily by the NBH instead of by the market. Commercial banks could access central bank funds at the official buying and selling rates (fixing rates)[13] once a day in every listed currency without limit on amount. The three major foreign exchanges (US Dollar (USD), Austrian Schilling (ATS), German Deutschmark (DEM)) were available during business hours and the NBH intervened at a ± 0.3% margin, instead of at the official margin of ± 0.25%. Prompt transactions lost their important role at the beginning and foreign exchange swaps (in prompt call - forward put deals) from one-month to one-year maturity became decisive. In March, 1993, a minimum limit of at least USD 1 million was introduced for transactions at the fixing rates. On June 1, 1993, the intervention band was extended to ± 0.5%. The development of market rates within the band reflected the expectations of devaluation and monetary policy had a new indicator. The quotation of fixing rates and the daily transactions at fixing rates were abolished on January 1, 1994. The minimum limit on transactions doubled in the middle of the year. The maturity of short-term swaps was decreased

---

[13] The NBH official currency fixing rate is a calculated exchange rate computed on a daily basis. At the moment, the most active 10 commercial banks are obliged to declare the USD/HUF exchange rate applied by them to the NBH at 11 o'clock each day. The average of these 10 exchange rates is the official fixing rate of the USD. Then the NBH computes the official fixing rate of other listed foreign exchanges by using the USD fixing and the other forex/USD cross rates valid at 11 o'clock. This kind of exchange rate is a well-known solution for computing an official exchange rate.

to three months in February and to one month in September.   This instrument was terminated in December, 1994.

Due to the rapid growth of the budget and of the current account deficit and due to the restrictive measures taken early in 1993, liquidity in the money market tightened and interest rates increased.   The stock of repurchase agreements with government securities as collateral began to increase significantly.   The limit on the amount of repo stock was too high to impede its growth.   In 1994, the NBH shortened the maturity of repos to two weeks and abolished the limit on the stock of repos.   While the main channel of access to central bank money was repurchase agreements in 1993, medium term swaps (with at least 15-months maturity) played a dominant role in 1994.   After a slight increase in repo rates, medium-term foreign exchange swaps became the cheapest source of central bank money.   A system of reverse repo tenders[14] was introduced in May, 1994.

Repo rates became the most important indicators of interest rate policy. The role of the central bank prime rate lessened, as it had an impact only on interest rates of special long-term refinancing credits.   In 1992 and 1993, commercial banks responded to policy with a lag of at least three months.   This reaction lag shortened remarkably in 1994.   The interest rate policy had a "following the market development" characteristic in 1993 and 1994 and interest rates had an upward tendency during these years.

While the development of other instruments continued to progress, exchange rate policy and especially its impact on the economy changed significantly period by period.   Between 1992 and 1994, the real effective exchange rate[15] remained as an intermediate target, but the NBH devaluated the HUF several times each year in small steps instead of large steps as was done formerly.   The precondition of this fixed but adjustable policy was the fact that most of the important steps of liberalization were completed.   The purpose of the policy of small steps was to curb expectations of devaluation and of inflationary expectations and via these, to cut inflation but maintain competitiveness.   In order to meet this requirement, monetary policy allowed a small appreciation of the HUF in 1992 and 1993.   Contrary to 1993, when the inflationary target was set, the

---

[14] NBH offered eligible securities for sale weekly for terms of two weeks, with repurchase obligation.

[15] The real effective exchange rate is computed on three bases: a) based on producer price indexes, b) on ULC basis and c) based on the CPI.   Under certain circumstances, these three figures would show different pictures.   The target in 1994 aimed at the real exchange rate based on producer price indexes.

external equilibrium became the final target in 1994 and the HUF was depreciated in real terms. As a result of the "small steps" policy, expectations of devaluation became stable and led to a continual growth of foreign deposits at the expense of HUF deposits.

There were a few developments regarding the exchange rate during this period. As a result of the EMU crisis in the summer of 1993, the ECU was replaced by the DEM in the currency basket to which the exchange rate of the HUF was pegged. The ECU was made part of the basket again on May 16, 1994, and its share increased from 50% to 70% according to the structure of foreign trade. The intervention band was widened to ± 1.25% in August 1994, and to ± 2.25% in December.

Third Period: March 1995 - 1996

The policy of a fixed-but-adjustable exchange rate regime was replaced by a crawling band system with a pre-announced crawl in order to rebuild the destroyed credibility of monetary (and economic) policy. Altering the exchange rate regime was based on the realized inability of monetary policy to keep the balance of payments account under control. Due to liberalization, the share of the public sector in total foreign debt of the country fell and that of the private sector increased. The decrease of monetary control on the balance of payments was a result of the growing indebtedness of the private sector to foreign entities. Monetary policy was able to control the domestic component of money creation, but not the foreign component. Therefore, in the case of an open Hungarian economy, monetary policy was able to control only a part of the money supply. This kind of regime can be preserved only if income, fiscal and monetary policies are harmonized and credible. If one element of this trinity works against the others, it sooner or later will lead to a forced adjustment of the exchange rate and a loss of credibility.[16]

Important preconditions of the crawling band regime included fiscal adjustment, especially the structural adjustment of expenses in order to reduce the budget deficit. The fiscal adjustment, the improvement of the

---

[16] Concerning the details of the introduction of the new exchange rate system, the government in agreement with the NBH devalued the exchange rate of the HUF by 9% on March 12, 1995 and announced a daily devaluation of the currency at 1.9% monthly average until the end of June, 1995, and 1.3% from the beginning of July. The rate of crawl was reduced to 1.2% on January 1, 1996, further to 1.1% on April 1, 1997, and to 1% on August 15, 1997.

current account, and the rapidly increasing liberalization that led to the high yields on government securities caused an extremely large capital inflow. This additional liquidity in a country with moderate inflation forced monetary policy to neutralize the growth of the money supply in 1995 and in the beginning of 1996. All elements of the system of monetary instruments were used on behalf of sterilization. As a result, the use of monetary policy instruments was fully determined by the exchange rate regime and sterilization efforts. The system required a high amount of government securities on the market in order to sterilize excess liquidity due to the lack of other collaterals for open market operations in the portfolio of the NBH. The bulk of the instruments of a central bank are able to curb the monetary base (high-power money) and the multiplication of central bank money, but not the growth of the broad money (M3)[17] stock. The reverse repo or any kind of deposit facilities with commercial banks are assets of commercial banks and liabilities of the central bank. In the consolidated balance sheet of the banking sector (in the banking survey in IMF-terms), these items offset each other and the capital inflow adds to the growth of the stock of broad money.

Regarding sterilization through outright selling of government securities from the portfolio of the central bank, there are two alternatives: (1) if these securities are purchased and held by the commercial banks, the result will be the same as that above. (2) If these government securities are sold to and held by the non-banking sector, net assets of the whole banking sector will be reduced and the stock of broad money will decline. If the sterilization is implemented by over-financing of the central budget and this growth of funds for the budget are held on the current account of the budget with the central bank, both the stock of monetary base and the broad money decline. Recognition of these problems was, of course, a result of a learning process.[18]

Due to excess liquidity, commercial banks did not need refinancing credits from the central bank. The stock of repos and short-term foreign exchange swaps decreased to zero and the stock of medium-term foreign exchange swaps declined. Until early 1997, the two main instruments to

---

[17] M3 in Hungary includes all kind of financial investment facilities offered by the banking sector, including current accounts, savings and time deposits, both in foreign exchange and domestic currency, and securities issued by the banking sector.

[18] A detailed explanation of the problem may be found in Barabas - Hamecz [1997].

sterilize excess liquidity were the outright selling of government securities from the portfolio of the NBH and the growing stock of reverse repos. As a result, the NBH had to make reverse repo rates attractive. Interest rates picked up in June-July 1995, when the interest rate differential on 90-day Hungarian T-bills over the average yield on the currency basket was more than 11% on an annual basis. As a consequence of the final and intermediate targets, monetary policy had to find the "adequate" interest rate differential as an operational variable that would stop the speculative capital inflow but not crush the growth of domestic savings. Moreover, policymakers should be able to channel the funds into the most effective investments in order to establish a sustainable path of economic growth. Therefore, the interest rate policy was strongly limited by the crawling band system and the struggle for credibility (that is, for keeping the exchange rate of HUF against the currency basket at the most appreciated edge of the intervention band). As a consequence, monetary policy tended to follow money market rates instead of determining them. The problem was complicated by the fact that money demand in Hungary had not been stable and monetary policy had to be careful of "over-sterilizing".

In order to cut interest rates and inflation, monetary policy allowed excess liquidity to grow in the market from the beginning of 1996. Interest rates had started to slump at the end of January, 1996, due to the excess liquidity in the system and was intensified further by the decline in the demand for credit. The improving budget balance (surplus in primary balance of the central budget) reduced the credit demand of the state and this was not replaced by the credit demand of the private sector. Monetary policy then faced a new problem: slightly declining nominal interest rates were in line neither with a slower decline of inflation nor the exchange rate path. During the rest of 1996, monetary policy had to increase nominal interest rates via central bank rates in order to avoid negative real interest rates on financial investments (and all of the negative consequences of such a situation). The yield curve had a strong negative slope indicating that the market participants expected a more powerful decline in inflation than the monetary authority. Economic growth started to accelerate during the last quarter of 1996, coupled with a significant growth of wages by the beginning of 1997. When it realized the possible inflationary pressure, the NBH decided to offer a 6-month deposit facility to commercial banks in January, 1997. The offered interest rate was the highest on the money market. It included the "price" of perfect illiquidity of this deposit due to the fact that banks could not withdraw it before maturity. Since the market did not adjust, the NBH did not decrease reverse repo rates on March 24, 1997, although market participants were sure of a decline. Moreover, a 12-month deposit facility was introduced in order to signal the inflationary expectations of the monetary authority.

The surprised market adjusted immediately and on the longer end of the market (over 1 year), a temporary "over-reaction" evolved. Since then, interest rates have fallen slowly. These 6-month and 12-month deposit facilities were followed by a 1-year NBH-bond on June 19, 1997. The NBH-bond is available both for commercial banks and brokerage firms. Since the stock of collateral in the portfolio of the NBH reduced significantly, reverse repo facilities were abolished and were replaced by a deposit facility with the same conditions as those of the former reverse repo on October 6, 1997.

The crawling band exchange rate regime was accompanied by a large conversion of foreign exchange funds into the HUF but the sources of conversion changed somewhat. In 1995, the main sources of conversion were the foreign exchange funds from abroad (usually direct borrowing of commercial banks and enterprises) and foreign exchange deposits of commercial banks with the NBH. In 1996, the stock of foreign exchange deposits of households began to decline, as did those of banks and businesses.

Since the market exchange rate of the HUF had been continuously at the lower (at the most appreciated) edge of the intervention band, the futures market provided a risk-free gain to both participants of futures. Banks opened long positions and sold foreign exchange funds in the spot market, and then loaned the funds to the government (T-bills) or deposited them with the central bank (reverse repos), essentially engaging in interest rate arbitrage. Speculators on the other side opened uncovered short positions and took two types of risk. One was that the central bank would depreciate the exchange rate over the crawl and the other was that the exchange rate would move up within the band. There was no reason to assume that either of these would really occur. As a consequence of declining interest rate differential, however, the opportunity for interest rate arbitrage disappeared by the third quarter of 1996. Conversion of foreign exchange into the HUF ceased until the introduction of the NBH bonds, which provided an attractive interest rate.

The introduction of the crawling band exchange rate system was a part of a stabilization-cum-reform policy package aimed at establishing both domestic and foreign equilibrium and a sustainable economic growth without accelerating inflation. The exchange rate system has served as a nominal anchor and has been promoted to create a stable and predictable financial environment. The results (for example, the accelerating growth, declining risk premium on HUF investments, or the improving graduation of the country's debt) show that monetary policy proved to be credible and was successful in achieving the above-mentioned goals.

Currency Convertibility[19]

Before the transition, the Hungarian Forint (HUF) was convertible only between 1926 and 1931. As a consequence of the Great Depression, a regime of extended foreign exchange restrictions was introduced in 1931 and remained in place until after World War II. Currency convertibility became a political symbol and was one of the main goals of the economic transition by the end of the eighties. Progress in the liberalization of some economic activities, the collapse of the East-European market and the black foreign currency market restrained the convertibility of the Forint. As a result of gradual liberalization, Hungary reached de facto convertibility regarding its current account transactions. With regard to capital movements, the HUF has been convertible in the case of direct investments of non-residents in Hungary since 1988 and capital outflow was linked to this. The Act of 1988 on Foreign Direct Investments of Non-Residents in Hungary provided a full-scale protection of foreign direct investments against any type of legislative damages (for instance, nationalization) and liberalized profit repatriation fully. The medium- and long-term portfolio investments of non-residents were also liberalized. A license obligation was attached to the portfolio investments of residents abroad and to short-term (less than 1 year) financial investments of non-residents in Hungary.

The 1995 XCV Act on Exchange Control Regulations (that came into force on January 1, 1996) met the requirements of Article VIII of the Agreement for the International Monetary Fund. Generally, the new Act says, "everything could be done free, which is not prohibited in the Act." There are three major principles of the new Code: (1) if the organization/activity is subjected to any kind of permission by other regulations, the getting of permission is a prerequisite for buying foreign

---

[19] I am grateful to Ms. Julia Facsady for her useful comments on this part.

currency; (2) residents are obliged to bring their foreign currencies to Hungary (with some exceptions); and (3) excepting international economic activities, settlements should be made in the HUF.

Non-residents were allowed to purchase longer than one-year securities in Hungary by this amendment. The purchase of the safest foreign securities against the HUF was allowed on July 1, 1996. This development offered an opportunity to diversify portfolios further and to cut transaction costs to investors. Non-resident investors have significant interests in the shares of Hungarian firms. They have been allowed to enter into BUX-forward deals[20] with residents since February, 1997. On the contrary, other forward and options contracts are prohibited and the range of Forint-related spot contracts on the exchanges is limited.

During the early years of transition, both benefits and burdens of rapid liberalization arose clearly and immediately. The slow increases in the household's foreign currency limit[21] and the liberalization of the household's foreign exchange accounts led to a large deficit in the travel balance in the balance of payments. The intense competition in the resident enterprise sector due to the liberalization of imports weakened the former structure of the tradeable sector and forced this part of the economy to reestablish themselves. The process was accompanied by a large decrease in production, while higher prices reflected the impact of liberalization on the business cycle. A wide variety of goods appeared. Savings were used to fuel a growing demand for new products, resulting in further growth of inflation. Increased liberalization led to a remarkable capital inflow and in a short period of time the amount of foreign direct investment (FDI) in Hungary exceeded the amount of FDI in the rest of the region. Convertibility was enhanced by the reduction of controls on the current and capital accounts and by the constraints on government policies to avoid capital flight.

Remaining restrictions on capital movements concern short-term flows and aim to avoid speculative capital movements and flight of domestic

---

[20] The BUX is the index of the Budapest Stock Exchange.

[21] Generally, the Hungarian people could have a very limited amount of foreign currency before 1988 for traveling purposes only ($50 in every third year). The limit was set yearly and the amount was increased continually after 1988, depending on the current account performance. Now the limit is high; moreover, citizens are allowed to have foreign exchange accounts with a commercial bank without any limit on the balance of the account. That is, the limit is not effective in practice.

savings. Since joining the OECD in 1996 and preparing to join the European Union, Hungary has undertaken further important liberalization steps. The planned amendment to the Act on Foreign Exchange, which is expected to come into force at the beginning of 1998, includes the most important steps. This amendment allows the settlement of payments in foreign exchange when the beneficiary is a non-resident counterpart. It allows non-resident companies (including financial firms) to open branches in Hungary but it treats these branches as resident entities.

The advantages and disadvantages of convertibility could not be separated from the impacts of other policy steps after 1995. The maintenance of the present crawling peg exchange rate regime requires coordinated fiscal, income and monetary policies. Such coordinated policies produce positive effects in the wake of increasing liberalization.

Concerning the transition period as a whole, the most important effect of the liberalization on monetary policy was the strongly limited scope for monetary instruments. Essentially, the private sector (enterprises, commercial banks and households) was able to offset the impact of monetary policy changes through foreign transactions. This restriction of monetary autonomy likely resulted in an "impossible trinity," when policymakers tried to build up a combination of fixed exchange rates, independent monetary policy and liberalization in Hungary. At least one of the three elements will not be able to work in the long run. Liberalization can lead to financing problems of the budget deficit when savings is done through financial instruments other than government securities. This has not occurred in Hungary so far, due to the relatively high yield on government securities that, in turn, has attracted foreign capital and resulted in a risk-free gain through interest rate arbitrage.

The main advantages of convertibility, together with liberalization, for the whole economy are the strong competition among firms and the growing supply of external resources of funds. The consequences include a sharp decline in transaction costs and a widened diversification of portfolios that increase yields and cut risks. Concerning the real sector, liberalization and competition in the tradeable sector resulted in a radical restructuring of the microeconomy. This created a stable basis for a well-established growth and healthy development for the rest of the economy, as reflected for example in the good performance of Hungarian (not only joint venture) firms on the stock exchange and in the growing export of manufactured products to developed countries.

Summary

The Hungarian financial system was transformed completely during the 1990 - 1996 period. The former tools and mechanisms of administrative credit policy were abandoned and an independent monetary policy with indirect instruments was established. However, the increase in liberalization limited the scope of monetary policy, financial intermediation became more complex and the private sector was able to offset the effects of monetary policy by changing its behavior. Investors now are able to diversify their portfolios and adjust to monetary policy changes. Liberalization forced the government and the central bank to conduct a permanently credible policy based on economic instead of political concerns.

Given the development of the financial sector and the economic performance during the last ten years, monetary policy may be described as successful. The external financial situation appears to be under control, the stock of net foreign debt is decreasing and international reserves are stable at desired levels. The deficit in the balance of payments is financed by capital inflow. The former speculation against the HUF turned into speculation in favor of the HUF. The ratio of short-term foreign debt to total foreign debt fell and liquidity in the country is stable. However, it should be noted that, parallel to the increasing liberalization, the impact of monetary policy on the balance of payments has been reduced sharply.

The main field of responsibility of a central bank according to the Central Bank Act and the present target system is to cut inflation. High inflation was due partly to the adjustment of the price level to that of the world market, to new taxes, to the change in relative prices and to high inflationary expectations. The NBH was not able to reduce inflation entirely and this failure is related to its target system. In the case of a pegged exchange rate, economic problems are reflected in the deficit of balance of payments and/or inflation (apart from the budget). If monetary policy monitors development of the exchange rate in order to improve the current account, it is able to stabilize but not reduce inflation. Hungary does not have an explicit inflation target announced as a figure or a target band and concerns about inflation are eclipsed by concerns about the balance of payments deficit.

Other issues are linked to realized or expected membership in different international organizations. Hungary has been committed to further liberalization of its financial system since joining the OECD. Prospective

EU membership necessitates the further harmonization of Hungarian financial regulations with EU standards. The central bank has to prepare for these changes in its functions, instruments, organization and in monetary regulation.

References

Act XXIV of 1988 on the Foreign Direct Investments of Non-Residents in Hungary (available in Hungarian, in Torvenytar [Code of Laws] Statutory Rule I of 1974 on Foreign Exchange Management (available in Hungarian, in Torvenytar [Code of Laws]).

Act XCV of 1995 on Exchange Control Regulations (available in Hungarian, in Torvenytar [Code of Laws] and Executive Decree 161/1995 on the Implementation of the Act XCV of 1995 on Exchange Control Regulations and Executive Decrees 92/1996 and 222/1996 on the Amendment to the 161/1995 Decree (available in Hungarian, in Torvenytar [Code of Laws]).

Annual Report [1990-1996]. National Bank of Hungary.

Barabas, Gy and I. Hamecz [1997]. "Capital Inflow, Sterilization and Money Stock I-II," (available only in Hungarian: Tokebearamlas, sterilizacio es penzmennyiseg), Kozgazdasagi Szemle, July-August, pages 653-672 and September, 1997, Budapest, Hungary.

Fuhrer, J.C. [1997]. "Central Bank Independence and Inflation Targeting: Monetary Policy Paradigms for the Next Millennium?" *New England Economic Review*, January-February, pages 19-36.

Rogoff, K. [1985]. "The Optimal Degree of Commitment to an Intermediate Monetary Target," *Quarterly Journal of Economics*, November, pages 1169-1190.

Zsoldos, I. and E. Voros [1997]. "Estimation of a Demand for Money Function in Hungary," manuscript, National Bank of Hungary (available only in Hungarian).

Table 7.1 An Overview of Monetary Policy Between 1987 and 1997

	1987 Re-establishment of the two-tier banking sector	1987 – 1991	1991 The Central Bank Act	1991 - March 1995	March 1995 Stabilization-cum-reform policy package	After March 1995
Main features of the period		**Early Period of Transition:** institutional and legal changes + priority of the foreign financial equilibrium + search for new mechanisms and tools of monetary policy + political constraints of the transition ⇓		"Independent" monetary policy without fiscal adjustment → strictly limited scope for monetary policy in achieving monetary goals due to the lack of fiscal adjustment		Crawling band exchange rate regime + Beginning of fiscal adjustment ⇓ Chance of independent monetary policy on the basis of policy coordination and macroeconomic results. Strictly limited scope for monetary policy due to the exchange rate system
Main problem of the period		*Erratic Monetary Policy*		Efficiency of monetary policy in Hungary on the basis of the less-developed (but quickly developing) Hungarian financial sector, without fiscal adjustment.		The effectiveness of monetary policy in general and in a transition economy supported by fiscal adjustment on the basis of a developed financial sector.
Target system of monetary policy		No explicit target structure		*Final target:* varying (inflation or foreign equilibrium) *Intermediate target:* real exchange rate *Operational target:* varying, (monetary aggregates or figures coming from the balance sheet of the NBH)		*Final target:* inflation *Intermediate target:* nominal exchange rate. *Operational target:* the interest rate differential (in order to reduce speculative capital flows but stimulate domestic savings)
Instruments of monetary policy		Establishment of the use of indirect tools but with dominance of administrative regulation		Stress on the use of indirect instruments (frequent and strict changes in the conditions of the single instruments)		Indirect instruments (establishment of a long-lasting structure of instruments based on the significant development of the financial sector)

8 Macroeconomic Stabilization in the Czech Republic

JAN FRAIT
RAMJI TAMARAPPOO

Introduction

The Czech Republic has been cited as a country that has made a successful transition from a centrally planned economy to a market economy. The official statistics for 1996 seem to support this view. With the exception of a growing deficit in the current account, all macroeconomic variables indicated a healthy economy. In 1996, real GDP growth was about 4 percent, inflation was just under 9%, the overall unemployment rate was 3.3% (one of the lowest in the whole of Europe), the government budget was nearly balanced, and the level of external debt was low. However, a closer look at the situation in the economy at the end of 1996 and the beginning of 1997 suggested that the era of success and stability was coming to an end and that the economic sky was obscured by many clouds.

This paper focuses on some important aspects of macroeconomic development in the Czech Republic during the 1991-1996 period. The first section describes the state of the economy prior to transition, the policy decisions made immediately after the transition, and the results thereof. The second section analyzes macroeconomic policy in the post-transition period focusing on the balance of payments and the exchange rate. The third section identifies problem areas in the economy along with their impact on macroeconomic development. Finally, the last section presents the conclusions of this study.

The Early Days of Reform

Before discussing the reform package, it is appropriate to describe the state of the economy in communist Czechoslovakia. Prior to World War II Czechoslovakia was one of the leading industrialized countries of the

131

world with private ownership of the productive means and a strong banking sector. During the era of socialism (1948-1990), industrialization of the economy continued, but in the wrong direction. Major emphasis was laid on developing heavy industries and as a result some traditional industries were sacrificed for sake of the cooperation within COMECON (Council for Mutual Economic Assistance, the communist trading bloc). Moreover, the infrastructure as well as services suffered from under-investment. The productive means were nationalized, the competitive banking system was replaced by a monobank system, the corporate sector was monopolized and market-based information processing was replaced by the information processing provided through a central-planning authority. These changes resulted in what was known as "extensive development." The economy had a relatively high yearly investment rate and a relatively high rate of GDP growth. However, the positive impact of high levels of investment was offset by inefficiency and low productivity in the corporate sector. This, in turn, led to a worsening of the terms of trade and slow growth of living standards.

In comparison to its East European neighbors, the government of CSFR (Czechoslovak Federation) faced relatively favorable conditions for instituting reforms. Fiscal policy during the socialist period was reasonable and the extent of the government debt was not excessive. "Monetary policy" of the socialist state bank was sound and the extent of monetary overhang was limited. Czechoslovakia, unlike Hungary or Poland, also had low gross foreign debt (15% of GDP at the end of 1989). At the microeconomic level, shortages arising from disequilibrium prices were not overwhelming.

The reform package launched at the end of 1990 and the beginning of 1991 consisted of the liberalization of prices, the sharp devaluation and partial convertibility of the currency, and trade liberalization. To counter potential inflationary pressures, these steps were accompanied by strict fiscal and monetary policy, and a fixed exchange rate. Privatization followed the initial stabilization phase.

The initial price liberalization resulted in a sharp jump in the price level which filled the inflationary gap created during the socialist period. The shock to the price level was also due to a large devaluation of the currency. Strict fiscal and monetary policy coupled with a fixed exchange rate allayed fears of spiraling inflation and lent credibility to the reform program. Given wide-spread political support for the reform process, the general populace accepted a decrease in real wages, pensions and social security benefits which further aided in the stabilization process. By the second half of 1991, the macroeconomy showed signs of fiscal and monetary stability which allowed attention to be directed toward stabilizing the situation in the corporate sector and in external trade.

As indicated in Table 8.1, the growth rate of real GDP was negative in 1990 and remained negative until 1993. These negative results have been blamed on the speed of reform (shock therapy), but it should be recognized that restrictive macroeconomic policy was pursued only through the first half of 1991 (see Table 8.2) and that the reform package was not implemented as rapidly as is sometimes claimed.

Table 8.1   Macroeconomic Indicators of Czechoslovakia and the Czech Republic

	1989	1990	1991	1992	1993	1994	1995	1996 [a]
Growth rate of Real GDP (%)	1.4	-0.4	-	-7.1	-0.9	2.7	5.9	4.1
CPI Inflation (%)	2.1	12.3	53.6	11.5	18.2	10.2	9.1	8.8
Unemployment (%)	-	1.0	6.6	5.1	3.5	3.2	2.9	3.5
Foreign Exchange Reserves (billion USD) [b]	2.5	1.3	3.4	1.2	3.8	6.2	13.9	12.4
Current Account (billion USD) [c]	0.4	-1.1	0.4	0.2	0.6	0.0	-1.5	-4.5
Capital Account (billion USD) [c]	0.3	0.3	0.1	0.0	2.5	3.0	7.5	4.0
Exchange Rate CZK/USD yr. avg.	15.1	18.3	29.5	28.3	9.2	28.8	26.6	27.1
Real Exchange Rate of CZK [d]	100.0	68.5	89.3	96.2	109.9	17.6	127.9	133.2
Gross Foreign Debt (bil. USD)	7.9	8.1	9.4	9.6	8.5	10.3	16.4	20.4

[a] Preliminary; [b] End of Period; [c] Convertible Currencies; [d] Basket DEM and USD, based on CPI, 1989=100.
Sources: Statistical Surveys of the Czech Republic, Czech Statistical Office, various issues from December, 1989 to December, 1996.

The drastic decline in production can be attributed directly to the fall of the COMECON, and the shortage of funds available to firms engaged in restructuring. Moreover, there were other, not so apparent factors, that contributed to the decline in the rate of growth of GDP. Among these factors were the inability of firms (managers) to adapt quickly to free market conditions, a misalignment in foreign trade, poorly defined property rights, a lack of restructuring before privatization, and the virtual nonexistence of capital markets.

Table 8.2 Some Indicators of the Czechoslovak Economy (1989-1992)

	1989	1990	1991	1992
Nominal GDP (bil. CZK)	758.7	811.3	977.8	1,059.9
Real GDP (bil. CZK, 1984 prices)	730.0	727.0	611.4	564.2
GDP deflator (increase in %)	1.2	8.7	61.1	11.0
Money supply M1(bil. CZK)	317.7	308.1	343.3	430.5
Money supply M2 (bil. CZK)	554.4	553.1	650.4	839.9
Real exchange rate vis-a-vis USD*	70.9	54.2	51.8	55.0

* (1985 = 100), an increase means real appreciation.
Source: Annual Reports of the Czech National Bank from 1989-1992.

Macroeconomic Development Since 1990

Introduction of the Czech Currency Convertibility

One of the challenges of transition was the implementation of an efficient exchange rate system. Two crucial decisions, the choice of exchange rate regime and the initial exchange rate level, had to be made. These decisions were particularly difficult given that policymakers could not rely on experience for guidance. The simultaneous liberalization in both the domestic and external spheres was accompanied by the implementation of partial convertibility of the Czechoslovak crown (for registered companies) on current account items.[1]

The Czechoslovak authorities opted for a fixed exchange rate regime mainly to control inflation by using the exchange rate as a nominal anchor of the economy.[2] The thin foreign exchange market, the absence of a

---

[1] Free and unlimited access to foreign exchange for imports, and proceeds from exports have to be transferred to authorized banks at the spot exchange rate.
[2] Fixed exchange rates can serve in unstable transitional economies as a substitute

forward exchange market, and the high risk of speculative bubbles eliminated a flexible exchange rate regime as a viable option. Moreover, it was believed that volatility of the exchange rate and potential misalignment could have harmful effects on an economy in transition.

In January, 1991, the Czechoslovak crown (CZK) was pegged to a basket of five currencies including the United States' dollar (USD), the German mark (DEM), the Austrian shilling (AST), the Swiss franc (CHF), and the British pound (GBP). After the break up of the CSFR, the CZK was pegged to a basket that included only the USD and DEM in March 1993. (Table 8.3 shows the currencies along with their weighting.)

Table 8.3 The Composition of the CZK Basket (%)

	USD	DEM	ATS	CHF	GBP
December 28, 1990	31.34	45.52	12.35	6.55	4.24
January 2, 1992	49.07	6.15	8.07	3.79	2.92
May 3, 1993	35.00	65.00	-	-	-

Source: Frait, J. *International Monetary Theory*, Ostrava, VSB-TU, 1996, p. 59.

As far as the initial level of the exchange rate was concerned, the decision was made to set the exchange rate at a realistically competitive level close to the market rate. In 1990 the commercial and non-commercial rates and special tourist rate were unified. This unification was accompanied by a gradual devaluation of the exchange rate vis-a-vis the purchasing power parity (PPP) rate. Three successive devaluations of the CZK vis-a-vis convertible currencies occurred in 1990, resulting in the following percentage declines: 16.6% on January 8; 55.3% on October 15 and 15.98% on December 28.[3]

While there were no further changes in the nominal exchange rate in 1990, the devaluations that did occur in that year resulted in a sharp undervaluation of the currency. After the last devaluation, the CZK/USD exchange rate was set at 28 CZK/USD whereas the PPP estimates would have placed the rate at approximately 12 CZK/USD. Even under socialism the CZK was undervalued vis-a-vis PPP and these devaluations extended

---

for traditional targets of monetary policy.

[3] The first devaluation was more or less an administrative correction associated with the removal of export subsidies. The second devaluation was unplanned and implemented under fear of depletion of foreign exchange reserves. The third devaluation was prompted by the fact that the pressure on reserves was not completely neutralized by the second devaluation.

the undervaluation of the CZK further. Some studies suggest that in 1997 the CZK remains significantly undervalued with respect to PPP or to the coefficient ERDI.

Table 8.4 Initial Official Exchange Rates in 1990-1997 (in CZK)

	USD	DEM	ATS	CHF	GBP
Dec. 28, 1990	28.000	18.230	2.590	21.340	52.500
January 2, 1992	27.840	18.350	2.610	20.570	5.370
May 3, 1993 to					
May, 1997	28.444	17.995	-	-	-

Source: Frait, J. *International Monetary Theory*, Ostrava, VSB-TU, 1996, p. 60.

Proponents of the effective exchange rate policy claim that the undervaluation was one of the "pillows" of transformation and that the primary aim of the devaluations was to make Czechoslovak exports competitive.   However, the "competitiveness effect" of the 1990 devaluations was in principle fully eroded by the inflation differential during 1993.   The nominal effective exchange rate has remained nearly constant while the real value of the CZK increased significantly in the period 1993 to 1996 (see Table 8.1).

The CZK/DEM exchange rate has remained nearly stable during the last few years, whereas the CZK/USD exchange rate has shown greater volatility. This is primarily due to a strategy that fixed the CZK exchange rate to a basket with a dominant weight placed on the DEM. Most Czech exporters and importers invoice their foreign trade in DEM and the stable CZK/DEM rate justifies a relatively low extent of currency derivatives hedging.

In retrospect it seems likely that the initial undervaluation of the CZK was excessive and caused an adverse shock to the economy. Policymakers should not be too severely criticized for this decision, however, since their decision-making was done under conditions of fundamental uncertainty and without a benchmark for a more precise evaluation of the equilibrium exchange rate. Nevertheless, after 1993 the economy was stabilized and there was no apparent reason to maintain a policy that undervalued the currency. A more reasonable policy alternative would have been to revalue the currency, than to manage the exchange rate according to the development of the inflation differential. Unfortunately, the government of Vaclav Klaus chose to designate the fixed (or more precisely "unchanged") exchange rate as a key component of its macroeconomic policy and refused to consider any adjustment in that policy.

In the period 1992-1994, the CZK remained a nonconvertible currency by International Monetary Fund (IMF) standards. Initially enterprises were allowed to keep foreign exchange accounts and borrow abroad nearly automatically. In 1994, the possibility of implementing full current account and limited capital account convertibility was increasingly discussed and eventually accomplished in the new foreign exchange legislation enacted at the end of 1995.[4] Since that time, the CZK has been a convertible currency, barring certain restrictions and controls.

Table 8.5 Czechoslovak Balance of Payments (1990-1992, convertible currencies, mil. USD)

	1990	1991	1992
Current Account	-1,105	356.5	225.6
Trade balance	-785	-447.4	-1,575.6
Service balance	37	827.4	1,652.4
Income balance	-316	-65.4	8.8
Unilateral transfers	-40	41.8	140.0
Capital Account	326	47.0	40.6
Foreign direct investments	181	592.4	1,054.9
Portfolio investments	-	-	-42.6
Other long-term capital	718	1,731.7	471.4
Short-term capital	-573	-2,277.1	-1,443.1
Errors and omissions	-324	494.4	-386.3
Change in official reserves	1,102	-879.9	120.1

Source: Czech National Bank.

The Balance of Payments in the Czech Republic After 1990

The main aim of the 1990 devaluations was to prevent the economy from falling into a balance of payments crisis. The introduction of internal convertibility was another step in that direction. In both 1991 and 1992 there was a surplus in the current account. The situation thus proved to be more favorable than had been expected and deficits in the trade balance[5]

---

[4] The Foreign Exchange Act, No. 219, 1995.

[5] The sharp increase in the deficit of the trade balance in 1992 can be attributed mainly to biased expectations of domestic and foreign subjects caused by the

were covered by service account surpluses (growing receipts from the tourist industry, in particular).

Table 8.6 Current Account and External Debt of the Czech Republic (bil. USD)*

	1/93	12/93	12/94	12/95	9/96	1/97
External liabilities	7.08	8.50	10.29	16.36	18.1	20.4
External assets	8.44	11.03	13.89	22.78	25.85	26.4
Net external debt	-1.36	-2.53	-3.59	-6.42	-7.75	-6.00

* In Convertible Currency, end of period.
Source: Annual Reports of the Czech National Bank from December, 1993 to December, 1996.

Table 8.7 The Czech Balance of Payments (1993-1996, mil. USD)

	1993	1994	1995	1996
Current Account	114.6	-49.7	-1,362.3	-4,475.8
Trade balance	-311.7	-888.9	-3,677.9	-5,971.8
Service balance	1,010.8	732.9	1,842.0	1,785.0
Income balance	-117.5	-20.1	-105.6	-679.9
Unilateral transfers	-467.0	126.4	579.2	390.0
Capital Account	3,024.8	3,371.1	8,225.9	4,071.7
Foreign direct investments	552.1	748.0	2,525.6	1,387.9
Portfolio investments	1,600.6	855.5	1,362.0	725.5
Other long-term capital	816.2	1,108.7	3,367.1	2,716.2
Short-term capital	55.9	658.9	971.2	-757.9
Errors and ommitions	-110.1	-949.8	594.5	-423.9
Change in Official Reserves	-3,029.3	-2,371.6	-7,458.1	828.0

Source: *Annual Reports* of the Czech National Bank from December, 1993 to December, 1996.

The competitiveness of Czech exports in 1991-1992 can be attributed mainly to the undervalued crown. As mentioned earlier, by 1993 the inflation differential had almost fully eroded the effect of the undervalued currency. The results for 1993 suggest that there were non-monetary and

forthcoming split of Czechoslovakia. There were significant uncertainties about the future monetary and trade regimes between the Czech Republic and the Slovak Republic, and regarding the values of their currencies.

non-price factors, other than the undervalued crown, that had a positive impact on exports. The sharp annual increases in exports to developed countries (about 20%) in 1991-1993 can be explained by factors such as an improved quality of exported goods, entry into new markets, and successful marketing by exporting companies. These forces helped to offset the effect of the rising real exchange rate of the CZK.

The balance of payments continued to be favorable even after the split of the federation in 1993. However, as shown in Table 8.7, the situation changed dramatically in 1994. The declining current balance between 1994 and 1996 signaled deterioration of the macroeconomic situation in the Czech Republic, mirroring the mistakes of the government and the central bank in the period after 1992.

The overall balance of payments was positive in 1993, 1994, and 1995, showing 3 billion USD, 2.4 billion USD, and 7.5 billion USD, respectively. The foreign exchange reserves of the Czech National Bank (CNB) increased from 0.8 billion USD in January, 1993, to more than 6.2 billion USD in December, 1994, and to 13.9 billion USD in December, 1995, despite deficits in the current account in 1994 and 1995. A dramatic reversal of this trend occurred in 1996 when the overall balance of payments showed a deficit of 0.8 billion USD and foreign exchange reserves declined to 12.4 billion USD by year's end.

The balance-of-payments developments in 1995 and 1996 led to lively discussions about devaluation and import restrictions. Such discussions focused mainly on the trade balance. In 1995 the deficit in the trade balance totalled 104 billion CZK and was approximately 175 billion CZK in 1996. The government argued that a deficit in the trade balance was typical of an emerging economy in transition, and was, to a certain extent, linked to economy-wide restructuring and growth in national income. This is, however, only part of the story. The sharp increase in the trade balance deficit (see Figure 8.1) was also caused by excessive growth of the money supply, a real appreciation of the CZK, sharp increases in nominal and real wages, and politically motivated regulation of some non-tradables prices. [6]

---

[6] The low competitiveness of Czech exports and growth in real income were reflected in high increases in imports with relatively small increases in exports. The deficit in the trade balance was only partially eliminated by the surplus in the services account. There is evidence that the worsening of the current account can be only partially explained by the real appreciation of the CZK. Jonáš (1996) explains that if we consider the import demand, the relevant real exchange rate is the one based on the consumer price index. With respect to this, one can say that

Figure 8.1 Trade Balance
          (monthly results, 1993-1996, current prices)

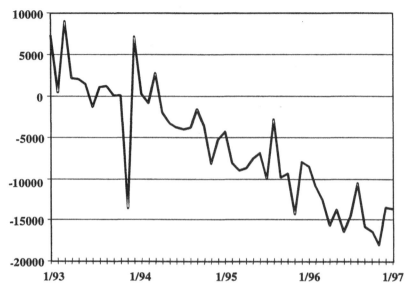

Source: Statistical Surveys of the Czech Republic, Czech Statistical Office, various
     issues from 1993-1997.

The current account deteriorated along with the trade balance. In 1995
the deficit was approximately 35 billion CZK (3% of GDP) and in 1996 it
was approximately 120 billion CZK (8% of GDP). The results from the
first six months of 1997 indicate that the deficit is nearly 55 billion CZK.
This created fears of sharp growth in foreign debt and the worsening of the

the imported goods were 21% cheaper in 1995 compared to the end of 1990.
Nevertheless, for the export demand, the real exchange rate based on the unit labor
cost index is more relevant. In this case, the Czech export was cheaper by more
than 10% at the of 1995 compared to the end of 1990. One can conclude that the
effects of the 1990 devaluations were still not eliminated, if the growth in labor
productivity were taken into account, until the end of 1995. The analysts of the
central bank concluded that the prime cause of the deficit was the growth of
domestic absorption which switched the production from exports to domestic use
and to the growth in investment demand which required high imports of capital
goods. The sharp rise in nominal wages in 1996 caused the sharp increase in real
unit labor costs.

balance-of-payments crisis in the future. Although the gross foreign debt has been growing steadily, the net foreign debt is still negative. Unfortunately, a significant part of foreign assets are probably unrecoverable and the country can hardly be viewed as a foreign creditor. If the above described trend continues in 1997, the situation will become unsustainable and a drastic change in macroeconomic policy will be inevitable.

Problem Areas and Their Impact on Macroeconomic Development

Capital Flows and Money Supply in the Czech Republic in 1993-1996

In the 1993-1996 period, the Czech Republic lost control over the net foreign assets of the banking sector, a problem similar to the one faced by the rapidly expanding economies of Asia and Latin America in the 1980s. This problem stemmed directly from the exchange rate policy of the government, which was a fixed exchange rate, maintained at the same level since the end of 1990 and used as a nominal anchor of the economy.

In a small open economy like the Czech Republic, developments in the balance of payments inevitably influence macroeconmic policy in general and monetary policy in particular. The unchanged exchange rate, the absence of expectations for devaluation, and relatively high nominal CZK interest rates had the predicted effect of attracting foreign investors. This resulted in a large influx of foreign capital and, in turn, created significant surpluses in the capital account. Moreover, the large inflow of foreign exchange created pressures for excessive growth in the money supply. The response of the central bank (CNB) was to sterilize the inflow. However, beginning with the second half of 1994, sterilization became increasingly difficult and, in 1995, discussions concerning the potential inflationary impact of foreign capital inflows were added to the macreconmic policy agenda.

Capital account surpluses for the four years, 1993 through 1996, amounted to 3.025 billion USD, 3.371 billion USD, 8.225 billion USD, and 4.071 billion USD respectively. The inflow of foreign capital in the form of direct and portfolio investment totalled 100 billion CZK in 1993 (10% of GDP), 119 billion CZK in 1994 (12% of GDP), 230 billion CZK in 1995 (18% of GDP) and 113 billion CZK (8.5% of the GDP). The amount of foreign direct investment grew rather slowly causing portfolio investment and foreign credits to the corporate sector to dominate the total inflow of capital. This was reflected in the growth of money supply, which accelerated in 1997 (see Table 8.8).

The inflow of capital and credit creation which was partially financed from abroad are important sources of the growth in money supply. Money supply growth was in response to an increase in the demand for money which the CNB claims is the result of a decline in the income velocity of money.[7] However, the fast growth in the money supply has not manifested itself in the price level.

The CNB decided to tackle the problem of excessive capital inflow by sterilizing the growing foreign exchange reserves. Large-scale sterilization has been conducted since the second quarter of 1993. Due to low government debt, a surplus in the government budget, and a relatively low stock of government treasury bills, the CNB decided to draw liquidity from the money market by issuing its own CNB treasury bills. In 1994 the CNB also used treasury bills of the Fund of National Property (FNP). The stock of CNB treasury bills peaked in July, 1995, at 105 billion CZK.

Table 8.8 Monetary Survey 1993 - 1997 (end of period, bil. CZK)

	IV/92	IV/93	IV/94	IV/95	IV/96	II/97
M2	599.4	722.1	877.3	962.4	1120.5	1135.2
M1	306.9	361.1	426.5	416.8	475.3	397.3
Net foreign assets	75.2	129.9	219.9	337.4	281.7	292.3
Net domestic assets	524.2	592.2	657.8	625.0	838.8	842.9
Currency	58.9	59.8	84.0	95.1	118.9	113.9
Demand deposits	248	301.3	342.5	321.7	356.4	283.4
Time deposits	236.6	303.6	390.0	458.7	559.5	606.5
Foreign currency dep.	55.9	57.4	60.8	86.9	85.7	131.4

Source:　Selected Indicators of Monetary Development, Czech National Bank, December, 1993 to December, 1997.

---

[7] According to the quantity theory, money demand is a function of the number of transactions and the income is used only as a proxy. It can be a reliable proxy in a stable economy, since the two variables are correlated, but this might not be the case of an economy in transition. We can identify several reasons for the increase in the number of transactions in the Czech Republic after 1990: a dramatic increase in the number of companies; a great array of new transactions in the financial markets, increased use of CZK abroad, etc. In our opinion this might be the reason for the increase in money demand and not so much the drop in the velocity.

In August, 1994, the minimum reserve requirements on sight deposits (from 9% to 12%) were lifted, while the reserve requirements on term deposits were kept at 3%. These actions removed about 10 billion CZK from the market. Similar actions were taken in 1995 when the minimum reserve requirements were unified at 8.5% on all deposits resulting in a 13 billion CZK withdrawal from the market. There were three more specific sterilization measures applied in 1995: (1) the transfer of FNP deposits from commercial banks accounts to CNB accounts; (2) the freezing of the proceeds from STP Telecom privatization in CNB accounts; and (3) a significant decrease in refinancing (discount and Lombard loans).

Figure 8.2 Net Foreign Assets (NFA) and Net Domestic Assets (NDA) in Monetary Base (bil. CZK)

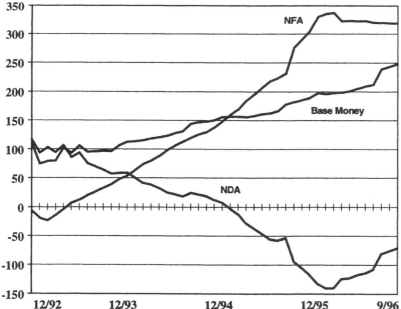

Source: Selected Indicators of Monetary Development, Czech National Bank, various issues from December, 1992 to December, 1996.

In April, 1995, the CNB introduced a 0.25% spread for sales and purchases of foreign exchange with commercial banks (up to this date, the deals were done at the mid-rate). The exchange rate fluctuation band was extended from ± 0.5% to ± 0.75%. In July, 1995, some restrictions on capital flows were imposed. These regulations were aimed at limiting the short-term open positions of banks toward nonresidents.[8] Banks were required to maintain the structure of short-term assets and liabilities holdings against foreign subjects in such a way that the short position could not overlap the total value of short-term liabilities by more than 30% or 500 million CZK. This measure was not very effective because regulated subjects responded by extending the maturity of foreign sources, which resulted in an overlap of slightly more than one year.

It is well known that in a fixed-exchange rate regime, sterilization has limits and these were encountered in the Czech Republic. Issuing treasury bills and drawing liquidity from the money market led to an increase in interest rates and the widening of the interest rate differential, which *ceteris paribus*, attracted additional foreign capital. This circular pattern rendered the CNB's sterilization policy ineffective and did not provide a solution to the problem. Moreover, the above described chain reaction lends support to the idea that under a fixed-exchange rate regime, the central bank cannot control the overall level of monetary base, but only its division between net domestic assets and net foreign assets.

Let us now consider the development of the monetary base and its components since 1993. Figure 8.2 traces the monetary base from December 1993 to October 1996 and shows the division of the monetary base into net foreign and net domestic assets. It is evident that the one-way flow of capital to the economy caused nearly the entire increase in money supply. Net foreign assets grew faster than the monetary base in this period. Consequently, the share of domestic credit in the monetary base declined significantly. Therefore it is clear that under a fixed exchange rate, the money supply is determined by the balance of payments.

As a solution to this problem, the majority of macroeconomists recommended the widening of the band for exchange rate fluctuation. The central bank responded in February, 1996, and the fluctuation band was increased to ± 7.5%. The measure had the expected effect and the inflow of capital slowed. At the same time foreign investors reduced the extent of their portfolio investments in the country due to the bad state of the capital

---

[8] A short-term position of the bank towards nonresidents is the difference between the value of short-term assets and liabilities against foreign subjects. This is foreign exchange as well as CZK assets and liabilities with a maturity of less than one year.

market. As a result, the capital account surplus in 1996 was relatively small compared to 1995. The rapid growth of net foreign assets abated and the CNB was able to get the money supply under control.

The central bank has been overshooting the targeted money supply growth every year, and the M2 measure grew at a rate of 20% in the last three years (see Table 8.9). The CNB claims that growth in the money supply has not manifested itself in the form of inflation due to the decline in income velocity. This explanation may not be completely accurate, however. In a fixed exchange rate regime, excessive money demand is diverted initially to imports (which is confirmed by the growing trade deficit). Only after the trade deficit forces the devaluation of the domestic currency can the inflationary effect of excessive money supply growth be felt.

The results for 1996 and 1997 indicate a slowing down of the money supply growth. After the widening of the exchange rate band and the decline in foreign investors, confidence in the domestic market the inflow of foreign capital dropped and the crisis in the banking sector slowed the growth of domestic credit. The M2 aggregate growth is projected to be 13 or 14 percent which is acceptable, but may be not sustainable.

Table 8.9   Actual and Targeted Money Supply Growth

	M2 growth rate (%)		
	Initial Target	Modified Target	Actual Growth Rate
1992	12	17.5	20.3
1993	17	19	20
1994	12-15	17	21
1995	14-17	14-17	20.2
1996	14-17	-	14
1997	7-11	-	9 (August)

Source: Selected Indicators of Monetary Development, Czech National Bank, December, 1993 to December, 1997.

Those who are concerned about the growing deficit in the current account recommend either devaluation of the CZK by 10-20% during 1997 or a switch to a crawling peg as applied in Hungary or Poland, accompanied by strict monetary and fiscal policy. Both government and CNB officials argue that the fixed exchange rate is the anchor of macroeconomic policy, and devaluation would not improve the current account but rather would cause inflation and the postponement of the restructuring of industry.

If the deterioration in the current account continues, devaluation would be a solution. However, this is a rather complicated solution for a country using a fixed exchange rate as a nominal anchor of the economy. Instead, we maintain that the authorities should drop their insistence on maintaining an unrealistic fixed exchange rate and evaluate the trend in the real value of the currency. A viable solution is to slow down the real appreciation by relatively frequent small nominal devaluations as in Hungary or Poland.

An additional argument for devaluation is the fact that the authorities have hardly any other instrument in the short or medium term. If we accept the idea that the Czech economy slipped into recession in the second half of 1996 (despite the fact that the current account is worsening), we have to accept that the only viable policy is devaluation and domestic demand restriction. Such a cure is, of course, unpleasant in the short run. However, the alternative would be to face a balance-of-payments crisis which could enforce a large devaluation and ferment an economy-wide financial crisis. The threat of being trapped in an inflationary spiral would then require very restrictive macroeconomic policy. This would mean returning to square one, to the very beginning of the transition, and the process of macroeconomic stabilization would have to be started once more.

Unemployment

As mentioned earlier, the Czech Republic has one of the lowest unemployment rates in the whole of Europe. Unemployment rose to 6.6% in 1991 from 1% in 1990. The unempoyment rate dropped after the reform package was instituted and with the successful privatization of the state-held companies. The unemployment rate is estimated to have been 3.3% in 1996 and is projected to be around 4.3% for the 1997-2000 period.

The low rate of unemployment may be attributed to the following:

- As a result of the rapid and successful privatization of state-owned enterprises, most of the workers displaced from the state and cooperative sectors were absorbed by the private firms (especially medium-size and small firms).
- There has been a great deal of growth in the informal sector since

1991. It is estimated that the share of the informal sector is approximately between 10% and 15% of the GDP. The Institute of Labor and Social Affairs in Prague estimates that roughly 250,000 individuals were employed in the informal sector.

• There is rampant over-employment in the Czech labor markets. There is evidence of labor hoarding by firms and many of the former state enterprises still behave "uneconomically."

• Active labor market policies adopted by the government in the wake of transition, the decline in real wages in the 1991-1992 period and the increase in labor productivity in 1995 and 1996 are also cited as reasons for the fall in unemployment in the post-transtion period.

General Macroeconomic Issues

Table 8.10 shows macroeconomic results in the Czech Republic for the period, 1990-1995. By comparision, in 1996 the economy seemed to grow at a satisfactory pace. However, one has to be careful when evaluating the statistical figures. The GDP growth of 4.1% and the industrial production of 6.8% cannot be viewed as signs of unambiguous success. In reality, the growth of GDP and industrial production seemed to slow in the second half of the year. One also must not forget that these indices declined sharply in the transitional years (see Table 8.3). As a result we have a low statistical base from which to evaluate current performance. In addition, if we theoretically accept the inefficiency and low productivity of the socialist enterprises, we should expect the liberalized and privatized capitalist economy with satisfactory resource endowment to grow faster than 4.4%.

There were some signs that in 1995 the economy had become overheated. However, this trend seems to have changed in 1996. Despite the official proclamations, the GDP growth rate was lower in 1996 (4.1%) compared to 1995 (5.9%). The growth rate of industrial production of 6.8% in 1996 was lower than that in 1995 of 9.2%. This was confirmed by discouraging results in the last months of 1996 and first months of 1997.

There are significant inflationary pressures that will prevent inflation from declining. The government's reluctance to allow some controlled prices to rise (electricity and heating prices, railway fares, housing costs etc.) only has the effect of delaying inflation. The sharp rise in the retail turnover in the end of 1996 was indicative of the rise in inflationary expectations. The growing deficit in the current account, despite the relatively low net foreign debt (see Table 8.5), sooner or later will force devaluation[9] which would fill the inflationary gap (created by high money supply growth in the previous years).

Table 8.10 Demand and Output in the Czech Republic[a]

	1990	1991	1992	1993	1994	1995	1996	1997[b]
Gross Domestic Product	-1.2	-	-6.6	0.9	2.7	5.9	4.1	1.2
- Consumption	6.7	-	9.1	2.9	5.3	6.2	6.3	5.6
- Govt Expenditures	0.9	-9.1	-4.7	-0.1	-2.3	0.4	3.1	1.7
- Gross Capital Formation	3.7	-	-	-2.2	22.1	20.6	17.2	-10.1
- of which: Fixed Capital Formation	-2.1	-	6.3	-7.7	17.3	22.3	8.6	-4.8
- Exports	-7.0	-8.8	0.9	7.5	0.2	15.9	3.3	15.4
- Imports	3.2	-	11.2	10.0	7.8	21.7	11.7	10.5
Industrial Production	-5.0	-	-	-5.3	2.3	9.2	6.8	3.6
Average Real Wage	-5.6	-	10.1	3.5	6.5	7.7	8.5	4.3

[a] Changes in % against the same period of the previous year, constant prices;
[b] 1997 Quarter 2.
Source: Statistical Surveys of the Czech Republic, Czech Statistical Office, various
     issues from 1990-1997.

There are problems on the fiscal front too. Thanks to the revenues from privatization, the government was able to balance the budget over the last few years. This is not likely to continue in the future as privatization has almost been completed. Furthermore, some public sectors such as education, railways, and health care are underfunded and are facing growing budget deficits. The budget deficit in 1996 is predicted to worsen in 1997, especially if the government still insists on subsidizing some industries in the public sector.

Conclusions

The initial macroeconomic stabilization in the former Czechoslovakia, in the aftermath of the velvet revolution in 1989, was undoubtedly

---

[9] There is some support for the use of a crawling peg regime as applied in Hungary or Poland.

successful. In 1993 the economy seemed to be stabilized and the proponents of the transition began to celebrate the "end of transition". Unfortunately, the stabilization has become a victim of its own success. The proponents of the transition seem to have ignored the fact that macroeconomic stabilization is a medium-term process and that the economy has to be stabilized at the microecomic level to achieve long-term growth. The development in the Czech Republic supports the idea that if the transition is not conducted rigorously and in a consistent fashion, the improvement in the macroeconomic situation might be only temporary and the desired rapid growth in the long run will not occur.

Available statistics for 1996 and 1997 suggest that the economy may not be headed in the right direction and that a period of recession may be at hand. The remedy would be to follow a strict macroeconomic policy in consonance with an economically sound exchange rate policy. This should also be accompanied by further privatization, reform of the banking sector and capital markets, deregulation of the non-tradeables sector, and the creation of a relevant institutional framework to define and enforce property rights.

References

CNB: *Annual Report*, Czech National Bank, various issues.

CNB: *Selected Indicators of Monetary Development.* Czech National Bank, various issues.

CSO: *Statistical Surveys of the Czech Republic*, Czech Statistical Office, various issues.

Dedek, O. [1995]. "Currency Convertibility and Exchange Rate Policies in the Czech Republic," *Politická ekonomie*, No. 6.

Desai, R. [1995]. "Financial Market Reform in the Czech Republic. The revival of repression?" CERGE, Working Paper No. 86.

Frait, J. [1996]. *International Monetary Theory*. Ostrava, Technical University.

Gottvald, J. and Simek, M. [1996]. *International Baseline Study - Czech Republic.* Institute of Employment Studies, July, The University of Warwick.

Hajek, M., et al. [1995]. "Macroeconomic Analysis of the Czech Economy: 1990-1994," *Prague Economic Papers,* Vol. IV, No. 2, pp. 101-147.

Hrncir, M. [1993]. "Exchange Rate and the Transition: the Case of the Czech Republic," *Politická ekonomie*, No. 4.

Hrncir, M. [1993]. "Financial Intermediation in Former Czechoslovakia," *Prague Economic Papers,* Vol. II, No. 4, pp. 312-330.

Janacek, K. et al. [1996]. "Czech Economy at the Start of 1996," *Prague*

Economic Papers, Vol. V, No. 2, pp. 103-121.

Kouba, K. [1994]. "Systemic Changes in the Czech Economy," *Prague Economic Papers*, Vol. III, No. 4, pp. 311-322.

Mertlik, D. [1995]. "Czech Privatization: from Public Ownership to Public Ownership in Five Years," *Prague Economic Papers*, Vol. IV, No. 4, pp. 321-336.

OECD Economic Surveys. The Czech Republic [1996]. OECD, July.

9 The Third Wave of Privatization: A Search for True Owners?

ERIC R. HAKE

Introduction

One of the most important issues in the process of privatization and transition is corporate governance. After the privatization of state enterprises, who will coordinate the process of restructuring industry? In Central Europe, this debate has focused on the role of banks and financial intermediaries in the emerging corporate structure. Should institutional investors be able to control large blocks of stock or should strict diversification rules be established? Should the emergence of "true owners"--long term investors with control of industry management--be supported or repressed? While some authors (Blanchard and Dornbusch 1996, 43-47; Roe 1994, 9-19) have outlined the benefits of strong financial intermediaries and bank ownership in industry, other authors have argued that the principal/agent conflicts and dangers of insider dealing make active financial intermediation a dangerous option (Dittus and Prowse 1996, 55-56).

The current situation in the Czech Republic, where investment groups and banking subsidiaries have consolidated control over large blocks of stock and routinely sit on the supervisory and management boards of industry, makes this debate somewhat outdated. It has been estimated that majority shareholders control approximately 50 percent of the 1,700 companies listed on the Prague Stock Exchange (King 1996, 9). While some of these investment groups originated in the private sector, investment groups founded by partially state-owned commercial banks wield substantial influence. Instead of addressing the relative merits of diversification and concentration strategies by institutional investors, or their right to exist, this paper focuses on the origin and role of these investment groups. How did the current situation emerge? Are investment groups behaving as "true owners?" Does the behavior of independent investment groups differ from those under partial state control? This paper benefits from the theoretical framework of recombinant property established by David Stark, who argues that privatization in Central Europe represents a transformation of property rights that merges private and state property in a web of cross-ownership. This perspective is more relevant to the situation of the Czech Republic than earlier analyses of corporate governance structure which assume a strict division between public and private property (Stark 1996, 111-112).[1]

After a review of the history of the Czech government's voucher privatization program and the privately-organized Third Wave of privatization in the next section, a description of the legal forms of financial intermediaries, their methods used to accumulate assets, and the evidence of industry-financial cross ownership is presented in the third section. The fourth section explains the different investment strategies adopted by financial intermediaries and the conversion of more aggressively-managed investment companies into holding companies during mid-1996. The changing structure of the Czech banking industry, and its impact on the financial intermediaries industry is discussed in the fifth section, which provides an introduction to a more detailed section on the third wave of privatization--the consolidation of ownership shares by larger financial intermediaries during late 1995 and 1996. In the seventh section, a comparison of changes in the largest financial group's portfolios from September, 1996, to January, 1997, suggests that the consolidation of share-ownership associated with the Third Wave represented a short-run strategy to consolidate ownership before profit-taking. The results, however, are mixed and reflect the different strategies of more aggressive private investment groups and the partially state-owned bank investment groups. In conclusion, the last section reviews the possible future strategy and role of financial intermediaries in the evolving industrial structure of the Czech Republic.

From State to Private Ownership: Voucher Privatization

The desire to reduce government ownership of industry quickly presented a series of problems in Czechoslovakia.[2] Conventional methods of auction

---

[1] Although Stark has dealt primarily with the development of Hungary, his work has broader relevance to the region.

[2] The division of the Czech and Slovak Federal Republics in the Velvet Divorce

or direct sale and the requisite determination of property values would have prolonged the process and favored foreign investors over the domestic, albeit nascent, business community. Privatization methods that would have favored the existing management of state-owned enterprises (SOE's) were also unacceptable. The concept of voucher privatization, championed by then Federal Finance Minister Václav Klaus and organized by Vice Minister Dušan Tøíska, provided an alternative that promised to be quick and politically viable. By freely distributing state property to the population, transition from state to private ownership would be rapid. Czechoslovakia was uniquely well-suited for this approach. Unlike Hungary or Poland, the lack of pre-revolution reforms had allowed the state to retain clear ownership of public property. The mass privatization of property would therefore not be influenced by the interests of incumbent management or the labor councils of State-Owned Enterprises. Voucher privatization was formally adopted by Act 92/1991, On Conditions and Terms Governing the Transfer of State Property to Other Persons, to be carried out in two waves that would privatize the majority of large-scale enterprises.[3]

The method of voucher privatization was relatively straight forward. SOE's slated for voucher privatization were corporatized (turned into joint-stock companies) and their stock was deposited with the Fond narodního majetku (National Property Fund, FNM) during the transitional period. Corporatized SOE shares were assigned a par value of CSK 1,000, with the number of shares issued being determined by the book value of property.[4]

For a purchase price (CSK 35) and registration fee (CSK 1,000), adult Czechoslovaks in the first wave of privatization received a voucher booklet of 1,000 points. In a series of auction rounds, participants used these voucher points to bid for the shares of the privatizing companies. To begin the process of equilibrating voucher points with enterprise shares, the initial investment point-share ratio was set at 3 points per share. If demand for shares in a particular enterprise (denominated in voucher points) exceeded supply by more than 25 percent, no trades would take place, and the investment point-share ratio would be increased for bidding

---

(January, 1993) will not be dealt with in this paper.

[3] For a complete description of the voucher privatization program, see Federal Ministry of Finance, 1992.

[4] All currency values prior to January 1, 1993 are in Czechoslovak Crowns (CSK). After January 1, 1993, the unit of currency changed to Czech Crowns (CZK).

in the next round. If the demand for shares did not exceed supply by 25 percent, shares would be allocated to the investors and any remaining shares would go to the next round, with a lower investment point-share ratio.

The first wave of privatization began in 1992. Close to 6 million Czechs took part in the distribution of shares in 943 enterprises, with a book value of CSK 200.8 billion privatized through vouchers (Frydman, Rapaczynski and Earle 1993, 85). The second wave of privatization, ending in late 1994, involved 6.15 million Czechs and the privatization of 861 companies.[5]   Table 9.1 provides a summary of the results of privatization. While property worth CZK 474 billion was privatized through the voucher method, the FNM still owned property worth CZK 230 billion at the end of 1995. As the result of the continuing ownership in enterprises held by the FNM, the government retained the ability to influence the emerging relationships between industrial and financial groups. Despite this continuing stake, government ownership of industry dropped from 86 percent to 10-35 percent in less than three years (Coffee 1996, 114, 119).[6]

Table 9.1 Results of Privatization, December, 1995 (billions of CZK)

	Shares Privatized through the Fond narodniho majetku (FNM)	Restitutions, Direct Sales and Auctions
Privatized Property	474.63	111.37
Still Owned by State	230.12	32.71
Not Yet Converted to Shares	1.69	--
Total	706.44	144.08

Source: Oldrick Rejnus and Radek Schmied, Czech Republic, in *Capital Markets in Transition Economics: Central and Eastern Europe*, p. 8.

While voucher privatization largely achieved the goal of distributing former state property, several problems have emerged. The rapid entrance of a large number of stocks onto the fledgling Prague Stock Exchange has

---

[5] Only 185 of these 861 companies had already been partially privatized in the first wave of privatization.

[6] These were the boundaries of estimates in 1994.

produced a relatively illiquid stock market. As of July, 1996, it has been estimated that only 20 percent of the securities listed on the Prague Stock Exchange were regularly traded (Babiak, 1996). Additionally, the wide distribution of shares--approximately 80 percent of the adult population in the Czech Republic became shareholders--has resulted in the ongoing concentration of share ownership. Individual shareholders, wishing to liquidate their holdings, have produced a condition of excess supply that kept share prices low[7] (Rejnuš and Schmied 1996, 9-10). These conditions allowed larger investors to consolidate their holdings by purchasing stock at significant discounts. This process is typified by the "Third Wave of Privatization," that began in late 1995 and continued through 1996. With limited shareholder protection, the acquisition of controlling blocks of stock allowed majority shareholders to cancel outstanding shares. Failing this, the appearance of majority shareholders has reduced demand for trading stock and dampened prices considerably.

While the strong position of control maintained by the Czechoslovak government was initially regarded as beneficial to the process of rapid privatization, its continuing influence has produced unforeseen difficulties. Favoritism towards the partially-state- owned banks and their investment subsidiaries can be regarded as either unnecessary government interference or a form of industrial policy. Similarly, the slow development of a comprehensive legal framework for the capital markets can be interpreted as either the prudent behavior of a classically liberal government (adopting general guidelines and then regulating in response to specific violations) or a smokescreen that obscures the true relationship between industry and the state and limits the opportunities of foreign investors.

---

[7] Following early enthusiasm, the official index of the Prague Stock Exchange PX-50 reached a peak of 1244.7 points on March 1, 1994. It then declined consistently until reaching its lowest point of 387.2 on June 29, 1995. Quotation of the PX-50 began on April 6, 1994 with a base value of 1000. The series was then generated back to September, 1993. Several differences exist between the introduction of first-wave shares (July, 1993) and second-wave shares (March, 1995). The introduction of first-wave shares was staggered and shares were generally perceived to be undervalued. Second-wave shares were entered onto the Stock Exchange simultaneously and were perceived as overvalued.

The Emergence of Financial Intermediaries

From the beginning of voucher privatization, the investment activities of banks and independent financial intermediaries were significant. Financial intermediaries were allowed to enter privatization in an attempt to reduce the fragmentation of share ownership which was expected to occur. While other countries, such as Poland, only allowed government ownership of investment companies, the Czech case is unique because the creation of investment companies was not limited by the state.

In most cases, a founding company (frequently a bank) would establish an investment company, which in turn would establish several investment privatization funds. While investment companies are joint stock companies according to Articles of Incorporation and Statutes, investment funds can either take the form of joint stock companies or, according to Act 248/1992, the form of unit funds (podílové fondy) which are not separate legal entities and have only Statutes which describe the types of activities in which the funds can engage[8]. Investment companies and investment funds issue shares with ownership rights, while the participation certificates issued by unit funds have no ownership rights. As a result of these differences, it is possible to gain control over investment companies or investment funds but not unit funds by acquiring shares on the secondary market.

While the legislation allowing the creation of unit funds was not adopted early enough to affect the first wave of privatization, the ability to keep unit funds under the control of the founding investment company made them significantly more attractive to the management of such companies. Consequently, the majority of new funds created for the second wave of privatization took the form of unit funds.[9]

In addition to ultimately gaining large amounts of stock by acting as intermediaries for individual investors, investment companies are also credited with the promotion and success of voucher privatization in its early stages. At the original deadline for registering voucher booklets, December, 1991, less than 5 percent of the eligible population had registered. It initially appeared that voucher privatization would suffer from a lack of popular participation. To provide additional opportunities

---

[8] Unit funds are not incorporated and, therefore, are dependent on their founding firm. They cannot exist independently or adopt a new management.

[9] The number of unit funds operating in December, 1994 was 275. The number of investment funds was 280.

to register, the deadline was delayed to the end of February, 1992 (Frydman, Rapaczynski and Earle 1993, 85).

Led by the advertisements of Harvard Capital and Consulting, the largest independent investment company in the Czech Republic, investment companies offered significant rewards to individuals willing to invest their points through intermediaries rather than engaging directly in voucher privatization.[10] Harvard Capital and Consulting's original promise in November, 1991, to redeem voucher booklets in one year at a price equal to ten times its cost (CSK 10,350) prompted similar promises by the investment companies founded by major Czech financial institutions. První Investièní a.s. (First Investment Company, PIAS), established by Investièní banka (Investment bank), offered a CSK 15,000 loan for voucher booklets; Kapitálová investièní spoleènost (Capital Investment Company, KIS), founded by Èeská pojištovna (Czech Insurance Company), offered CSK 15,000 for a voucher booklet; and Spoøitelna investièní spoleènost (Savings Investment Company, SIS), founded by Èeská spoøitelna (Czech Savings Bank), offered CSK 11,000[11] (Coffee 1996, 124). In terms of the voucher privatization program, individual investors accepting these offers would deposit all or a portion of their investment points into an investment fund in the so-called 'zero round' prior to the actual bidding on stock which would start in the 'first round'.

The creation of investment companies began shortly after the government decree 383/1991 established the basic rules, which were later extended and codified in amendments 67/1992 and 69/1992. An additional act, 248/1992, On Investment Corporations and Investment Funds, further clarified the rules but was adopted too late to affect the first wave of privatization. In addition to the general requirements for organizing investment companies and funds, these acts provided basic diversification guidelines. No investment fund could own more than 20 percent of any company's stock, while no single holding of stock could represent more than 10 percent of the investment fund's assets. Limitations on cross-ownership prohibited investment companies from

---

[10] Harvard Capital and Consulting is the registered name and not a translation. It has no affiliation with Harvard University, although the founder of HC&C did attend the school.

[11] Concern generated by these promotional activities led Parliament to hold a special session to adopt new amendments regulating investment companies. This resulted in the revision 248/1992.

owning shares in other investment companies, while investment companies and their founders could not hold each other's shares.

Regulations on cross-ownership were designed to produce independent management structures within the framework of founding firms, investment companies, and investment funds. In practice, close relationships have emerged for two reasons:

(1) A loophole in the legislation allows cross-ownership of shares between investment funds and the firms that founded the investment companies. As investment funds were founded by investment companies, and not by the creators of the investment companies, they are not technically direct subsidiaries and therefore are not subject to the restriction against cross-shareholding between parents and subsidiaries. The "grandparent" founding company can own shares in the subsidiaries of its investment company without breaking the law. Some investment funds have also been active in purchasing the shares of its "grandparent" founding bank or other financial institutions. This has been done, arguably, to protect the banks from hostile takeovers.

(2) The promotional commitments made by the largest investment companies (to repurchase investment fund shares from the public) ultimately allowed the banks to gain controlling stakes in the investment privatization funds. While this exists to some degree in several of the larger banks, it is most apparent in the case of Investièní a poštovní banka (Investment and Postal Bank, IPB).[12]

This inter-relationship between founding firm, investment company, and investment and unit fund also allows a circumvention of the restriction on shareholdings in a single company. While the investment funds of a single investment company are not allowed in total to hold more than 20 percent of the stock of any company, the combined unit funds are allowed to own 20 percent of stock in the same company. Adding to this the possibility that founding firms and investment companies may own stock provides the opportunity for investment groups to gain majority control.[13]

In the first wave of privatization, 260 investment funds were involved, ultimately collecting 71.8 percent of all investment points. In the second wave of privatization, 353 investment funds accumulated 64 percent of all

---

[12] Investièní banka merged with Postovni banka in 1994, greatly increasing its share of Czech deposits and providing a retail network of local banks.

[13] For the purposes of this paper, the term "investment group" will be used to refer to the combination of founding firms and their affiliated investment companies, investment funds, and unit funds.

Table 9.2 Top 15 Investment Funds and Holdings, August, 1996

Name	Manager	Market Capitalization (million CZK)	Former Fund Name	Affiliation
Investment Funds				
Restituèní investièní fond	PIAS	8,650.18	-	Gov. Owned, managed by IPB
Komerèní banka IF	IKS KB	6,846.70	-	Komerèní banka
SPIF cesky	SIS	6,517.12	-	Ceska sporitelna
SPIF vynosovy	SIS	2,849.16	-	Ceska sporitelna
PIF	KIS CP	2,794.62	-	Ceska pojistovna
1.IF Zivnobanka	ZB-Trust	1,922.86	-	Zivnostenka banka
SPIF vseobecny	SIS	1,614.20	-	Ceska sporitelna
Rentiérský IF	PIAS	1,167.64	-	Investièní a poštovní banka (IPB)
Holding Companies				
Harvardsky prumyslovy holding	HC&C	2,180.09	HIF Divid.	Harvard Capital and Consulting (HC&C)
Bank Holding	PIAS	1,607.96	Banko. IF	Investièní a poštovní banka
Harvardsky financny spolecnost	HC&C	1,505.08	HIF Rusto.	Harvard Capital and Consulting (HC&C)
PPF investicny holding	PPF-IS	1,115.63	PPF Prvni Cesky	Prvny Privatizacni Fond
YSE	Linh Art	1,082.12	IF YSE	YSE
1.CS holding	Optimus	758.80	Credit-anstalt CEIF	Originally Creditanstalt. Acquired by Motoinvest
Total Capitalization		40,512.15		

Source: Atlantik Financial Markets Financial Services Research Group, Funds Sector Research and Selected Funds, p. 6.

investment points (Atlantik Financial Markets 1996, 4). The accumulation of voucher points was also concentrated in the largest funds. In the first wave, the 13 largest investment funds gained 42.8 percent of total investment points. In the second wave, the 15 largest investment funds gained 40.6 percent (Coffee 1996, 136).

Table 9.2, Top 15 Investment Funds, shows the relative importance of the largest bank and independent funds. The top 15 funds represent 82 percent of total market capitalization for all funds listed on the Prague Stock Exchange as of August, 1996. The largest, Restituèní investièní fond (Restitution Investment Fund, RIF), was established by the government to satisfy obligations associated with restitution. The government owns a golden share in RIF, allowing it to control its activities, although actual management of the fund is carried out by the investment company of Investièní a poštovní banka, PIAS. Government ownership of RIF will continue to decline, however, as restitution claims are satisfied through the allocation of RIF shares to individuals.

The funds founded by PIAS, Rentiérský IF and Bankovní IF, also performed well during privatization. The strategies of these funds, and their grandparent affiliate (Investièní a poštovní banka), have produced a significant degree of cross-ownership, as well as a concentration of holdings in the other large banks. Through its promotional obligations at the beginning of the first wave of voucher privatization, IPB provided loans to individuals who deposited their voucher booklets with its funds, using the investment fund shares as collateral. The lesser value of the investment fund shares in comparison to the original loan led many small investors to default on their loans. IPB, therefore, retained ownership of its investment funds' shares.

As of September, 1996, IPB owned more than 30 percent of the shares in five of its investment funds.[14] These investment funds also acquired shares in IPB. Through a series of purchases by affiliated funds, IPB's controlling block in itself surpassed the holdings of the FNM. As of February 1997, the FNM owned 31.5 percent of IPB. The second largest shareholder was IPB's Bankovní holding, with 10.7 percent. Although direct stock holdings of this nature disagree with the intent of the law, this case is not considered illegal as Bankovní holding was founded by PIAS,

---

[14] Bankovní Holding (43.86%), IF Obchodu (47.68%), Køištálový IF (35.24%), Potravinvá0ský IF (35.24%), and Prùmyslový IF (33.81%). IPB also owns controlling interest in two other subsidiaries: IF Bohatství (29.76%) and Rentiérský IF (29.62%).

which in turn was founded by the IPB owned company, Domeana. In addition to the stock owned by Bankovní holding, IPB also indirectly holds another 26.2 percent through Vojenské stavby (90 percent owned by IPB), Charouz holding (founded with loans from IPB), and three PIAS funds: IF Bohatství, Rentiérský IF, and Privatizaèní IF. (Calbreath 1997, 5, 9) As a result of these holdings, IPB is considered to be under independent management.

While Restituèní investièní fond is the single largest fund, the three funds managed by Spoøitelna investièní spoleènost (SIS), the investment company of Èeská spoøitelna, have a greater combined market capitalization. SIS acquired the largest percentage of investment points in the first wave of voucher privatization, 10 percent of the total, and originally carried out its investment activities through a single fund, SPAS. Due to its size and resulting unmanageability, this fund was divided into three funds in June, 1995, (SPIF Èesky, SPIF Výnosový, and SPIF Všeobecná) with SPIF Èesky receiving the most liquid shares. SIS is considered to have one of the most widely- diversified portfolios, primarily due to its very large size. By the end of voucher privatization, SIS subsidiary funds owned shares in over 500 companies.

The investment fund (PIF) managed by the Èeská pojištovna investment company (Kapitálová investièní spolecnost, KIS) was originally established as an independent fund. KIS CP gained control in the first wave of privatization by purchasing its shares from individual investors in early 1992 (Atlantik Financial Markets 1996, 43). Èeská pojištovna has also been quite active in purchasing the shares of smaller domestic banks. At one time, it owned a controlling stake in Velkomoravska banka and majority stakes in Kreditní banka and Pragobanka. On the other hand, Komerèní banka, controlling the single largest non-state investment fund, Komerèní banka IF, has not actively sought to purchase controlling stakes in the domestic banking sector. This lack of interest is probably because Komercni banka is already the largest bank in the Czech Republic, controlling some 27 percent of total bank assets as of June, 1996.

While the main financial institutions of the Czech Republic are well represented among the top investment funds, independent investment companies were also able to attract enough voucher points to become major players. Most notably, these include YSE, Harvard Capital and

Consulting, and První privatizaèní fond (PPF).[15]   Harvard Capital and Consulting (HC&C) has received a great deal of attention, primarily because of its lack of transparency.[16]   During voucher privatization, HC&C adopted an aggressive strategy, concentrating its ownership in key companies.   HC&C has also developed a close relationship with Michael Dingman's Stratton Invest which appeared on the Czech capital markets in late 1995.   Like Harvard Capital and Consulting, the other large independent investment funds have typically adopted a strategy of concentration instead of diversification.[17]

Different Funds, Different Strategies: The Rise of Holding Companies

The independent funds, and to some extent IPB, adopted a different strategy than the funds of the partially state owned banks.   Instead of widely diversifying their shareholdings, they actively sought to gain controlling blocks of stocks in individual companies.   To continue pursuing this investment strategy, many of the important independent funds (as well as Bankovní IF of IPB) converted to holding companies in the middle of 1996.   Their primary motivation was to circumvent the diversification requirements of investment funds.   By calling extraordinary shareholder's meetings on relatively short notice, investment funds were able to pass motions changing their Articles of Incorporation.   While

---

[15] YSE is not an acronym.

[16] After allegedly purchasing industrial information from a former employee of the state intelligence agency, the founder of HC&C, Viktor Kozený, left the country in 1994 to avoid possible prosecution.

[17] Other funds of some importance that are not included in the top 15 investment funds include the Kvanto and Zluty funds of Ceskoslovenska obchodni banka (Czechoslovak Commerce Bank, CSOB), the fourth largest domestic bank which is also partially state owned.   The largest private bank, Agrobanka, and its investment company, A-Invest, also did not make this list.   Its unit fund. AGB podilovy fond, acquired the largest percentage of investment points in the second wave of privatization (320 million voucher points, 5.2 percent of the total).   Agrobanka's success is largely credited to their promotional policy of providing immediate loans to individuals depositing their voucher books with AGB podilovy fond.   As these loans were collateralized with the shares acquired during the second wave of privatization, they essentially were unsecured at the date of disbursement.   Similar to the case of IPB, this program resulted in Agrobanka becoming the majority owner of AGB podilovy fond participation certificates.

changes in Statutes require approval by the Ministry of Finance, changes in the Articles of Incorporation supersede the Statutes and do not require acceptance by the Ministry. Investment companies and privatization funds, therefore, can convert to holding companies, while unit fund transformation is not possible. Because only limited shareholder protections existed prior to July 1, 1996, the management of the new holding companies was under no obligation to buy out dissenting minority shareholders.

The flurry of conversions (72 holding companies were created between March and July, 1996) was largely the result of the new amendments to the Securities Act, Commercial Code, Act on Investment Companies and Investment Funds, and the Stock Exchange Act (Czech National Bank 1996b, 39). While adopted in April, the majority of these provisions did not become effective until July 1, 1996. These new amendments made conversion much more difficult. In addition to requiring a qualified two-thirds majority of all shareholders to adopt changes in the Articles of Incorporation, dissenting minority shareholding stakes have to be purchased at a price equal to the net asset value (NAV) of the fund's shares. Because fund shares trade at a substantial discount to NAV, the cost of buying out minority shareholders has become prohibitively expensive.

The increased risk and loss of minority rights associated with holding companies has resulted in the rapid decline of their stock prices. One example of this is the conversion of Harvard Capital and Consulting investment funds. In the three weeks following the announcement of its conversion at a March 26, 1996, general meeting, the share price of Harvardský dividendový fond (Harvard Dividend Fund) dropped 30 percent. Subsequently, Harvard průmyslový holding (Harvard Industrial Holding), which merged six of HC&C's investment funds and SKLO Union, merged with Stratton Invest in July to form the largest private financial company in the Czech Republic, Daventree Holding, with assets of CZK 37.8 billion. These funds also experienced a rapid decline in stock prices. The collapse of share prices is not, however, only associated with the funds of Harvard Capital and Consulting. While the average price of investment funds remained relatively stable during 1996, the average price of converted investment funds dropped 42 percent from February 1, 1996 to July 4, 1996.[18]

---

[18] This information was based upon data from the top 15 investment funds and

The Evolution of the Czech Banking System

In addition to the privatization of industry, the financial sector of the Czech Republic has undergone substantial transformation since 1990. These two processes are not in fact separable, as privatization and consolidation in the banking sector have been intimately involved with the rise and fall of key players in industry ownership.

Prior to 1990, Statní banka Èeskoslovenska (State Bank of Czechoslovakia, SBCS) operated as both the central bank and commercial bank. Two other banks, Èeská spoøitelna and Èeskoslovenksá obchodní banka (CSOB) were also in operation. A two-tier banking system was created in 1990 by dividing the SBCS into a Central Bank (Czech National Bank) and transferring its commercial functions to the newly created Komerèní banka and Investièní banka, while Èeská spoøitelna and CSOB were given universal banking licenses. In addition, entry to the banking sector was liberalized. An additional state bank was created in 1991, Konsolidaèní banka. Konsolidaèní was established as a repository for the classified loans (loans with a high probability of default) that the state banks had created during the preceding period of soft-budget constraints.

Table 9.3 Banks in the Czech Republic

Year	State Institutions	Private Domestic	Foreign Participation			
			Partial	Total	Branches	Total
1990	4	10	3	1	0	18
1991	5	16	4	6	0	31
1992	1	25	7	9	6	48
1993	1	24	8	10	10	53
1994	1	15	14	11	10	51
1995	1	13	14	11	10	49
1996*	1	13	13	14	10	51

* As of September, 1996.

Sources: Czech National Bank, Annual Reports [Prague: CNB] 1993-1995, 1-30 1996. Passim. Czech National Bank, Banking supervision in the Czech Republic, [Prague: CNB, 1996], 13.

holding companies with a benchmark of March 21, 1996 at 1000 points for both indices (Atlantik Financial Markets 1996, 10).

Up to 1994, when the Czech National Bank stopped granting operating licenses, the private commercial banking sector grew rapidly.[19] Table 9.3, Banks in the Czech Republic, shows that this growth was particularly rapid in the private domestic sector. The peak number of 25 banks was reached by the end of 1992. Due to the lax regulatory environment, a number of these banks engaged in self-dealing, issuing loans to management and affiliated concerns, such that the share of classified credits produced by smaller banks increased rapidly. From 1994 to 1996 more formal regulatory procedures were adopted that required increased provisioning for bad loans, an increase in the required reserve ratio from 8.5 to 12 percent, as well as closer evaluation of banking activities (Czech National Bank 1996a, 5-12). These actions accelerated the consolidation of the banking sector. As of September, 1996, 13 domestic banks were still operating, 5 banks had undergone acquisition (3 by Union banka) and 10 banks had experienced either liquidation, receivership, or forced administration. While the classified portion of total bank credits peaked in 1994 at 38.6 percent, consolidation has lowered this share to 34.5 percent as of June, 1996. Taking into account the new laws on provisioning and classification of credits, the actual decline in the riskiness of bank portfolios has been more extreme. As noted in the 1997 First Quarter Report of the Czech National Bank, the ratio of classified credits to total credits continues to decline (although no precise figure is provided).

Tables 9.4, 9.5 and 9.6 summarize the situation of domestic banks as of September, 1996. Coop banka provides an example of the self-dealing engaged in by some of the other small commercial banks. This bank was originally founded in 1991 by a group of cooperatives using CSK 300 million of their own capital. The management increased its share capital to CSK 500 million in 1992, despite complaints by some of the member cooperatives. The bank then began to accept investments from outside the cooperatives. Under the guidance of the general director, loans worth CZK 200 million were granted to two businessmen, who then used the loans to acquire a two-fifths stake in the bank. Their subsequent default led to the bank's repossession of shares and a search for new investors. A partnership was then developed with several other firms and investment funds, which borrowed CZK 300 million to buy the outstanding shares in Coop banka. Additional purchases gave the partnership a 52 percent stake in the bank, after which time the bank began to grant millions of crowns in

---

[19] The Czech National Bank began granting licenses again in September, 1996.

bad loans. At the time of its forced administration in 1996, Coop banka had created bad debt worth CZK 500 million. Its ratio of classified credits to total loans was greater than 40 percent (Friedrich 1996a, 5).

Table 9.4   Domestic Commercial Banks: Receiverships, Liquidations and Mergers

	Size* by Bank Assets	Date of Decision	Decision, Relationship with Rescuer
Receiverships and Liquidations			
Kreditní a prumyslova bk	-	Sept. 1993	Forced administration-license revoked Aug. 1995.
AB banka	-	May, 1994	Decrease in basic capital, CS received deposits.
Banka bohemia	-	July, 1994	Liquidation, CSOB received deposits.
Ceska banka	-	Dec. 1995	License revoked.
Prvni slezska banka	25	May, 1996	License revoked-liquidation.
Podnikatelska banka	19	June, 1996	Forced administration, receivership.
Realitbanka	24	July, 1996	Forced administration.
Velkomoravska banka	21	July, 1996	Forced Administration, CP majority ownership.
Kreditní banka Plzen	9	Aug. 1996	License revoked-liquidation, CSOB acquired CP stake.
Agrobanka	6	Sept. 1996	Forced Administration, Motoinvest controlled.
Mergers			
Posta banka	-	1994	Acquired, merged with Investicni banka.
Bankovní dùm SKALA	16	Feb. 1996	Recrship, taken over by Union banka.
COOP banka	18	Apr. 1996	Recrship, taken over by Foresbank.
Ekoagro banka	11	Apr. 1996	Recrship, taken over by Union banka.
Evrobanka	15	1996	Recrship, taken over by Union banka.

* As of June, 1996.

Source: Ekenem, no.46, 1996, 84. Czech National Bank, Banking Supervision in the Czech Republic [Prague: CNB, 1996], p. 30.

Two banks that were managed more prudently, Foresbanka and Union banka, were able to increase their assets through mergers negotiated by the Ministry of Finance and the Czech National Bank. Foresbanka, with a classified credit ratio of 4.4 percent, purchased a 98 percent stake in Coop banka for CZK 499 million in June, 1996. Union banka, with a classified credit ratio of 4 percent of all loans, purchased three banks: Bankovní dům Skala, Ekoagrobanka, and Evrobanka. Union banka was formerly the sixth largest private bank in the Czech Republic with assets of CZK 13.89 billion, which should increase to CZK 30-40 billion upon completion of the mergers (Union banka 1996, 14).

Despite the rapid growth of private domestic banks and the introduction of foreign banks and their branches, the majority of bank assets are still concentrated in the four partially state owned banks, Komerèní banka, Èeská spoøitelna, Èeskoslovenksá obchodní banka, and Investièní a poštovní banka. As of June, 1996, they owned 75 percent of the CZK 1,560 billion in bank assets, with Komerèní banka controlling 27 percent.[20]

The two largest banks to undergo forced administration, Plzeòská banka and Agrobanka, were both associated with the independent financial company, Motoinvest. Their history shows the types of behavior engaged in by more aggressive financial intermediaries and the incompatibility of different investment strategies.

In the fall of 1995, Motoinvest gained control of Plzeòská banka by purchasing shares from the government. Taking advantage of the large

---

[20] Several of these larger banks, most clearly IPB and CSOB, have been involved in the consolidation of the small bank sector. IPB has owned large blocks of stock in Velkomoravska bank, Kreditní banka Praha, and Pragobanka. CSOB, which has long been interested in entering the retail commercial sector, was initially interested in purchasing Ekoagrobanka, which was later sold to Foresbank. CSOB was eventually successful in entering the retail commercial sector as a result of the government coordinated sale of Pragobanka and Kreditní banka. The majority owner of these two banks had previously been Èeská pojištovna. The large losses of Kreditní banka (CZK 5.5 billion) would have overwhelmed the CZK 2.28 billion in base capital held by Èeská pojištovna if Kreditní had been allowed to fail. Rather than allow this to happen, the Banking four (CNB, FNM, and the Ministries of Privatization and Finance) allowed CSOB to buy Èeská pojištovna's 83 percent (Pragobanka) and 61 percent (Kreditní banka) stakes for CZK 1. To cover the losses of these banks, CSOB sold its 14 percent stake in Èeská pojištovna to the independent investment fund, První privatizaèní fond (First Privatization Fund, PPF). PPF in turn financed this purchase through loans from IPB (Friedrich 1996b, 7).

discounts at which investment fund shares traded, Motoinvest began to use the assets of Plzeòská banka to purchase shares in several investment funds, beginning with Zivnobanka 1.IF. While the Zivnobanka fund was successful in thwarting the efforts of Motoinvest by raising registered capital and selling it first to the existing shareholders of Zivnobanka IF, other investment funds were not so successful (Atlantik Financial Markets 1996, 34). The investment funds of Agrobanka, Komerèní banka, Creditanstalt, and CSOB were also targeted by Motoinvest, which eventually acquired majority stakes. These activities, which placed Plzeòská banka's share of assets in stock above 60 percent, attracted the attention of the Czech National Bank authorities, who advised divestiture. While retaining ownership in Agrobanka and several of the Creditanstalt funds, Motoinvest sold its other stakes to their previous owners. It is interesting to note that Motoinvest was unable to acquire stakes in the funds of Harvard Capital and Consulting, Èeská pojištovna, Spoøitelna banka and Investièní a poštovní banka because these funds were already securely controlled by their grandparent founding firms (Schmied, 1997).

Table 9.5   Domestic Commercial Banks: Banks with Increases in Basic Capital (BC)

	Size* by Bank Assets	Date of Decision	Decision, Relationship with Rescuer
Universal banka	20	1996	BC increased by new investors.
Moravia banka	14	1996	BC increased by present shareholders.
Banka Hana	8	1996	Multiple-fold increase in BC.
Pragobanka	10	1996	BC increased by shareholders, SCOB acquired CP stake.
Zemska banka	23	1996	Restructuring finished, activities curtailed.
Pizenska banka	22	1996	BC increased by present shareholders, Motoinvest.
Foreshanka	13	1996	BC increased by present shareholders.
Prvni mestska banka	17	1996	No need to increase basic capital.
Union banks	12	1996	BC increased to execute mergers.

* As of June, 1996.

Source: Ekenem, no.46, 1996, 84. Czech National Bank, Banking Supervision in the Czech Republic [Prague: CNB, 1996], p. 30.

Table 9.6 Domestic Commercial Banks: Solvent Banks

Bank	Size by Bank Assets[a]	Acronym	State Share[b]	Acquisitions
Komerèní banka	1	KB	48%	None
Ceska sporitelna	2	CS	45%	Received Deposits of AB banka.
Ceskoslovenka obchodny banka	3	CSOB	66%	Acquired Pragobanka, Kreditni for CZK 1.
Investièní a poštovní banka	4	IPB	32%	Large stakes in Pragob., Kreditni, and Velkem.
Konsolidacni banka	5	KoB	100%	Temporary Owner: Ekoagrobanka
Zivnestenka banka	7	-	0%	None

[a] As of June, 1996. [b] In November, 1996.

Source: Ekenem, no.46, 1996, 84. Czech National Bank, Banking Supervision in the Czech Republic [Prague: CNB, 1996], p. 30.

Agrobanka, the largest private domestic bank in the Czech Republic, fell under forced administration in September, 1996. The events that precipitated this action, however, were not strictly the result of Agrobanka's economic status. Its attempt to borrow money on the interbank market in order to cover short-term debts was ignored by the larger domestic banks. The failure to raise funds on the interbank market caused Agrobanka to turn to the Czech National Bank. It has been alleged that this behavior by the other banks was in response to Motoinvest's earlier activities involving the acquisition and resale of the larger bank's investment funds. This shortfall in meeting its obligations resulted in a temporary condition of forced management by the Czech National Bank (Sedlák 1996, 7; Czech National Bank 1996b, 43).

Since the acquisition of Agrobanka by Motoinvest, their activities have become closely intertwined. Several of the funds under their joint management have been transformed into holding companies to avoid investment fund diversification requirements, with the largest being AGB IF I (Apollon Holding) AGB IF II (AGB Holding) Creditanstalt CEIF (1. CS Holding) and IF YSE 2 (4. CS Holding). Following these conversions, the investment fund of Agrobanka, A-Invest, was sold to Motoinvest. It is the intention of Motoinvest to consolidate its remaining unit funds and IPF's under the management of A-Invest (Agrobanka 1996, 14).

The Third Wave of Privatization

While the consolidation of ownership shares by the larger financial intermediaries has been ongoing since the beginning of voucher privatization, the conditions of the capital market, the emergence of holding companies, and the threat of increased shareholder protections accelerated the process in late 1995 and 1996. This struggle to establish controlling ownership stakes by the intermediaries is fundamentally the result of competitive pressure. While some funds have attempted to diversify their holdings, they have had to adopt defensive measures to protect their portfolios from the more aggressively managed financial groups.

The third wave of privatization, which is not affiliated with the government programs of voucher privatization, refers to the attempts of investment funds to accumulate shares by directly buying out smaller shareholders.[21] While several of the more aggressive investment funds were involved in this activity, the most obvious was the advertising campaign of Motoinvest, carried out through Plzeòská banka, which offered to buy out small shareholders.

Two other activities have had the same result of concentrating share ownership, although they are not referred to specifically as being a part of the third wave. The first involves the accumulation of controlling blocks by purchasing shares from individual investors through the stock exchange. The second type of activity has been the sale of the accumulated blocks of stock through direct trades, as different investment groups bargain for ownership of operating companies.

The purchase of shares from individual investors has occurred primarily through the RM-S, the over-the-counter trading system. On the RM-S, the excess supply of small shareholdings depressed prices and provided an opportunity for arbitrage between the two official exchanges.

---

[21] The opposition party (Czech Party of Social Democrats, CSSD) and Prime Minister Václav Klaus have both issued negative statements about the third wave (Lidové Noviny, 1995).

The RM-S system has become a primarily buyer's market, with sales then being carried out on the Prague Stock Exchange.

The transfer of large blocks of stock through direct trading involves a specific contract between two investors. It does not affect the prices on the Prague Stock Exchange. While direct trades can be settled on either the RM-S or Prague Stock Exchange, an ad-hoc market has emerged at the Støedisko cenných papírù (Central Securities Register, SCP). All ownership transfers ultimately must be registered at the Central Securities Register. For negotiating direct trades off-market, the simplest procedure is merely the transfer of ownership titles at the SCP, avoiding the formal mechanisms of the two regulated markets. Prior to July 1, 1996, direct trades carried out through the SCP were notoriously opaque, as it was very difficult to determine the buyers and sellers. The new regulations, however, require that the SCP publish the names of owners who hold 10 percent or greater in any issue of stock.

This new requirement, while increasing the information about ownership to a certain extent, is unfortunately incomplete. The wording of the law has been taken literally, so that the true level of ownership remains hidden. This can occur if a company has more than one issue of initial capital. As ownership is reported in terms of 10 percent in any single security issue listed on the Prague Stock Exchange, the possibility of maintaining control through unlisted issues of initial capital remains. Additionally, the reporting of ownership based on the percentage held in individual security issues, rather than a percentage of the total securities issued by each company, further obscures the extent of ownership by individual shareholders (Czech National Bank 1996b, 39).

Accurate total figures for the level of activity carried out on the Central Securities Register and/or through direct trades is difficult, primarily because of the lack of consolidated reporting. As the Prague Stock Exchange has grown, direct trades carried out at the Securities Center have declined from 80 percent (1994) to 58 percent (1-3 Quarter 1996) of total direct trades. The overall importance of direct trades, however, has not declined. As late as September 1996, direct trading was still responsible for 80-90 percent of all security transactions (in volume of shares) (Czech National Bank 1994, 55; 1996b, 39).[22]

---

[22] There are five different methods of trading stock in the Czech Republic and three different agencies through which trades take place. For a more complete description of these intricacies, see Rejnuš and Schmied 1996, 10-14.

Harvard Capital and Consulting, which in many ways has been a leading innovator among the investment funds, targeted key companies during voucher privatization, resulting in a portfolio which includes majority ownership in some 15 companies. While the secretive nature of Harvard Capital and Consulting makes it difficult to determine the extent of its holdings, its majority stakes in Èeská Námoøní plavba, Sepap, and Fatra are common knowledge (Calbreath 1996b, 7).

Many of the larger bank funds, such as Èeská spoøitelna's funds, have also been undergoing a consolidation of holdings. This is primarily the result of having over-diversified their holdings during voucher privatization. While the combined funds managed by SIS owned shares in 490 companies in December, 1995, this number has steadily declined. As of May 1996, SIS funds held shares in 220 companies. Their ultimate goal was to continue their reduction to some 140 shares by the end of 1996. (SIS Funds 1996). In the case of SIS, however, it does not appear that this decline in the number of items in their portfolio is associated with an attempt to gain majority control over individual companies.

Investièní a poštovní banka, which has also been decreasing the number of items in its portfolio, has simultaneously attempted to increase its ownership in key companies. This trend became apparent in their public announcement of June, 1996, which outlined their majority purchases in Biocel, Plzeòský Prazdroj, and Jihoèeské mlékárny. These purchases were preceded in that year by other majority stake purchases in February and May, in Elektro-Praga Hlinsko and Kablo Energo (Calbreath 1996a, 1).

These acquisitions tested the legal revisions that had been passed in April, 1996. While the majority of the regulations were slated to become effective on July 1, articles dealing with the buying out of minority shareholders had actually become effective on May 1. Faced with the realization they would have to buy out the minority shareholders in Plzeòský Prazdroj, Biocel, and Jihoèeské mlékárny, IPB backtracked. IPB announced it did not actually own more than 50 percent in the companies directly, but was holding some of these shares for another investor (who remained anonymous) (Atlantik Financial Markets 1996, 14-15). This early test of the new regulations did not prove promising for future regulatory diligence. As a result of its disclaimer, IPB was not forced to buy out the minority shareholders.

While the investment funds of Èeskoslovenksá obchodní banka have typically adopted a pattern of diversification, CSOB has taken advantage of legal ambiguities to purchase a formerly independent investment fund turned holding company, FINOP, which has a highly concentrated portfolio. Since its acquisition by CSOB, FINOP has not fundamentally altered its strategy. This action by CSOB can be considered an attempt to engage in the process of concentration without increasing the riskiness of the investment funds that it founded. As the law on diversification and cross-ownership pertains to funds that were founded by investment companies, the purchase of a previously independent investment company allows circumvention of these rules (CSOB, 1995).

Are Investment Funds the "True Owners?"

Consolidation of investment funds' portfolios was clearly evident in 1995 and 1996. To a large extent this can be considered the natural response to the over-diversification that occurred during voucher privatization. Consolidation has also been spurred by the competitive environment that allows some funds to engage in hostile actions against the holdings of other investment funds. If they chose to ignore this threat, diversified investment funds would risk a decline in the value of their portfolio as other funds could accumulate majority stakes, diminishing the value of outstanding shares. Under the conditions of an illiquid stock exchange, share prices do not appear to respond to the continual evaluation of expected future earnings. Instead, the value of stock apparently is derived from its ability to allow corporate control.[23] The long run impact of the process of consolidation, however, has not been discussed. Will investment funds maintain majority holdings into the future and behave as the "true owners" of industry, investing in reorganization and adopting strategies for long-term growth?

Interviews with company management carried out in 1994 by John C. Coffee, Jr., Professor of Law at Columbia University, do not support the view that investment fund management is capable of playing a positive role in the long-run strategies of industry. While fund managers are able to secure positions on the managing boards where decision making is concentrated, they have not taken an assertive role, save their predilection for replacing management. The tendency to replace management teams

---

[23] While the Prague Stock Exchange does have several large issues in which trading responds to the value of future expected earnings, the vast majority of shares listed do not behave in this manner. For further discussion of the alternative sources of stock value, see Mayer 1994, 190-193; Hake 1996, 53-55.

rapidly, it is suggested, is because IPF directors do not have any other strategy to improve company profitability. Restructuring has caused employee layoffs and employees have been laid off in many companies due to the inability to make payrolls. However, the importance of IPF management in making these decisions is not significant. Indeed, many of the managers interviewed suggested they were still waiting for a "true owner" to appear before implementing long-run strategies such as selling off assets or establishing subsidiaries. This is true even in those

Table 9.7   Portfolio and Ownership Stakes: Based on Holdings Greater than 10 Percent of Share Issue -- Part A

	Number of Titles in Portfolio		Average Ownership Stake by Title		Number of Companies in Portfolio	
	Jan., 1997	Change since 9/96	Jan., 1997	Change since 9/96	Jan., 1997	Change since 9/96
Decreasing Ownership Stake						
Daventree	6	-1	27	-4	6	-1
Motoinvest	9	-13	20	-3	9	-13
YSE	32	+8	26	+1	24	+7
Investièní a poštovní banka	91	-12	19	-1	68	-11
Zivnostenka banka	16	-1	17	-1	14	-1
Stable Ownership Stake						
Fond narodniho majetku	338	-26	41	0	338	-26
Ceska pojistovna	56	-10	19	+1	54	-9
Komerèní banka	72	-3	16	-1	66	-5
Increasing Ownership Stake						
Agrobanka	83	-22	22	-1	68	-21
PPF investièní spoleènost	15	-7	26	+2	13	-6
Cecks sporitelna	146	+2	17	0	115	-12
Ceckest. ohchodny banka	61	+6	29	+1	41	0

Source: Stredisko cennych papiru (Central Securities Register), Czech Republic. Available at http://stock.eunet.cz/hcpp_e.html#scpms.

Table 9.8 Portfolio and Ownership Stakes: Based on Holdings Greater than 10 Percent of Share Issue -- Part B

	Average Ownership Stake in Companies		Holdings > 33.3%		Holdings > 50.01%	
	Jan., 1997	Change since 9/96	Jan., 1997	Change since 9/96	Jan., 1997	Change since 9/96
Decreasing Ownership Stake						
Daventree	27	-4	1	-3	0	0
Motoinvest	20	-3	1	-2	0	-1
YSE	34	-1	14	+2	8	0
Investièní a poštovní banka	25	-1	20	-5	5	-2
Zivnostenka banka	19	-1	2	-1	0	-1
Stable Ownership Stake						
Fond narodniho majetku	41	0	170	-7	103	-4
Ceska pojistovna	19	0	9	+3	3	+1
Komerèní banka	17	0	5	0	0	0
Increasing Ownership Stake						
Agrobanka	27	+1	22	-6	5	-1
PPF investièní spoleènost	30	+3	5	+2	3	0
Cecks sporitelna	22	+3	16	+5	10	+9
Ceckest. ohchodny banka	43	+5	29	+4	15	+5

Source: Stredisko cennych papiru (Central Securities Register), Czech Republic. Available at http://stock.eunet.cz/hcpp_e.html#scpms.

companies in which large stock holdings by financial investment groups already exist (Coffee 1996, 152-156).

Further support for the view that investment groups are not behaving as "true owners" of industry can be found in a comparison of investment group portfolios from September 1996 and January 1997. Results from this period, which coincides with the decline of "Third Wave" activity, suggest that consolidation of ownership stakes represented a short-run strategy to consolidate ownership before selling off their stakes to other investors.

While some groups are still concentrating their holdings in individual companies, a larger number have actually seen a decline in their average ownership stakes in companies.   Tables 9.7 and 9.8, Portfolio and Ownership Stakes, summarize the portfolio holdings of the largest banks, independent holding companies, and their subsidiary investment funds (referred to collectively as investment groups), from September, 1996 to January, 1997.

It appears that investment funds have been engaged in the consolidation of majority stakes for the purpose of selling off these stakes to outside investors.   As a result of the low liquidity of the stock exchange and the wide dispersion of ownership shares, outside investors would have been unable to engage in single large block purchases of shares without the intermediary activities of the investment funds.   For this reason, investment funds have provided a useful function in the ongoing process of privatization and consolidation of ownership.

This does not mean, however, that investment fund and banking ownership of industry will cease to exist in the short run. Their continued presence is possible for two reasons:

(1) The FNM still owns a significant portion of company shares. As the FNM divests these holdings, their purchase by investment funds is likely.   This presents a problem for the continued sale of government assets, as the FNM may be hesitant to allow certain funds to gain more comprehensive stakes in key industries. This concern is clearly evident in the FNM use of its 26.3 percent stake in Èeská pojištovna to block further purchases of Èeská pojištovna by První privatizaèní fond, PPF (Atlantik Financial Markets, 1997, 17).

(2) Some investment funds may retain partial ownership even if they sell a controlling block of stock to an outside investor. The fact that some majority holdings in companies have approached 80-90 percent of shares makes this a likely scenario. The investment funds would then be able to retain positions on the managing boards of industry and establish secure customer relationships for the banking services of their parent or founding firms.[24]

---

[24] Because Tables 9.7 and 9.8 were compiled using the public information provided by the Central Securities Register (SCP), it should be interpreted with caution and not compared with other sources of information dealing with portfolios and ownership stakes. As the information provided by the SCP only includes

While 9 of the 12 investment groups described have experienced a decrease in the total number of titles in their portfolios, it should be realized that this figure ignores multiple holdings in single operating companies. Taking into account these multiple holdings, it is possible to determine the number of companies held in the portfolio of each investment group (Number of Companies in Portfolio). The number of companies in portfolio has declined in 10 of the investment groups. YSE was the only investment group that saw an increase in the number of companies in its portfolio.

Taking into account these multiple holdings, it is possible to determine the average ownership in companies held in the combined portfolio of each investment group (Average Ownership Stake in Companies). Five investment groups experienced a decline in their average ownership stakes during this period, three remained unchanged, while four investment groups experienced an increase.[25]

The most surprising result, and worthy of further description, is the behavior of Èeskoslovenksá obchodní banka (CSOB). While actively involved in the consolidation of the banking sector, CSOB had not typically been associated with an aggressive portfolio strategy. As of January, 1997, however, it held the largest average ownership stake of all groups described, 43 percent, surpassing the concentration of the government's FNM. This is largely the result of the purchase of FINOP

---

holdings of 10 percent or greater in any security issue listed on the Stock Exchange, the possibility for hidden ownership remains. This sample also skews the summarized results, increasing the average ownership ratio and reducing the total number of listings in the portfolios by ignoring all holdings less than 10 percent of individual security issues. Due to these limits in reporting, it is not possible to compare these results with institutional ownership stakes from other countries. Because the information provided by the SCP has not changed during this time, however, comparison of the two periods does provide valid results.

[25] In terms of the five investment groups that experienced a decline in their average ownership stake in companies, it should be realized that they include the investment funds most associated with aggressive management strategies. For this reason, it appears that their earlier attempts to gain majority stakes in operating companies represented a transitory process. They are now engaged in some degree of liquidation and profit taking as they sell their majority stakes to outside investors. Due to the lack of transparency in the Stock Exchange, this conclusion is tentative. With the available information it is not possible to determine if the decline in average ownership stakes actually represents the sale of large blocks of securities to affiliated foreign companies or to non-financial domestic partners.

holding, whose average ownership stake is double the average of all other companies included in the CSOB investment group.[26]

Although Èeská spoøitelna experienced the second largest increase in its average ownership stake, it should be recognized that this increase is from a relatively small base (19 percent average ownership stake as of September 17, 1996). The increase of 3 percent in average ownership is, therefore, not as significant as the increase in the ownership stakes of the other investment groups, namely, PPF investièní spoleènost and Agrobanka.

Some general conclusions about the behavior of partially-government-owned banks, private banks, and private investment groups are possible. Different investment strategies (diversification or concentration) do not coincide with institutional classifications. While some of the larger partially-state-owned financial institutions have maintained diversified portfolios, such as Komerèní banka and Èeská pojištovna, Investièní a poštovní banka and Èeskoslovenksá obchodní banka have produced a higher degree of concentration. Similarly, smaller banks have not clearly adopted one or the other strategy. Zivnostenká banka has adopted a very prudent approach, while Agrobanka, clearly under the influence of Motoinvest, continues to concentrate ownership even during a period of forced administration. Independent investment companies have seen a higher degree of ownership concentration when compared to partially-state-owned bank groups, although they have also been active in the current phase of profit taking and liquidation. The lack of clarity between these different groups of financial intermediaries and their strategies suggests that individual management is most important in determining strategy. The existence of government ownership in the largest commercial banks has not produced a unified strategy vis a vis private banks or independent financial groups.

Conclusion

While the program of voucher privatization in the Czech Republic largely served its purpose of distributing a significant portion of the state holdings

---

[26] This comparison ignores multiple holdings in operating companies because the calculation of multiple holdings requires that the related investment companies be considered as a group.

in industry, it has been followed by a period of ownership concentration and the rise of powerful financial intermediaries. This has occurred primarily because the shares created by voucher privatization were, in total, converted into shares listed on the Stock Exchange. The result was very low liquidity and a stagnation of stock prices.

Financial intermediaries, operating in an environment of lax and indefinite regulation, were then able to engage in a range of investment strategies, ranging from the widely over-diversified shareholdings of the largest commercial banks, Èeská spoøitelna and Komerèní banka, to the aggressive concentration of share ownership by independent investment companies such as Harvard Capital and Consulting and YSE.

With ill-defined and poorly enforced laws on cross-shareholdings, founding companies and their subsidiary investment funds have created extensive networks of cross-ownership and multiple holdings in single operating companies. The lack of minority shareholder protections has produced a capital market in which majority or controlling stock ownership is necessary to maintain the value of the initial investment.

The concentration of share ownership and the fight for majority stakes in operating companies typified by the third wave of privatization, does not appear, however, to be the final result. During the period September, 1996 to January, 1997, many of the more aggressive investment funds were divesting their majority positions and selling their controlling blocks to outside investors. For this reason, it appears that active financial intermediation and the third wave of privatization represent a continuing phase in the search for the "true owners" of industry.

These results are not comprehensive--several investment groups are still engaged in the concentration of share ownership, including the investment companies of partially-state-owned banks. Large-block ownership by the financial community is likely to continue as long as the rewards for concentrated holdings outweigh the benefits of diversification. While the much anticipated revision of legal codes has not produced a completely transparent process for transferring stock ownership, it has improved conditions to a considerable extent. Further legislation and the more strict enforcement of existing legislation will not eradicate the process of holding large blocks of stock in the Czech Republic but could possibly supplant domestic financial ownership of industry with ownership by foreign or domestic industrial groups.

References

"Agrobanka Sells Company A-Invest" [1996]. *Mladá Fronta Dnes,* [Youth Front Today] 16 July,14.

Atlantik Financial Markets Financial Services Research Group [1996]. *Funds Sector Research and Selected Funds.* 16 August, Brno: Atlantik Financial Markets.

Atlantik Monthly [1997]. *Czech Capital Market Research March 1997,* Brno: Atlantik Financial Markets.

Babiak, Stefan, ed. [1996]. *Information Center of the Prague Stock Exchange Monthly Report,* July.

Blanchard, Oliver and Rudiger Dornbusch [1991]. *Reform in Eastern Europe,* Cambridge: MIT Press.

Calbreath, Dean [1996a]. "Buyout Spree is IPB's Bid for Freedom" *Prague Post,* 19-25 June, 1.

___ [1996b]. "Harvard Merger Breathes New Life Into Stock Exchange" *Prague Post,* 17-23 July, 7.

___ [1997]. "Good Luck in Following the IPB-Ownership Shell Game" *Prague Post,* 19-25 February, 5, 9.

Coffee, John C., Jr. [1996]. "Institutional Investors in Transitional Economies: Lessons From the Czech Experience" in *Corporate Governance in Central Europe and Russia, Volume 1, Banks, Funds, and Foreign Investors,* ed. Roman Frydman, Cheryl W. Gray, and Andrzej Rapaczynski, 111-186. Budapest, London and New York: CEU Press.

"CSOB Gains Control Over FINOP Holding" [1995]. *Mladá Fronta Dnes,* [Youth Front Today], 11 December, 15.

Czech National Bank [1994]. *Annual Report 1994.* Prague: Czech National Bank.

___ [1996a]. *Banking Supervision in the Czech Republic,* Prague: Czech National Bank.

___ [1996b]. *Report on Monetary Development in the Czech Republic for the Period January-September 1996,* Prague: Czech National Bank.

Dittus, Peter and Stephen Prowse [1996]. "Corporate Control in Central Europe and Russia: Should Banks Own Shares?" in *Corporate Governance in Central Europe and Russia, Volume 1, Banks, Funds, and Foreign Investors.* ed. Roman Frydman, Cheryl W. Gray, and Andrzej Rapaczynski. 20-67, Budapest, London and New York: CEU Press.

Federal Ministry of Finance (Prague) [1992]. "Coupon Privatization, an Information Handbook" *Eastern European Economics* 30, 4, Summer, 5-38.

Friedrich, Alex [1996a]. "One More Bank Down, Another Back Up Again as the CNB Moves to Save Coop Banka" *Prague Post,* 1-7 May, 5.

___ [1996b]. Large Banks Play the Tune for Small-Bank Mating Dance. *Prague Post,* 19-25 June, 7.

Frydman, Roman, Andrzej Rapaczynski, and John S. Earle [1993]. *The*

Privatization Process in Central Europe, Budapest, London and New York: CEU Press.

Hake, Eric [1996]. "Systems of Corporate Governance in the Czech Economy" in *Economic Growth and Restructuring in the Czech Republic: Proceedings of the Conference in Brno, Czech Republic, 16-17 May 1996*, by Mendel University. Brno, Czech Republic: Mendel University, 50-56.

King, Neil, Jr. [1996]. "Power Plays" Central European Economic Review, Vol. 4, No. 4 (May, 8-13.

Lidové Noviny. [People's Newspaper] [1995]. 3 November, 3; 11 November, 3.

Mayer, Colin [1994]. "Stock Markets, Financial Institutions, and Corporate Performance" in *Capital Markets and Corporate Governance*, ed. Nicholas Dimsdale and Martha Prevezer, 179-194, Oxford, New York, and Toronto: Clarendon Press.

Rejnuš, Oldrich and Radek Schmied [1996]. "Czech Republic" in *Capital Markets in Transition Economies: Central and Eastern Europe*, London: Edgar Elgar.

Roe, Mark J. [1994]. *Strong Managers, Weak Owners: The Political Roots of American Corporate Finance*, Princeton: Princeton University Press.

Schmied, Radek [1997]. Interview by author, 18 February, Brno, Mendel University.

Sedlák, Lubomír [1996]. "CSFB: Big Banks Getting Bigger, Weak Banks Grow Weaker" *Prague Post*, 17-23 July, 7.

"SIS Funds' Portfolios will be Further Reduced" [1996]. *Burzovní noviny*, [Stock Exchange Newspaper], 17 May.

Stark, David [1996]. "Networks of Assets, Chains of Debt: Recombinant Property in Hungary" in *Corporate Governance in Central Europe and Russia, Volume 2. Insiders and the State*, ed. Roman Frydman, Cheryl W. Gray, and Andrzej Rapaczynski. 109-150, Budapest, London and New York: CEU Press.

"Union Banka Takes Over Three Small Banks" [1996]. *Central European Business Journal* 1-7, November, 14.

10 Certain Specific Features of Monetary Policy in the Czech Republic[1]

STANISLAVA JANACKOVA

This article is concerned with selected, mutually dependent problems of monetary policy that demonstrate the specific position of the Czech economy, that is to say, an economy that is undergoing transformation. The first part is concerned with the effect of a stable exchange rate as a nominal anchor for an economy in transition, one that is undergoing notable changes in price relations. In the Czech Republic, where currency was not convertible for capital transactions (rate of exchange was undervalued due to purchasing-power parity), the anchoring role of the exchange rate was utilized by means of other mechanisms than are used in market economies with a completely convertible exchange rate. This, in turn, has implications for further steps toward the convertibility of the capital account in the balance of payments.

The second part of this article discusses the problem of indebtedness among different enterprises and stemming from that, their inability to pay. This phenomenon is interpreted as a definite specific pathological "financial innovation," typical for the initial stage of transformation in the Czech Republic and in other countries; the consequences of this phenomenon for monetary policy are discussed, particularly as they affect inflation.

Stable Exchange Rate as a Means of Anchoring Other Price Entities

Right from the beginning of transformation, but especially starting in 1991, the State Bank of Czechoslovakia and, later, the Czech National Bank, was faced with the task of finding an adequate monetary policy for

---

[1] Reprinted with permission from *Eastern European Economics*, January-February, 1996, pp. 60-74, published by M.E. Sharpe, Inc. (Armonk, New York).

an economy in which, due to the process of privatizing existing and newly-established enterprises, the numbers of such enterprises as well as the number of transactions were growing rapidly. Given new pressures and, as a result of new opportunities, new financial structures as well, the behavior of these enterprises was undergoing changes. For the first time after almost fifty years, prices were free. One effect that was expected was a drop in GNP on a scale that was difficult to predict. A limited internal currency convertibility was introduced for current account transactions. Foreign capital began flowing into the country.

In searching for an adequate and reliable monetary policy that in these difficult circumstances could assure both internal and external currency stability, the central bank found support from the IMF, the World Bank, and the European Union in the form of credits, stand-by credits, and expert advice. However, the fundamental capacity to develop a sound monetary policy while transforming the Czech economy naturally could not be implanted from the outside.

A stable currency rate was chosen as an anchor to assist in motivating other economic agents. Even though the rate was not officially set for the long term, the central bank from the start announced, and also successfully carried out, a policy of a stable exchange rate.[2] This stability, insofar as the Czech Republic was concerned, was not even threatened by the process of the breakup of the federation or the separation of currencies. In July, 1994, the Czech economy will begin the forty-second month of currency stability, which distinguishes it dramatically from almost all the other economies undergoing transformation.

The means by which the stable currency rate fulfilled its role as a nominal anchor were unique precisely because they were implemented during a transforming economy. It makes sense for market economies that have a fully convertible currency and a liberal capital account to use an anti-inflationary stance to attach the exchange rate firmly to the currency of some country, or group of countries, that has a low inflation rate. In conditions of liberalized capital flows, domestic monetary policy is forced to give up its independence. If it wants to maintain a fixed exchange rate, it must follow the monetary policy of the country (or countries) to whose

---

[2] The exchange rate for the Czech Koruna was defined *vis-a-vis* a basket of rates (USD, DEM, ATS, CHR, FRF); in 1993, the number of exchange rates in the basket was decreased to two (DEM, 65%; USD 35%), which reflects the rate structure of the majority of transactions of the Czech Republic with foreign countries.

currency the rate is bound; it must pay attention to differences in currency and, especially, in credit policy, for inattention would cause the flow of capital to react immediately, and through the balance of payments, this could very rapidly jeopardize the fixed rate. We then speak of "importing stability" or of the so-called disciplinary effect produced by a fixed rate on domestic monetary policy and, as a consequence, on domestic inflation. This mechanism naturally presupposes that inflation is primarily a monetary phenomenon that can be mastered by monetary policy. However, for the Czech economy, which is in the process of transformation, this assumption would be unsuitable and unrealistic.

First of all, a series of specific inflation impulses stemming from transformation took place that could not be completely mastered by monetary policy: fundamental changes in retail prices coupled with declining output under conditions of limited price flexibility; the specific situation in the labor market; and a number of institutional changes, such as the introduction of a new taxation system. Second, so long as the Czech currency remained inconvertible for capital transactions and some capital flows were regulated, the mobility of capital across frontiers remained limited. As a result, a stable rate cannot play its "disciplinary" role by means of its effect on credit management. Third, under these circumstances, any further potential "disciplinary" mechanism could not be utilized because it acts more slowly, by means of the current account in the balance of payments; there is a threat that inflationary differences *vis-a-vis* countries with which we have a fixed rate would undermine the competitive capacity of Czech products. This potential "disciplinary" effect was intentionally suppressed by undervaluing the rate of exchange in relation to purchasing-power parity.

Nevertheless, a stable rate of exchange was used as an anti-inflationary anchor in the movement of price entities. This concept was to be carried out by means of the current account of the balance of payments, thus a somewhat different type of mechanism. In the transformation concept, a stable rate of exchange served as an anchor for prices of imported goods and thanks to the opening up of foreign competition, also for prices of all kind of goods that pass through or could potentially pass through foreign trade (so-called 'tradeables'). Thus the exchange rate would have an anchoring influence on the whole price level.[3]

---

[3] In foreign literature, Williamson (1991) also implicitly distinguishes between these two concepts of the exchange rate as a monetary anchor.

The anchoring of price movements had a fundamental significance for the liberalization of prices in January, 1991, when the markets began to search for new, rational price relations that would reflect the structure of world prices as well. Even when the general market imbalance was lessened by stabilization policies in 1990, one had to expect certain changes in demand and upward pressure on price levels. Large changes in relative prices cannot, by themselves, occur without an increase in the total price level because at least some of the prices are less flexible downward. When there are large changes in relative prices in the Czech economy, that is exactly the time when a stable exchange rate has the task of providing a single firm point around which the new price structure can be created and that helps slow down the growth of the aggregate price level.[4] This effect was important even in the later years, including after the introduction of the new taxation system, when a wave of even more clearly institutionally-conditioned price movements occurred. It is naturally very hard to prove the efficacy of the exchange rate as an anchor empirically. However, an indirect proof may be obtained by comparing the rate of inflation in the Czech economy with that of Hungary or Poland, where, we know, they were unable to maintain a stable rate and carried out repeated devaluations.

A stable exchange rate also apparently helped inhibit inflationary impulses stemming from wage pressures. It is highly probable that the pressure of wage growth is stronger in a climate of repeated devaluations of the exchange rate. A stable exchange rate doubtless provided a proper framework for structural changes in the economy and helped to ameliorate the bad influence of the loss of traditional markets, as well as helping to introduce rapid reorientation to the market of developed countries.[5]

In spite of these mechanisms, which were used to slow down price increases, one had to count on the fact that the rate of inflation in the early transformation years would be greater than that in mature market economies. Therefore, the key question as to the reliability of the plan to hold on to a stable exchange rate was how to establish a correct initial rate;

---

[4] Klaus, 1993.

[5] The share of developed market economies in the exports of the Czechoslovak Federal Republic grew by 30 percent in 1989, by 52 percent in 1991, and by 64 percent in 1992; in 1993, it reached 70 percent, 55 percent to European Union countries. During 1993, Czech Republic exports grew by 20 percent, imports by 2.7 percent minus trade with Slovakia. The share of exports in GNP reached approximately 40 percent.

this rate had to provide a cushion for the subsequent gradual growth of the actual effective rate of exchange while avoiding the need for devaluating the currency, all the while renewing the capacity for competition.[6] The chosen rate, 28 Czech koruny to 1 U.S. dollar, was undervalued relative to the purchasing-power-parity rate, which, in January 1991, was roughly estimated to be 10 Czech koruny per U.S. dollar. Undervaluation helped maintain the trade balance; particularly in the beginning, the chosen rate had a marked effect against imports and in favor of exports.

Thus a distinct cushion of price competitiveness was created for the economy. A further cushion was created in 1991 by a decrease of 24 percent in real wages; thus real wages were temporarily kept under the level that was maintainable from the production standpoint. Thanks to the space thus created, the further decrease in productivity, which accompanied microeconomic restructuring, did not threaten the competitive capacity of the Czech economy directly. By these means, the inflationary effects of a simultaneous decrease in productivity and an increase in real wages that occurred in 1992 were to some extent mitigated.[7]

A modified mechanism of the effect produced by the exchange-rate anchor, at a time when the economy was being transformed, had varying implications for monetary policies. As was mentioned above, in a trans-forming economy it is not possible to "import" sufficient internal currency stability by fixing the exchange rate against the currency of a country with low inflation; a considerable part of inflation here was not purely a monetary phenomenon. Specific inflationary impulses, together with the ongoing transformation, could not be held in check by a restrictive monetary policy. The viewpoint that inflation could not occur as long as the central bank "did not accommodate" inflationary pressures will have to be considered an illusion under these circumstances.[8]

On the other hand, in *this* specific situation, there was an advantage in the fact that, even given a stable rate of exchange, the free space for

---

[6] The introduction of limited internal convertibility in January 1991 was preceded by three devaluations of the Czech Koruna *vis-a-vis* the convertible exchange rates during 1990. The Czech koruna was devalued by 16.6 percent on January 8, 1990, by 55.3 percent on October 15, 1990, and by 15.98 percent on December 28, 1990, so that its value *vis-a-vis* the USD sank practically by half.

[7] Klaus, 1993.

[8] This question also relates to the problem of inter-enterprise indebtedness and its influence on monetary policy. See below.

gaining an independent monetary policy adjusted to internal needs and goals was not closed off. Thanks to limited convertibility and partial regulation of the flow of capital, capital mobility across borders was lower and the influence of foreign conditions was much more accommodating and did not have a direct effect on curtailing domestic monetary policy.

Postponement of convertibility in the capital account of the balance of payments thus enable us to use the stable rate as an anchor without sacrificing an independent domestic monetary policy.[9] From the standpoint of the current account of the balance of payments, undervaluation of the rate during this middle period supported the possibility of an independent monetary policy. At the present time, a lower level of individual wages as compared with the wages of the chief trading partners works in much the same way.

Thus we can summarize that the Czech economy needed both an independent monetary policy as well as the right conditions for its application. Finding an adequate monetary policy was, of course, an immensely difficult task, in part because monetary authorities were faced with a substantial increase in the volume of transactions and parameter changes (such as speed of money circulation or credit attitudes of commercial banks), which in a normal market economy are considered more or less constant.

The monetary policy of the State Bank of Czechoslovakia and of the Czech National Bank has already been discussed in greater detail in a series of articles in specialized publications.[10] The results listed in them, insofar as internal and external currency stability is concerned, are considered by independent foreign specialists to be a notable success; inflation was seen to be substantially lower than in other economies undergoing transformation. The highest inflation rate during the first transformation phase in the Czechoslovak Federal Republic was in 1991, when it reached 57 percent. This can be compared to the highest annual rate of inflation in Poland, which reached 640 percent in 1989. In the Czech Republic, a cumulative increase of consumer prices in the course of the initial four years of transformation (1990-93) was 126 percent, thus considerably less than in Poland during only one year. In spite of the fact that Poland and Hungary initiated transformation processes sooner, they still had a higher inflation rate than the Czech Republic (see table 10.1).

---

[9]   Klaus, 1994b; Frenkel, 1986.

[10] For example, Bulir, 1993; Pospiss, 1993.

On the whole, in the Czech Republic, additional macroeconomic indicators were also more favorable, with the exception of growth of GNP, which in Poland in 1993 was already positive.

The development of the Czech economy was likewise characterized by two notable price jumps, which were quickly suppressed and did not grow into an inflationary spiral: after price liberalization in the first quarter of 1991, with a jump of roughly 40 percent; and after the introduction of the value-added tax at the start of 1993, with a jump of roughly 8.5 percent. A long-term measure that defined the "core" of inflation after the subtraction of these extraordinary influences did not, however, exceed 1 percent per month during the whole course of the transforming process; thereafter, annual levels of inflation remained below 10 percent. The nominal rate of exchange remained stable; the real effective rate, as measured by price indexes, increased during the period 1991-93 roughly by 65 percent; export data indicate, however, that this increase so far has not undermined the competitive capacity of Czech exports, the latter also being helped by relatively low wage costs.

Table 10.1 Basic Macroeconomic Indicators: Czech Republic, Poland and Hungary (1993)

Indicator	Czech Republic	Poland	Hungary
Growth of GNP (%)	-0.3	4.0	-1.5
Unemployment (%)	3.5	15.7	11.0
Inflation (%)	20.8	37.8	21.1
Surplus (+) or Deficit (-) of the State Budget (as % of GNP)	+0.1	-6.8	-5.1

Sources: Czech Statistical Bureau, Czech National Bank; OECD; *The Economist.*

Insofar as the "core" inflation in the Czech Republic in 1991-93 did not exceed 10 percent annually and no moves in 1994 are expected that would lead to price jumps, the Czech National Bank and the government estimate that this year it may be possible to hold inflation below 10 percent. A lower inflation rate strongly facilitates the maintenance of a stable exchange rate and thus opens the road as well for further steps in the area of exchange-rate convertibility.

In undertaking each further step toward convertibility, potential gains, costs, and risks must be weighed. In this area, we can deduce much from the experience of other countries. A specific question arises for the Czech Republic, among others, as a transforming economy, that concerns the steps toward convertibility in the capital account of the balance of payments. This is the aspect of compatibility of a stable rate as an anchor with monetary policy independent of the monetary policy of other countries.

Given full convertibility and liberalized transactions, the role of a fixed rate as a nominal anchor begins to function in an orderly manner. Maintaining a fixed rate will require that domestic monetary policy follow development in countries to which the Czech koruna is linked. For example, if the central bank decided to support domestic growth by decreasing interest rates as compared to foreign interest rates,[11] it would cause an outflow of capital, which would endanger a fixed rate; steps taken by the central bank in support of the exchange rate would decrease domestic money supply and also eliminate the effects of lower interest rates. A loss of independence for domestic monetary policy can be an argument against the introduction of full convertibility, given an economy in a state of transformation that has specific domestic goals.[12]

Of course, the question arises as to whether the already achieved level of liberalization of the flow of capital in the Czech Republic will not, in the near future, be seen as an obstacle to an independent monetary policy, given a fixed exchange rate. With the further development of domestic capital markets, potentially destabilizing capital flows, which are made possible by already existing legal structures, could become larger and force an adjustment of monetary policy. At the same time, this may cause a decrease in the effectiveness of regulations, which are still being used in relation to certain categories of capital.[13]   In that case, it would be necessary for domestic interest rates to show greater respect for developments in foreign capital markets; there would also be an increase in pressure to stabilize the exchange rate at a previously determined interval.

---

[11] For domestic subjects, real interest rates are the deciding factor.   For foreign capital, for a short time, the deciding factor could be nominal rates, but real rates do enter into their decisions as long as there is a large deviation of nominal rates from real ones caused by a high rate of inflation. This causes foreign investors in domestic markets to expect devaluation, then this is what they include in their decision possibly to shift their capital elsewhere.

[12] Klaus, 1994a and 1994b.

[13] Dedek, 1993.

In any case, an urgent interest of the Czech economy is to prepare itself for closer connections with the world economy in the area of capital flows. This means, in addition to other factors, a constant effort to lower the rate of inflation to the level existing in mature market economies. What is fundamental in this connection is further financial consolidation of the enterprise sphere, including the solution of the problem of inter-enterprise indebtedness.

Monetary Policy and Inter-Enterprise Indebtedness

During the whole four-year period of the first phase of transformation, the monetary policy of both the State Bank of Czechoslovakia and the Czech National Bank was based on the concept that it should be restrictive or neutral. In order to be able to judge objectively to what extent monetary policy was in fact restrictive, we would have to have at our disposal greater knowledge concerning the changes in the volume of transactions (transactional demands for money) as well as changes in the velocity of money circulation.

It is not hard to measure the velocity of money circulation ex *post* as related to GNP. However, such data may be erroneous as long as nominal GNP ceases being a good approximation of the total volume of transactions that this money must serve. This in fact is what happened in the Czech economy, where, in connection with the process of transformation, there was a marked increase in the need for transactional money per unit of nominal GNP.[14] With the emergence of private activities, there was an increase in the number of companies (in just 1990-91 their number grew from 1,500 to 11,000); many internal company transactions changed into intercompany transactions, when large enterprises were broken up into smaller ones; and changes in ownership generated a great many financial transactions whose volume did not have a direct relation to the size of GNP. It is possible that the actual speed of money circulation *de facto* grew even in periods when this speed as measured by nominal GNP seemed to be decreasing (M2 grew faster than nominal GNP). In spite of that, it is not clear whether growth in the speed of money circulation could be great enough to compensate fully for growth in the volume of transactions per unit of GNP. In other words, questions

---

[14] Klaus, 1994a.

arise: Did the financial system ensure sufficient liquidity for the economy? Did the specific form of involuntary trading credit, inter-enterprise indebtedness, in reality ensure such additional liquidity, which was otherwise missing in the economy? Was restrictive bank credit policy the primary reason for the large growth of inter-enterprise indebtedness and secondarily for the inability of enterprises to pay?

Let us begin with the second question. In spite of the fact that it is tempting to answer it in the affirmative, closer analysis of the reasons for the growth of inter-enterprise indebtedness in various economies undergoing transformation leads us, on the contrary, to a negative answer.[15] In the Czech Republic, the growth of inter-enterprise indebtedness showed us a by no means cheering microeconomic contrast to its successful macroeconomic policy; however, the same problem happened in the first stage of transformation in other countries as well. Practically everywhere, the main reason was a decrease in demand and growth of prices, a situation to which enterprises could not adapt quickly. Simultaneously, there was a collapse of financial discipline and a creation of a structure of stimuli that in practice rewarded enterprises for postponing their payments.[16]

Statistical data show a dramatic rise in inter-enterprise claims upon their reaching maturity in almost all economies undergoing transformation. In Czechoslovakia as well, the beginning of transformation was accompanied by this phenomenon, which led rapidly to chain reactions of secondary inability to pay. Overdue inter-enterprise claims, following a mild increase in growth in the second half of 1990, grew dramatically during 1991; their volume rose from 50 billion Czech koruny at the beginning of the year to more than 170 billion Czech koruny at the end of the year, which represented 25 percent of various banking credits in the enterprise sphere, or almost 18 percent of GNP.

In spite of the fact that the government undertook certain measures during 1991 to diminish the problem, the inability to pay (credits for constantly turning over supplies were transferred to the Consolidation Bank in March 1991 with maturity in eight years; in October 1991, 50 billion Czech koruny were issued for bank recapitalization and for the write-off of certain enterprise debts) and the volume of claims after

---

[15] Bigman and Leite, 1993; Clifton and Khan, 1993; Janackova, 1992; and Hrncir and Klacek, 1994.

[16] Bigman and Leite, 1993, p.5.

reaching maturity continued to grow. The growth of these claims stopped only during 1992; in the second part of the year, they slowly dropped to 58 billion Czech koruny. Comparable data for 1993 are unfortunately not available. Expert guesses indicate that from the second half of 1992 inter-enterprise indebtedness did not grow but, on the contrary, decreased somewhat, even in 1993.[17]

For comparison, we can mention certain data from a study undertaken by the Hungarian Monetary Fund.[18] In Hungary, a rough volume of overdue inter-enterprise debts achieved the level of approximately 8 percent of GNP in March 1992 and 17 percent of the broad money supply. Nonetheless, this item is undervalued because it includes only debts of enterprises that were actually declared insolvent by the Hungarian National Bank. The data for Polish overdue inter-enterprise claims are not available. As far as the total volume of inter-enterprise credits is concerned, in Poland at the beginning of 1990 it reached approximately 160 percent of total bank credits issued to enterprises; at the end of 1991, this decreased to 125 percent of total bank credits issued to enterprises, in other words, 17 percent of GNP. In Bulgaria, they succeeded in preventing an accumulation of overdue claims by using strict disciplinary measures. In Romania, gross overdue inter-enterprise debts increased during 1991 almost 18-fold and reached 53 percent of GNP and more than 200 percent of the broad money supply. In Russia, during the first half of 1992, overdue inter-enterprise debts increased from less than 3 percent to more than 150 percent of the broad money supply, thus roughly by 2 trillion rubles; this increase continued despite considerable efforts by the central bank to speed up payments and a large increase in bank credits. "Neither technical measures for speeding up payments nor credit operations can solve this problem by themselves. Not until they are accompanied by measures that introduce financial discipline into the system and speed up needed structural changes in state enterprises."

In Czechoslovakia, enterprises entered the period of transformation with a heavy burden of bad debts and with an inherent liquidity risk caused by the fact that, in the 1970s, a part of their own financial means was centralized and replaced by so-called credit for permanent turnover of supplies. At the start of the transformation, banks were undercapitalized. Approximately one-quarter of their credits represented bad or highly risky

---

[17] Hrncir and Klacek, 1994.
[18] Bigman and Leite, 1993.

credits. Because of this, banks during this period used a relatively hard credit policy: total credit volume was below the limit set by the central bank.

However, the chief reason for the sharp increase in inter-enterprise indebtedness was neither past debts nor a current lack of bank credits but a sharp decrease in demand and a threat of budgetary constraints. The problem as a whole was rooted in the behavior of enterprises. Enterprises dependent on state paternalism and used to conditions of scarcity in the economy, together with apparent boundless demand and soft budgetary constraints, reacted during the first stages of transformation in a way that only deepened their problems with liquidity; at the same time, they quickly realized that they were not going to be severely threatened for their lack of financial discipline.[19]

By the end of 1990, in expectation of price increases following their liberalization, enterprises started to accumulate supplies. This strategy turned out to be shortsighted. In 1991, for internal and external reasons, there was a marked drop in demand and a marked growth in the nominal interest rate. Simultaneously, budgetary constraints on enterprises were reinforced by a decrease in subsidies. Enterprises reacted by asking the state for help; thus they stopped paying their commitments to the tax offices, to banks, and particularly to their suppliers. Enterprises preferred to continue manufacturing and "selling" to their customers, who they knew were insolvent, rather than curtail production and employment under pressure of decreased demand when they did not succeed in finding new production and outlet possibilities.

Credit involuntarily provided by trading partners was much cheaper than banking credit. Involuntary creditors carried this burden backward onto their suppliers. Enterprise managers who could not fulfill their obligations were hoping that the government would reach in and help them financially.

This type of behavior was conditioned by the time privatization was just getting started and there were as yet no bankruptcy laws.[20] However, the lack of such a law was a problem not only for the legal side of the economy. It would have hardly been possible to "release" into the

---

[19] Janackova, 1992.

[20] The first version of the bankruptcy law was approved only in the fall of 1991, and its full validity was postponed. Only in April 1993, after corrections that were supposed to limit the danger of a chain reaction of bankruptcies, was the law fully implemented.

economy a bankruptcy law in a situation in which relative prices were still so distorted by forty years of irrationality that the financial situation of that particular moment in a given enterprise could not serve as a criterion for judging its quality and vitality. Thus the loosening of financial discipline was simultaneously a symptom of a period of searching for a new price structure and of a lack of criteria for selecting out less-than-effective enterprises.

Partly as a result of the deliberate nonpayment of obligations, the lack of payment capacity by enterprises, previously mainly due to bad credits from the past, began to grow. A long chain reaction of "secondary lack of payment capacity," brought about by forced inter-enterprise credits, came into being.[21] Involuntary inter-enterprise credit reproduced the soft budget constraints for debtors and contributed a specific form of "supplemental liquidity" to the economy. As mentioned by Clifton and Khan in an analysis published by the IMF, "Inter-enterprise credits, upon reaching their term of maturity, were obviously also a liquidity, one delivered to the general system over and above the normal money supply".[22]

The above-mentioned authors also concluded that the influence of this additional liquidity on the economy could be evaluated if we add the inter-enterprise indebtedness to the broad money supply, and they see it as emerging alternatively from the gross and the net inter-enterprise indebtedness. This leaves a series of questions. Nonetheless, one cannot deny that chains of mutual credits added a specific form of liquidity to the economy, by *de facto* facilitating the transactions between enterprises that had no ready money, deposits, or bank credits. This form of liquidity is pathological because its volume can grow out of control: forced credit need not be based on any kind of money assets of the creditor.

The lack of financial discipline was not limited to state enterprises. During the period when the criteria were just being established and were creating legal underpinnings for the selection of the inefficient enterprises that were a hotbed for expanding this sickness, inter-enterprise debts were expanded even into already privatized enterprises and into newly created private firms. Inter-enterprise indebtedness and secondary payment incapacity led to an increase in bank credits as old credits were renewed and interest was added to them. Additional liquidity was achieved by

---

[21] Voluntary inter-enterprise credit was nonetheless also reported as claims on reaching maturity, because, from the legal standpoint, standard commercial credit did not exist in the institutional arrangement.

[22] Clifton and Khan, 1993, p. 687.

stepping outside of the enterprise framework; enterprises "financed" their payments of wages, on occasion even taxes, by a forced credit from their suppliers. All this served to complicate the monetary policy of the central bank.

Thus we can conclude that forced inter-enterprise credit represents a certain specific "financial innovation" on the part of enterprises, typical for the first phase of transformation: it softened the toughness of budgetary constraints; it created additional liquidity in the economy; and it influenced negatively the capacity of the central bank to fight inflation by means of a restrictive monetary policy.

There remains an open question whether the durability of inter-enterprise indebtedness was also *supported* by a restrictive monetary policy, such as the credit policy of commercial banks, which gave the economy fewer credits than were permitted by the monetary policy rules of the central bank. However, this question has at least two aspects: on the one hand, one cannot exclude the possibility, for reasons listed above and connected primarily with the process of privatization, that the volume of transactions per unit of nominal GNP grew to such a size that the need for transaction money was not actually met by the growth in the money supply.

Even if it were possible to guess with sufficient accuracy what the growth of the transaction demand for money might be in these circumstances, there remains a second side to the story. At the time when the processes that brought about an increase in the number of transactions first started, the economy already contained widespread inter-enterprise indebtedness and secondary incapacity to pay. As long as enterprise behavior that reproduced these phenomena continued to exist, a loosening of the money supply could have led to the danger of uncontrolled inflation. It was not realistic to expect that "healthy money" would simply push out and replace such a pathological form of liquidity. This could not happen without substantial changes in the behavior of enterprises, reinforced by the very real threat of bankruptcy.

In spite of the above, the growth of inter-enterprise indebtedness ensured for the enterprise sector as a whole a higher, purer influx of funds. As regards the fact that debts upon reaching maturity caused a secondary widespread inability to pay, the government repeatedly undertook measures that were supposed to diminish this problem. These measures were directed both at inter-enterprise debts and enterprise debts in banks. Largely due to a partial write-off of debts, the enterprise sector was able to absorb a considerable number of additional financial means. Even seen from this viewpoint, the relatively small rate of inflation in the Czech Republic, in comparison with other economies that are being transformed, shows an obvious success.[23]

During the recent period, one may reasonably suppose that, thanks to continuing restructuring and consolidation in the enterprise sphere, the character of inter-enterprise indebtedness will be changing and will continue to change. In a situation in which, due to the slowness of court decisions, there is a real threat of bankruptcy, one can expect that the part of inter-enterprise indebtedness that reflects low financial discipline would start to decrease. And, on the contrary, the part that one could characterize as being voluntary trade credit supported by a healthy financial situation of the creditors would grow. At the same time, there is a presumption that a part of inter-enterprise debts could be replaced by bank credits or by financial means obtained in the capital markets, where one could gradually widen the spectrum of financial mechanisms, which the "enterprises would then be able to use.[24] Mutual credits of claims and debts have so far represented a rather temporary solution. Durability of results depends on the strengthening of financial discipline. Other ways that can alleviate this problem are a buyout of claims by special firms; extrajudicial measures by the state in the financial restructuring of some of the firms; and, in the most extreme cases, the bankruptcy of some enterprises. This would simultaneously strengthen the financial discipline of the remaining ones.[25]

From the standpoint of monetary policy, the most dangerous aspect is inter-enterprise indebtedness. It is less risky when the level is stabilized or

---

[23] There was certainly a whole series of reasons for the relatively low inflation rate in the Czech Republic. These depended not only on monetary but also on fiscal policies. One of the factors was the positive role of the stable exchange rate as an anchor, which was successfully maintained in the Czech Republic. Furthermore, there is a possible partial explanation in the fact that the influence of uncontrolled liquidity might have been less significant in the Czech Republic. Forced inter-enterprise credits added uncontrolled liquidity to all economies being transformed. In the Czech Republic, this influence was apparently compensated to a certain extent by faster privatization, which increased transactional demand for money and thus partially absorbed this additional liquidity.

[24] V. Kupka, in Janacek and Klvacova, 1994.

[25] In spite of that, it is a pity that for 1993 comparable data concerning inter-enterprise indebtedness are not available. Following this aspect separately from other debts in the enterprise sector made sense and was thus indicated in this report.

declines. Nonetheless, a gradual solution of the problem of inter-enterprise indebtedness would remove a significant complicating element facing monetary policy. It would also strengthen assumptions as to further decreases in the rate of inflation in the area controlled by monetary policy.

References

Bigman, D., and Leite, S.P. [1993]. "Enterprise Arrears in Russia: Causes and Policy Options," IMF Working Paper No.64, August.

Bulir, S. [1993]. "Ceskoslovenska monetarni politika po roce 1989" (Czechoslovak monetary policy after 1989), *Finance a uver*, No.5.

Clifton, E.V., and Khan, M.S. [1993]. "Interenterprise Arrears in Transforming Economies. The Case of Romania," *IMF Staff Papers*, Vol.40, No.3 (September).

Frenkel, J.A. [1986]. "International Interdependence and the Constraints on Macro-economic Policies," *Welewirischaflliches Archiv*, No. 4.

Greene, J.E., and Isard, P. [1991]. "Currency Convertibility and the Transformation of Centrally Planned Economies," *IMF Occasional Papers*, No. 81, Washington, DC.

Hrncir, M., and Klacek, J. [1994]. "Interenterprise Indebtedness and Performance of the Banking System--The Czech Case," Paper for the ACE workshop, Prague, February.

_____. [1991]. "Stabilization Policies and Currency Convertibility in Czechoslovakia," *European Economy*, special ed., No.2.

Janacek, K., and Klvacova, E. [1994]. "Restmktulizace, anebo banicroty" (Restructuring or bankruptcies), *Ekonom*, No.13.

Janackova, S. [1992]. "Microeconomic Aspects of Transformation," *Prague Economic Papers*, No.3.

Klaus, V. [1994a]. "Makroeconomicka stranka systemovych zmen: poucni z ceske zkusenosti" (Macroeconomic Side of Systemic Changes: Learning from Czech Experience). Lecture given when receiving an honorary doctorate, Prague.

_____. [1994b]. "Par slov o konvertibilite ceske koruny" (A few words about the convertibility of the Czech koruna), *Lidove noviny*, Vol.5, No.4.

_____. [1993]. "Transformacni pravidla: hypoteza dvou polstaru" (Transforming principles: The hypothesis of the two cushions). Lecture given for the Czech Economic Society, Prague, November.

Mathieson, D.J., and Rojaz-Suarez, L. [1993]. "Liberalization of the Capital Account," *IMF Occasional Papers*, No.103.

Pospisil, J. [1993]. "Vychodiska ceske menove politiky V WCC 1993" (Results of Czech Monetary Policy in 1993), *Finance a uner*, No. 5.

Williamson, I., ed. [1991]. *Currency Convertibility in Eastern Europe,* Washington, DC: Institute for International Economics.

Wolf, T.A. [1991]. "The Exchange Rate and the Price Level in Socialist Economies," in *Managing Inflation in Socialist Economies in Transition,* edited by S. Commander, Washington, DC: The World Bank.

11 Restructuring of the Banking Sector in Slovakia

ZORA KOMINKOVA
VIKTORIA MUCKOVA

Introduction

The beginning of the economic transformation in Slovakia is related to the former Czecho-Slovak Federation (CSFR). After the political breakdown in 1989, the transformation developed under "shock-therapy" within the framework of the Economic Reform of 1991. Simultaneously, the two-tier banking system was created and new financial structures emerged. On January 1, 1993 the Federation dissolved and two successor States were established, the Slovak Republic and the Czech Republic. Despite popular rhetoric, the macro-economic policy of the Slovak government continued in the direction of the stabilization program of the former Czecho-Slovak government. The development of the Slovak banking sector progressed after the establishment of the central bank, the National Bank of Slovakia.

The aim of this paper is to present the main development trends in the Slovak banking sector during 1993-1997. The description of the banking sector and the issues regarding restructuring are introduced after a short overview of the macroeconomic development in Slovakia in the next section. The third section is focused on the monetary policy of the National Bank of Slovakia, while the fourth section presents the foreign exchange policy and exchange rate regime for the country. The current landscape of Slovak commercial banks is presented in the fifth section. The last section contains information regarding the progress made in the financial restructuring process and a summary.

Macroeconomic Development Trends

During the first four years of the national independence, economic growth in Slovakia changed from the transformation recession of 1993, toward

201

high rates of growth during 1994-1996. Stabilization of the macroeconomic environment progressed rapidly as inflation decreased and the external stability of the Slovak currency was reinforced by growing foreign exchange reserves of the National Bank of Slovakia (NBS). An overview of the main macroeconomic indicators is given in Table 11.1.

Table 11.1 Main Macroeconomic Indicators in Slovakia, 1993-1997[a]

Indicator	1993	1994	1995	1996	1997
GDP (%, 1993 prices)	-3.7	4.9	6.8	6.9	6.0[b]
Industrial production					
(%, constant prices)	-13.5	6.4	8.4	2.5	3.5
CPI (%, annual average)	23.2	13.4	9.9	5.8	6.1
Government budget					
deficit (%GDP)	-7.3[c]	-1.2[c]	-1.6	-4.4	-4.3
Fiscal deficit (surplus)					
(% of GDP)	7.1	2.6	-0.5	0.8	--
Balance of trade and					
services (USD million)	- 619	762	570	-2106	-999
Current account					
balance/GDP (%)	5.0	5.5	3.7	-10.2	-10.9
Unemployment rate (%)	14.4	14.8	13.8	12.4	13.1

[a] First half of the year. [b] Constant prices, December, 1995. [c] Cleared from the clearing balance with the Czech Republic.
Source: Statistical Office of the SR, National Bank of Slovakia.

The establishment of an independent State came with an adjustment period in the economy. The economic recession in 1993 continued and GDP decreased by 3.7%. The economic development in this year was affected by various economic and non-economic factors, such as a smaller domestic market and the costly process of reconstituting the State infrastructure, as well as the introduction of a new tax system (VAT base), and a new system of health and pension insurance. This, together with devaluation expectations after the breakup of the monetary union with the Czech Republic (on February 8) and the devaluation of the Slovak currency by 10% (on July 10) caused an acceleration of inflation to a yearly rate of 23.2% in 1993.

Due to the extraordinary conditions of the year, the government budget deficit reached 7.3% of GDP. Unsatisfactory development in the external sector contributed to a huge slowdown in trading with the Czech Republic and resulted in a deficit in the balance of trade and services in the amount of USD 619 million. The deficit in the current account was USD 559 million.

Economic revival began in 1994. GDP growth reached 4.9%, the average inflation rate was cut to 13.4%, and the Government budget deficit slowed to 1.2% of GDP. The leading sector of economic growth was foreign trade, as export performance was enhanced by growing external demand and by the effects of the Slovak crown devaluation. On the other hand, imports were slowed by the 10% import surcharge imposed in March, 1994. As a result, the balance of foreign trade and services reached a surplus of USD 762 million and the current account amounted to USD 712 million.

In 1995, economic growth accelerated to 6.8%. The average annual rate of inflation reached 9.9%, while Government spending resulted in a budget deficit of 1.6% of GDP. The balance of foreign trade and services generated a surplus of USD 570.2 million and the current account had a surplus of USD 649.5 million. An important development in 1995 was the increase in consumer and investment demand in the domestic economy. Though the dynamics of gross fixed capital formation had not been restored, economic growth was due primarily to the utilization of free capacity in production. Despite internal expansion, the driving force behind economic growth remained in the export sector.

A different picture of economic development arose in 1996. Domestic demand increases, fueled by an increase in gross fixed capital formation, became the leading factor in the continued expansion of GDP, which reached 6.9%. Favorable as well was the further decrease in the inflation rate that reached 5.8%. On the other hand, serious imbalances occurred in the foreign trade sector. Rapid growth of domestic demand, supported by accelerated increases in wages, caused a huge increase in imports. Simultaneously, export growth slowed due to a worsening of international trade conditions and the diminishing effects of devaluation from the spring of 1993. As a result, the deficit in the balance of trade and services reached USD 2.1 billion and the current account deficit was USD 1.9 billion (10.4% of GDP and 10.2% of GDP, respectively).

In the first half of 1997, economic growth slowed moderately to 6.0%, while inflation accelerated to 6.1%. Due to the possibly dangerous developments in the external sector, the Slovak government re-introduced import surcharges at a 7% level, enlarged the duties in the certification of imports and imposed regulations on wages in the last quarter of the year.

While these measures may slow the growth of imports, they do not resolve the issue of unsatisfactory growth in Slovak exports. Serious issues of macroeconomic stability remain, including the growing amounts of government spending and the government budget deficit.

For a small open economy as Slovakia, the development in the external sector represents one of the key factors that influences the conditions of overall macroeconomic stability. Unfortunately, due to the fact that (1) the main proportion of Slovak exports is formed by semi-products and products with a low level of manufacturing, (2) the technological development in general has been slow, and (3) the dynamics of the business cycle abroad have been lower, the competitiveness of Slovak exports has been slow since the second half of 1995. On the other hand, import requirements of the Slovak economy are very high (close to 70% of GDP) in general. In fact, there are many items (apart from energy, raw materials and consumer goods) that are fully dependent upon imports since there are no substitutes in the domestic market.

An alternative source of new technologies that could moderate the import requirements to a large extent is foreign direct investments (FDI). The FDI inflow to Slovakia remains at an unsatisfactory level, although its level has accelerated since the second half of 1995. The amount of foreign capital invested in the Slovak economy reached around USD 1 billion at the end of 1996. However, most of the FDI went to the trade and banking sectors, leaving relatively small amounts going toward strategic investments for economic restructuring.

Management structures in the enterprise sector continued to develop, conditioned by the privatization process. Data on the private sector in the Slovak economy in 1996 show that it contributed 76.8% to the GDP, generated 68.2% of the industrial production (including co-operatives), and employed 59.8% of the total labor force.

Monetary Policy of the National Bank of Slovakia

The National Bank of Slovakia (NBS) was established by the Act of the National Council No. 566/1992 as the central bank of the Slovak Republic (SR) and began its operations on January 1, 1993. The major role of the NBS is to ensure the stability of the Slovak currency (Slovak crown, SKK) and keeping inflation under control. To meet this task, the following main activities fall under the Bank's jurisdiction: (1) determination of monetary policy and of its main instruments of monetary regulation; (2) issuance of banknotes and coins; (3) money supply management; (4) coordination of payments and settlement of accounts between commercial banks and ensuring efficiency of these operations; (5) supervision of banking activities and the prudential performance of the banking system. The NBS represents the SR in international monetary institutions and world financial markets, and coordinates the tasks arising from this representation.[1]

The NBS performs its main tasks independently[2] of the Government. However, within the limits of the Act on the NBS, the Bank must support the government's economic policy. The Governor or an appointed Bank Board member informs the Government of approved decisions of the Bank Board and participates in meetings of the Government. The NBS advises the Government in the areas of monetary policy and banking. The NBS

---

[1] The supreme bodies of the NBS are the Bank Board and the Directorate. The Bank Board is the highest management body of the NBS outlining Slovakia's monetary policy and the instruments for its implementation, and making decisions on regulations to be imposed by the Bank in order to control the money supply and inflation. The members of the Bank Board are the Governor, two vice-governors and five other members. The Governor and vice-governors are appointed for a 6-year period by the President of the SR upon the proposal of the Government and endorsement by the Slovak National Council. Other members of Bank Board are appointed for a four-year period by the Government upon the proposal of the Governor. During the membership on the Bank Board, members cannot perform the functions of a Parliament deputy nor a member of the Government. The executive body of the NBS is the Directorate, which is responsible for implementing the Bank Board decisions.

[2] However, as with the independence of any other central banks, the independence of the NBS is not absolute. First, the fixed exchange rate regime does not enable the NBS to make wholly independent monetary policy decisions. Second, as stated by Bruni (1995), the independence *de jure* (given in the Slovak case by the Act on the NBS) is not the exhaustive characteristic of central bank independence. One may state that because of the very successful disinflationary monetary policy strategy of the NBS in the first year of Slovak independence (1993), the NBS played a key demonstrative role in the process of overcoming the unrealistic vision of a more permissive (as compared with the CSFR period 1990-1992) budgetary policy of the First Slovak Government. As a result, a satisfactory level of harmonization of monetary and Government finance policies was reached, contributing to a rapid stabilization of the macroeconomic environment in the country.

must present half-year and annual reports on monetary development to the Parliament and publish information on quarterly monetary developments.

Regarding foreign exchange management, the NBS trades in gold and foreign exchange with domestic and foreign banks, establishes the conditions for the regulation of the balance of payments, sets the conditions for trading in gold and foreign exchange by banks and other persons, and issues securities denominated in foreign exchange.

The Bank enjoys legislative powers as well. It submits bills pertaining to currency and the money supply to the Government and, together with the Ministry of Finance, proposes bills pertaining to foreign exchange operations and banking.

By law, the monetary policy goal of the NBS is ensuring the internal and external stability of the Slovak currency. The main monetary policy target is to control the rate of inflation, which is performed through two intermediate targets: (1) a fixed exchange rate of the Slovak crown (as a longer-term target) and (2) the annual growth of the money supply expressed by the monetary aggregate, M2.[3] The operational variable is central bank money, the monetary base, defined as a sum of bank reserves with the NBS and the cash-currency in public and commercial bank holdings. The monetary base is regulated by changes in the discount and Lombard rates, open market operations, and minimum reserve requirements.

Since the beginning of its operations, the NBS has had a strategy to decrease the importance of direct instruments (namely credit limits) and to increase the use of indirect instruments with a growing role for open market operations. However, the importance of individual instruments grew with the monetary development in Slovakia, which recorded substantial changes since 1993.

The monetary environment in 1993 was quit unstable, marked by the establishment of national independence of the country, the emerging Slovak financial market, and the introduction of the first, single Government Budget Act of the Slovak Republic.[4] Due to the lack of

---

[3] The aggregate, M2, is defined as a sum of narrow money, M1, and quasi-money, or as a sum of notes and coins in circulation, demand deposits, time deposits including deposit certificates and deposits by building societies, and foreign currency deposits.

[4] In the years 1990-1992, there were three Government budgets in the former Czech and Slovak Federative Republic: a Czech, a Slovak and a Federal one. Through the Federal budget, a redistribution of resources between both Republics

liquidity in the banking sector, refinancing from the NBS through auction refinance credits and rediscount credits reached relatively high amounts. Credit limits played an important role in this year, prescribed originally for all commercial banks and later used to a limited extent. With regard to the new monetary environment, changes in the discount rate had remained at its original rate of 9.5% until December when it was increased to 12.0%, in order to influence public expectations of a disinflationary monetary policy of the NBS. The development of open market operations, after repurchase agreements were introduced, was rather slow in 1993.

During 1994-1995, monetary development stabilized, enabling more systematic selection of the monetary policy instruments. The importance of credit limits decreased as their general use was canceled. Limits were set only for banks with credit activities exceeding SKK 20 billion since the second half of 1994 and finally were abolished as of January 1, 1996.

More operative monetary policy management through changes in the indirect instrument parameters has been applied since 1995. In order to support economic growth, the discount rate was decreased to 11% on March 17. As the disinflation process continued throughout the year, a second cut in the discount rate to 9.75% occurred on October 6, followed by another cut to 8.8% on January 13, 1996. In addition, several changes were made in the minimum required reserves (RMR) in order to withdraw the excessive liquidity in the banking sector that became a serious issue in the second half of 1994. Apart from setting the RMR on building savings deposits at 1% (as of April 1, 1995), a more important step was taken to combine the former 3% and 9% ratios on time and demand deposits, respectively, at the single higher level of 9% as of August 1, 1996. The RMR on building savings deposits was increased to 3% on October 24, 1996. On this date, the interest on the RMR paid by the NBS was set at a level of 1.5%.

The dynamic development of open market operations of the NBS began in the second half of 1995. Their importance in controlling the money market increased in 1996. Apart from REPO and re-REPO operations, an important part of open market operations became the purchasing of its own bills by the NBS. Issuing NBS-bills for sterilization purposes became a regular activity of the NBS during 1996, since, given a relatively favorable government budget performance, the limited amounts of T-bills were not

---

was accomplished. Balances from the Federal budget deficits were to be repaid by the successor States.

able to take care of the growing liquidity of the banking sector. In 1997, the NBS continued the tight monetary policy that was begun in 1996. The REPO rates for individuals REPOs were canceled and REPO tenders became the only means of monetary policy in early 1997, depriving banks of automatic access to refinancing by the NBS.

The NBS adopted a two-target monetary policy orientation, the targets being a fixed exchange rate of the currency and the growth of the money stock, M2. At times these targets were difficult to meet simultaneously. The conditions of the regime of internal convertibility of the Slovak currency resulted in substantially lower requirements in foreign exchange reserves and interventions of the central bank. A relatively high level of monetary protection was preserved after liberalization of the current account of the balance of payments (on October 1, 1995), as well. Another supporting factor for continuing the monetary targeting practice was the gradual extension of the fluctuation band of the exchange rate of the Slovak crown (to the current ±7% against the basket parity).

Table 11.2 Monetary Targets of the NBS

	Monetary Program		Actual Values	
	M2 (in percent)	inflation (CPI)[a]	M2 (in percent)	inflation (CPI)[a]
1993	12	17.0	18.3	25.1
1994	13.2	10.0 - 13.2	18.9	11.7
1995	12.3	8.0	21.2	7.6
1996	11.6±0.6	6.0-7.5	15.7	5.6
1997	10.7	4.9-5.8	12.8[b]	6.2[b]

[a] Yearly indexes December/December; [b] September 1997/September, 1996.
Source: National Bank of Slovakia.

A dynamic inflow of foreign exchange resources supported by favorable foreign trade development occurred during 1994-1995. In 1996 there was an enormous increase in foreign bank loans and in enterprises financing large amounts of imports. These developments resulted in an excessive growth of liquidity in the Slovak banking sector that put great pressure on the growth of the money stock. In spite of the sterilization activities of the NBS and an unconvincing level of stability of the money velocity, the money stock growth target was exceeded each year (see Table 11.2).

Due to the fixed exchange rate, foreign exchange policy requirements given a safe level of foreign exchange reserves of the NBS were the leading criterion in evaluating the importance of the fulfillment of the external and/or internal intermediate monetary policy target. The fact that the final disinflationary goal was successfully achieved during this time period without any serious disturbance to the growth of M2 confirms the crucial function of the fixed exchange rate as a nominal anchor.

From this viewpoint, one may state that monetary policy was successful. Since the 1993 devaluation, foreign exchange (FX) reserves of the NBS have grown gradually. While at the end of 1993 they represented the value of 0.7-month Slovak average imports of goods and services, the 1995 year end level covered 4-month average imports. However, growing import requirements in FX resources caused some decreases in the FX reserves/imports ratio, resulting in 2.8 monthly average imports in June, 1997.

An important issue of NBS monetary targeting is the ability of the NBS to control the money supply. This ability relies partially upon its control of the development of the resource (assets) side of the monetary base and/or upon the effectiveness of regulations undertaken towards the use of the monetary base. A recent study showed that the ability of the NBS to control the monetary base resources directly was lacking in practice[5] as movements in the monetary base have been significantly influenced by net foreign assets, which are not directly controllable by the NBS. In addition, control requires a stable (or predictable) value of the money multiplier between the monetary base and the targeted monetary aggregate (M2, in our case). The stability of the money multiplier has been found rather doubtful, as well.

Increases in bank lending to the enterprise and personal sectors were relatively low in 1993 and 1994 due to tight regulation via credit limits (see Table 11.3). However, in 1995-1996, after partial releasing of the regulation (it remained in force only at the five largest Slovak banks with lending activities exceeding SKK 20 billion), the growth in bank lending accelerated mainly due to the growing lending activities in banks not subject to credit limits. Total credit to enterprises and households increased by 18.2% in 1996 (although it is to be stressed that a

---

[5] See for example, Kominkova, Z., "Regulation of the Money Stock and Issues of Monetary Targeting in the Slovak Republic," *Biatec*, 4, 1996, No.8, pp. 29-36.

considerable part of the increase in crown loans comprised interest on non-performing loans), and credits in foreign currency increased by 35.7%. Apart from the abolishment of the credit limits (since the beginning of 1996), the main factor that caused such a high increase in lending was growing domestic demand supported by rapid wage growth. The almost twofold rise in credits denominated in foreign currency (as compared with the total credit to enterprises and households) was related to a huge increase in imports and, consequently, to the need of financing the current account deficit. In 1996, personal lending increased for the first time since 1993. However, the share of enterprise sector loans of total enterprise and household crown loans remained at the 1995 level of 94.6% (as compared with 92.7% in 1993). Credits in foreign currency (extended exclusively to legal entities) have grown substantially. Their share of total lending reached 8.8% in June, 1997, compared to 3% in 1993.

In order to slow down the lending activities of banks that were the main factor of the money supply expansion (close to 40 % toward the end of 1996), the NBS adopted measures in July, 1996, oriented against both domestic and foreign currency credit expansion: the ratio of required minimum reserves was increased (and unified) to the level of 9%, and the Lombard rate was increased to 15% (i.e., by 2 points). In addition, the NBS introduced the so-called *bank foreign exchange position for monetary purposes.* This regulation imposed upon banks a required foreign exchange assets/liabilities ratio, adjusted with regard to resident and non-resident origins.[6] Announced in mid-July, it came into force on December 31, 1996. By this date banks were obliged to reach the ratio of 0.65.[7] For 1997, the ratio was increased to 0.70 on March 31 and to 0.80 on June 30.

Despite rapid progress in the disinflationary process in the Slovak economy and despite a gradual decrease in the discount rate of the NBS, lending and deposit interest rates of commercial banks remain relatively high in Slovakia. While the yearly rate of inflation decreased from 25.1% in 1993 to 6.2% in mid-1997, the decrease in average interest rates was

---

[6] The ratio was constructed with the numerator representing the bank's total foreign exchange assets minus foreign exchange assets with residents and the denominator representing the bank's foreign exchange liabilities plus liabilities with non-resident banks denominated in Slovak crowns.

[7] In fact, banks reached the ratio of 0.663 on December 31, 1996. The remaining uncovered position would be penalized by increasing minimum reserve requirements.

substantially smaller. The average deposit rate on deposits in domestic currency (both demand and time deposits) decreased from 8.67% in December, 1993, to 7.75% in June, 1997. The average lending rate decreased from 14.01% in December, 1993, to 13.22% in December, 1996 and increased again to 14.94% in June, 1997.

The development of deposit and lending rates of the Slovak commercial banks may be dominated more by the policies of the largest Slovak banks than by the inflation development and discount and Lombard rates of the NBS. This may be due to the fact that the balance sheet structure of these most powerful banks contain the highest amounts of non-performing loans that influence the banks' behavior in the direction of maintaining interest rates at a high safety level.

Interest rates in the interbank deposit market were increasing as well. During 1995, the official BRIBOR[8] rates moved from 4.5% to the discount rate level of 9.75% (December, 1995) and continued to rise, reaching the Lombard rate of 15% (December, 1996). The main factors in the BRIBOR rates development in 1996 were: (1) the high sterilization activity of the NBS via the issuance of large amounts of NBS-bills, and (2) the increase in the required minimum reserve ratio that resulted in withdrawing additional amounts of banking sector liquidity equal to SKK 13 billion, which increased the RMR volume with the NBS by approximately 70%.

Table 11.3   Bank Credit to Enterprises and Households
(yearly % changes)

	1993	1994	1995	1996	1997*
Total credit to enterprises and households	10.8	0.4	14.7	18.2	7.9
- credits in SKK	9.1	-1.6	12.3	16.8	9.7
- enterprises	10.4	-0.8	13.6	16.9	8.9
- households	- 6.1	-11.3	-6.7	16.3	25.3
-credit in for. currency	118.9	77.8	57.6	35.7	-8.0

*June 1997/June 1996
Source: Monetary Survey of the NBS 1993-1996; in current exchange rate.

---

[8] BRIBOR = BRatislava InterBank Offering Rate. Since July 1995, BRIBOR on overnight, 1-month, and 3-month deposits are announced. In March 1996, a 6-month BRIBOR was introduced, as well.

A dramatic development in the interbank rates occurred in 1997. A general rise in the rates was accompanied by their enormous volatility. By the end of May, a lack of liquidity, related to the critical development in the foreign exchange market in connection with the foreign attack against the Slovak currency, caused a limitation in interbank market trading. Banks temporarily stopped the BRIBOR rates quotation.[9] Despite a remarkable stabilization of the rates (to around 20% generally) in a short period of time, the foreign exchange market was cleared, though the quotation of the BRIBOR rates was not renewed until recently.

Foreign Exchange Policy and Exchange Rate Regime

The main characteristics of the foreign exchange policy and the exchange rate regime of the National Bank of Slovakia have their origin in the foreign exchange experience from the beginning of the economic transformation within the former Czecho-Slovak Federation. The setting of a new exchange rate level implied a series of devaluations, which resulted in the depreciation of the crown by about 100% (from 7.20 CZK/1USD to 28 CZK/1USD). The exchange rate was fixed against a basket of five currencies (USD, DEM, ATS, CHF, FFR).[10] From a systemic point of view, the choice of the initial level of the exchange rate was critically conditioned by the declaration of internal convertibility of the currency that defined the starting point for external sector liberalization. The internal convertibility of the currency was introduced on January 1, 1991.

The fixed exchange rate experience from the beginning of the transformation proved to be successful mainly in two ways. (1) The exchange rate depreciation under conditions of a fixed regime created room for the exchange rate to work as a nominal monetary anchor, which resulted in a rapid slow down in inflation. (2) The performance and territorial restructuring of the export sector toward market economies was promoted after the CMEA-market (Council for Mutual Economic Assistance) breakdown. However, the adopted exchange rate (of 28

---

[9] During this period, the highest interbank rates were reached. The overnight rate was 185.0%, the one-month rate was 62.5% and the six-month rate was 45.0%.

[10] USD=US dollar; DEM=German mark; ATS=Austrian schilling; CHF=Swiss franc; FFR=French franc.

CZK/1 USD) put the Czecho-Slovak crown among the most depreciated currencies within the group of Central European transition countries.

At the beginning of 1993, the National Bank of Slovakia aimed to follow the foreign exchange and exchange rate policies of the former State Bank of Czecho-Slovakia. Therefore, the precondition was to maintain the internal convertibility of the new Slovak currency which, together with reaching a suitable level of inflation, became the main monetary policy goal for 1993. Only when the internal convertibility was in place was the maintenance of the fixed rate declared an intermediate target of the monetary policy of the NBS, which became part of the monetary program for 1994.

The NBS was obliged to introduce some administrative regulations into foreign exchange management finally to accede to a 10% devaluation of the Slovak crown on July 10, 1993.[11] The devaluation proved sufficient to improve the situation. The behavior of economic entities became more stable and the outflow of foreign exchange was slowed, so that administrative regulations were canceled gradually. The stabilization effect of the devaluation was supported by additional measures adopted to restrict imports.[12]

An important step regarding the Slovak crown exchange rate definition was taken in July, 1994, when the currency basket was simplified from five to two currencies (DEM and USD) in a 60:40 ratio.[13] At the same time the fluctuation band of the SKK exchange rate was enlarged to ±1.5% (with a maximum daily deviation of ±1%) against the cross-exchange rate of DEM/USD.

---

[11] After the devaluation, the weight ratios of individual currencies in the currency basket were: USD 49.09%, DEM 36.16%, ATS 8.07%, CHF 7.79%, FFR 12.92%.

[12] There were obligatory consultations on payment conditions of imported goods, an introduction of the import surcharge of 10% in March, 1994 (in force until the end of 1996), and certificates for foodstuffs in inter-republic Czecho-Slovak trading. Regarding the protectionist measures, on the other hand, the Slovak economy has a very low level of customs protection (the average amount of customs duties is around 4 - 5%). In addition, joint-venture companies were liberated of the customs duty on technological imports, and the customs duty on imported cars up to 1,500 cu cm was cancelled for the period 1995-1996.

[13] The absolute value of the currency basket is defined as 1 IDX = 0.012817 USD + 0.029663 DEM.

During 1994-1995, the balance of payments developed favorably and the foreign exchange reserves of the NBS (and of commercial banks as well) grew significantly due to a rapid expansion in export sector activities. Possible methods of current account liberalization were discussed in the beginning of 1995. After the Czech Republic announced its intention to retire from the Payments Agreement[14] with the Slovak Republic (motivated by the same current account liberalization goal and the related fulfillment of the non-discriminatory payment conditions of the IMF's Article VIII), a new foreign exchange act introducing convertibility[15] of the Slovak crown on current account transactions was put into force on October 1, 1995.

The convertibility on the current account was an important milestone in the development of the exchange rate regime. Within the framework of the new foreign exchange act, the monetary program of the NBS for 1996 recommended enlarging the role of foreign exchange policy, especially in the direction of a more flexible exchange rate policy. As of January 1, 1996, the fluctuation band of the SKK was extended from ±1.5% to ±3%. Further extensions[16] to ±5% and to ±7 % followed on July 16, 1996 and January 1, 1997, respectively. Thus, the maneuvering space for the exchange rate policy was significantly enlarged so that the NBS could react more flexibly on the balance of payments development, especially with regard to control of short-term foreign capital inflows.

Innovations in exchange rate trading between the NBS and commercial banks at the foreign exchange setting by the NBS were adopted, as well. In order to support the development of the interbank foreign exchange

---

[14] In order to promote foreign trade relations between the Czech and Slovak enterprises, the payments agreement included a clearing regime in current account payments between both Republics. Other important agreements between the Republics, concluded in order to avoid an undesirable unrestrained breakdown in mutual Czecho-Slovak economic relations, were the currency union and the custom union. The currency union broke down on February 8, 1993, approximately one month after the CSFR split. The custom union is still enforced at present.

[15] The act enables a gradual liberalization of the capital account transactions as well (excluding the final stage of transition toward full convertibility).

[16] The NBS through the "Auction Committee" weekly determines in what part of the fluctuation band the exchange rate of the SKK should move during the next week. No limitation for daily fluctuations against the basket parity are in force presently.

market, a currency band of ±0.25%[17] for commercial banks trading at the foreign exchange fixing was introduced, minimum required amounts traded on the foreign exchange market were increased to USD 300,000, or DEM 500,000 respectively,[18] and some of the obligations of banks to comply with the currency band set by the NBS for trading on behalf of clients in foreign exchange were removed.

As a sort of safety fuse, regulation limiting the amount of foreign exchange that banks are allowed to sell for tourist purposes remains in the foreign exchange policy. In 1993, the regulation allowed citizens to purchase hard currency equivalent to SKK 7,500 (per capita) from financial institutions. During 1994-1995, the tourist limit was increased gradually to an amount equivalent to SKK 60,000 (USD 2, 000, approx.) which is the current limit. Its removal is being discussed.

One may state that during 1993-1996, the NBS was successful in maintaining the fixed exchange rate regime of the national currency. An important feature of its performance has been the fact that no intervention of the NBS on the foreign exchange market in favor of supporting the fixed rate was required. The exchange rate policy made flexible use of the fluctuation band. In the NBS's determination of the exchange rate of the SKK, a main role is played by the commercial banks' supply and demand for foreign exchange and by the development of the current account.

In October, 1996, the negative balance in the foreign exchange account of the NBS most likely resulted from the outflow of foreign speculative capital after the fluctuation band was enlarged from ±3% to ±5%. In December, the commercial banks' intention to reach the 0.65 ratio in its foreign exchange position by the end of the month by purchasing foreign exchange resulted in a depreciation of the exchange rate by 1.33% over one month. As of December 31, 1996, the exchange rate of the SKK was 1% below the basket parity.

With the approval of the new Foreign Exchange Act on October 1, 1995, the current account transactions were liberalized. Capital flows were liberalized with regard to non-resident investments in Slovakia, including capital transfers and earnings from these investments (in the

---

[17] This means that the NBS sells foreign exchange for an exchange rate that has increased by 0.25% and buys for a rate that has decreased by 0.25%, compared to the exchange rate value that was set by the NBS.

[18] Before 1996, the minimum required traded amount was set at the level of 100,000 currency units in USD or DEM, respectively.

form of share and bond purchases, and other direct financial investments). With the movement of Slovakia toward membership in the OECD, the NBS in cooperation with the Slovak Ministry of Finance developed a schedule for capital account liberalization, which was approved by the Slovak government in June, 1996. The time and subject schedules of the capital movement liberalization were arranged with regard to the economic restructuring conditions in Slovakia.

The fluctuation band of the exchange rate of the Slovak crown was further widened to ±7%, as of January 1, 1997. This theoretically allows a band of 14% for exchange rate fluctuations. However, recent developments characterized by close exchange rate movements around the central parity reduced, in practice, the band to about half in scope (7%). This might be enough to stop undesirable speculative capital inflows due to the high interest rates in Slovakia. Apart from the possible appreciation of the exchange rate and the devaluation expectations, one might see a similar result given the expected and unavoidable deficit in the current account in 1997.

From a longer-term view, maintenance of the fixed rate will be dependent upon the speed of overcoming the current "unproductive" development of the balance payments. In other words, it will depend upon how fast the balance of payments will witness a reversal of the present current account deficit and reflect a technological recovery of the economy and, thereby, a higher performance of Slovak exports.

An important factor in the required changes in the capital flows structure is an increase in foreign direct investments (including portfolio investment) in the Slovak economy. Apart from improvements in legislation that are forthcoming, their faster inflow is expected in connection with a new wave of ownership restructuring via the sale of new private enterprises (cheaply acquired from the State) abroad.

Given the conditions of the Slovak economy, the application of a fixed nominal exchange rate pegged to a basket of currencies, extended by a fluctuation band, proved to be satisfactory and successful in general. Thus, discussion about changing the exchange rate regime is not being regarded as useful at present. Nevertheless, maintaining the current level of the fixed rate should not be seen as an ultimate final policy goal.

Banking Sector Developments in the 1990s

Until 1989, the Czecho-Slovak banking system existed in a form that only marginally resembled the current two-tier system. The so-called mono-banking system in Slovakia consisted of the following:

The State Bank of Czecho-Slovakia [SBCS] that fulfilled the function of the central bank of the State within the centrally-planned economy. It functioned as the largest commercial bank, administered the vast majority of financial resources and was the main creditor and organizer of the entire payment system in the country.

The Czech State Savings Bank in Prague and the *Slovak State Saving Bank* in Bratislava administered almost all saving deposits of individuals (the deposits were fully guaranteed by the State) and were the main suppliers of loans for individuals (in particular, special loans to newlyweds, for housing construction projects and the purchase of household equipment);

The Czecho-Slovak Commercial Bank [CSOB] secured operations and transactions denominated in foreign currencies between domestic trading companies and foreign subjects and represented the State in international financial markets;

The Entrepreneurial (Merchant) Bank [Zivnostenská banka] secured foreign exchange transactions for individuals.

After January 1, 1990, within the framework of the transformation of the economy, the banking system experienced substantial changes. The State Bank of Czecho-Slovakia was transformed in two parts: (1) the SBCS situated in Prague as the central bank of the State retained the functions of the issuing bank and, (2) by separating the commercial bank functions of the former SBCS, three commercial banks were created, as follows:

Commercial Bank Prague [Komerèní banka Praha] assumed one part of the deposits and credits, in particular those of entities located in the Czech Republic. It assumed the respective technical equipment, premises and personnel from the SBCS.

General Credit Bank [Všeobecná úverová banka] in the Slovak Republic, did the same as the Komerèní banka in the Czech Republic.

Investment Bank [Investièní banka Praha] assumed a part of long-term credits, in particular those that were given to enterprises to finance large investment and housing projects in Czecho-Slovakia. On January 1, 1992, the Slovak organization units were disconnected on the grounds of which the *Investment and Development Bank [Investièná a rozvojová banka*

Bratislava] was established.

Changes in banking regulations brought about more radical changes in the banking system, specifically concerning the powers of the central bank, the position against the government, monetary instruments, the role and position of commercial banks, and the framework of their activities in the banking sector. Furthermore, a partial privatization of the four main domestic banks started and the banks were transformed in joint-stock companies. Foreign banks were allowed to begin their banking activities.

After the central bank was established, Slovak commercial banking developed independently. The number of banks increased continually. From a total of 29 banks operating presently in Slovakia, there are 25 domestic institutions (with and without foreign capital participation), 4 branches of foreign banks and 10 representative offices of foreign banks. As of July 1, 1997, there were 1,186 organizational units of banks, 17 of which operated within the local branches of foreign banks. The character of their territorial distribution is influenced by the fact that the head offices of 20 banks are located in Bratislava, the capital of the Slovak Republic.

The prevailing form of Slovak commercial banks is that of joint stock companies (23 banks). Two banks are public financial institutions that fulfill special banking functions. The *Slovak Guarantee Bank* (*Slovenská záruèná banka*) and the *Consolidation Bank* (*Konsolidaèná banka Bratislava*) engaged in activities that are concentrated primarily on servicing the pre-transformation credits and loans, and facilitating loans for specific transformation purposes.

Of the total number of domestic banks, twenty-one banks have been granted a universal banking license and four are holders of specialized banking licenses for specific activities (building savings banks, guarantee and consolidation banks). Fifteen banks are licensed to conduct foreign exchange activities. The other banks have a limited license in this field.

The first data concerning the amount of equity capital of commercial banks were officially published on April 1, 1993. The subscribed equity capital of commercial banks increased from SKK 13.8 billion on April 1, 1993 to SKK 30.6 billion on July 1, 1997. The participation of foreign investors in the Slovak banking sector increased from 10.6% to 38.3% of the total volume of subscribed equity capital for this same period.

Slovak commercial banks provide basic banking services, such as the receipt of customer deposits, the granting of loans and advances, and other services. With regard to deposit operations, various types of deposits are accepted (demand deposits, savings deposits, time deposits, certificates of deposits, and bank obligations) from various depositors (corporate customers, households, central and local governments, other banks, etc.). On the basis of concentrated resources, banks conduct business activities mainly by granting loans and making investments. Differences arise mainly within the range and the quality of banking services provided. Offers of services depend largely on the level of automation and computerization within the banking sector.

On the Slovak financial market, banking institutions render financial services in both Slovak crowns and foreign currencies. Interbank payments and settlements are the largest operations carried out by banks and involve practically all corporate entities. The opening of bank accounts and the conditions of their administration and termination are governed by the Commercial Code (No. 513/1991 Zb.). At present, payment cards are still in the process of development; they are used only in ATMs and at filling stations in exceptional cases. The number of domestic payment cards has increased, while the number of international cards is relatively low. With an increase in the number of such cards, the number and volume of transactions concluded through ATMs will also increase. A precondition for the widespread use of payment cards is the development of telecommunication and computer networks.

In addition, banks provide foreign exchange operations. They keep accounts for customers, make international payments, conduct foreign exchange transactions, make loans abroad, and deal in foreign securities. Most banks operate in Slovakia on the basis of a full or limited foreign exchange license. Large banking institutions render various services in the field of investment banking, namely, capital market operations, products and services in the field of financial and investment consulting, and services in the field of market research and analysis. Other services rendered by Slovak banks are: safety deposit services, factoring, forfeiting, and financial leasing.

The issue of financial sector privatization concerns the limited, though powerful group of four State financial institutions that were created within the first stage of forming the two-tier banking system during 1991-1992, as indicated above. Every other new commercial bank that emerged, excluding the two specialized public financial institutions (the Consolidation Bank and the Slovak Guarantee Bank) was established exclusively as private companies. By the Act on Large Privatization, banks were transformed into joint-stock-companies.[19]   The current share of bank's subscribed equity capital (excluding the NBS) held by the National Property fund and by the State amounted to 40.6% of total equity at the end of 1996.

The third Meciar Government in its Program Declaration from January, 1995, emphasized the stability of the development in the Slovak economy. To this end, the Government would specify the interests of the State in the privatization of strategic enterprises, including the banking sector. The enactment of related legislation since 1995 was a major part of the package of new legislative powers regulating the privatization process.

The second wave of voucher privatization in Slovakia was replaced by the so-called bond method.[20] This amendment increased the powers of the NPF, and considerably accelerated the process of privatization in the form of direct sale, public tender and the sale of shares on the capital market. Subsequent to this legislation, a law was passed to secure the interests of the Government in the privatization of strategically important State enterprises and corporations. This law (NC SR No. 192/1995 Z.z.) defined which companies could be privatized only with government approval.

The need to restructure the banking sector and solve the bad debts problem, as expressed in the Government Program Declaration, initiated considerable discussion regarding what step to take first: privatization or restructuring.   After an intermediate period of declarations that banks would be privatized until the end February 1996, the present legislation conserves the existing ownership structure in the banks until the end of March, 1997. As a result, the expected fast process of bank privatization has been slowed.

---

[19] The shares of the joint-stock companies became the ownership of the National Property Fund (NPF). As the companies gradually were privatized (or sold by the NPF to new private owners), the NPF collected earnings from the sales and the share of the NPF in the capital ownership of individual companies decreased.

[20] According to this, each individual registered in the second wave of the voucher privatization is entitled to a bond issued by the National Property Fund (NPF) at a par value of SKK 10,000. These bonds have a maturity of December 31, 2000 and may be used for specific purposes. A shortening of the maturity date to December 31, 1997 was made for pensioners by an amendment to the Act in October, 1996.

Trading in bonds started in August, 1996. High supply was met with low demand in the first weeks. By mid-1997, 15.7% of the total number of bonds were redeemed.

Foreign capital participation in the subscribed banking capital in Slovakia developed rapidly compared to its very low starting amounts. While the participation of foreign investors in the Slovak banking sector represented 13.6% of the total banking equity in Slovakia, as of June 30, 1993, their share amounted to 38.3% by mid-1997. The major part of this increase occurred during 1995, as the growth in equity capital as a whole before 1995 was rather moderate. Foreign capital participation was reported in 14 domestic commercial banks operating as of June 30, 1997. To this date, four branches of foreign banks operate in Slovakia. By June 30, 1997, the Czech Republic had the largest share (37%), followed by Austria (21%), Netherlands (19%), Germany (7%), USA and France (4% each), Great Britain and Italy (3% each) and Russia (2%).

Banks with foreign capital participation (banks with foreign capital participation under 10% are classified as bank with no foreign participation) are mainly medium-sized entities, with equity capital between SKK 0.5 billion to SKK 1.85 billion. The equity participation ranges from 10% to 100%.

Process of Financial Restructuring

The restructuring of the banking sector, which is a basic condition for the recovery of financial flows between commercial banks and their economic environment, must continue to take place in two areas. On the one hand, banks must strengthen their internal resources in order to cover loan losses. On the other hand, it is necessary to establish standards with regard to the financial flows of enterprises. The cleaning up of the banking sector's balance sheet especially with regard to long-term loss-making entities will lower the risk involved in lending operations. Improving the banks' loan portfolios solely by writing off loss-making loans to the detriment of bank reserves represents only a short-term solution that could solve the consequences but not the causes of the bad loan problem. The worsening trend in the quality of loan portfolios and the related problem of high interest rates would persist. Therefore, through financial restructuring it is necessary to solve the causes of the generally high rate of credit risk and the frequent failures in inter-firm financial flows.

The development of the restructuring process in the Slovak banking sector is analyzed below with special attention paid to following: (1) the causes of the loan portfolio problem in Slovakia; (2) the measures prepared and adopted to take care of this problem; and (3) the restructuring program.

Causes of the Loan Portfolio Problem

The transformation process of the Slovak Republic towards a market-oriented economy was characterized by (a) changes in relative prices, (b) the collapse of former CMEA export markets, (c) the sudden tightening of import competition, (d) reduced state subsidies, and (e) an inappropriate industrial structure with only a marginal share of value-added products. These conditions resulted in the large number of enterprises becoming unprofitable and burdened with high volumes of debt. Many enterprises were capable of covering their operating costs, but servicing their debts was more difficult since they inherited a volume of "out-of-market, long-term credits" that were extended to enterprises between 1967 and the late 80s. A certain amount of the bad loans, especially those granted in the more recent period, became 'classified' due to insufficient experience of credit officers and imprudent credit policies of commercial banks. The Slovak banks' capital-to-total-assets ratios were low (ranging from 0.84% to 1.22%) compared to banks in advanced market economies. The capital adequacy ratio, which may not fall below 8% according to the Basle capital adequacy standards, reached an average of 1.72% in the banking sector. The exceptions were banks operating on foreign markets (CSOB and Zivnostenská banka) which reached a 4% to 5% ratio of capital to risk-weighted assets.

There are several reasons for these developments: (1) There was an intensive need to create a banking sector rapidly that would conform with the needs of a transforming economy. Many new business entities had been established in the economy and the undersized banking sector, which was undergoing a slow reform at the end of the eighties, was unable to handle this development. (2) There was an absence of adequate personnel qualifications for a rapidly expanding banking sector. The experience required to evaluate a business plan properly was scarce and many important characteristics regarding the qualifications of a client were not available. (3) It was necessary for banks to support the process of privatization, the development of small and medium-sized enterprises, and other activities called for by the society, and which were among the priorities of the economic policy pursuing economic transformation. A common denominator of these pressures was the criticism that banks were not flexible enough in supporting business activities. (4) It was relatively easy to enter the banking sector[21] (this is particularly evident in comparison with the current situation in which entry into this sector for new entities is very complicated and is subject to very demanding licensing procedures). (5) The implementation of guarantees on performing and non-performing loans was complicated. An essential factor in the whole issue of loan guarantees and their resolute implementation, which was frequently a reason for only a formal role of guarantees in the loan relationship, was the fact that the existing legal environment and court procedures created a situation which is in favor of a debtor and detrimental for a creditor. The positions of debtors and banks are uneven. (6) In some cases, the lack of experience resulted in unstable bank development, as well as shortcomings in assets and liabilities management. (7) Insufficient experience with trading in the capital market caused banks, trading on their own behalf and into their own portfolio, to purchase shares at times when prices were falling. This caused losses that further aggravated the negative consequences of the bad loan transactions.

The Measures Prepared and Adopted

The first attempt to deal with the bad loan problem dates back to the former Czecho-Slovak Federation and was based upon a general "debt forgiveness" of enterprises. All enterprises were broken down into the following three categories in order to assess their financial strength: (a) viable enterprises with the sufficient capability of servicing their indebtedness; (b) potentially viable enterprises with positive operating cash-flow but heavily burdened, with debt that is not being repaid; and (c) loss making enterprises.

The government had put aside approximately 15 billion crowns to solve the problem. One part of these funds (11 billion crowns) was mainly dedicated to the potentially viable companies. The National Property

---

[21] While at present the minimum required capital (initial capital) is 500,000 million SKK and, given the NBS Provision from December, 1993, that the whole amount must be deposited in monetary form, the 1990 required starting level of capital was only 50,000 million CZK (i.e. 1/10 of the present one). The starting level was increased to 250-280 million CZK by the end 1992. By the SBCS Provision from 1992, it was augmented further to 300 million CZK.

Fund swapped its bonds for credits of viable enterprises with commercial banks. The remainder of funds (4 billion crowns) was to be used for strengthening the capital of banks. These measures, however, did not have the expected effect. The primary and secondary inter-company indebtedness did not drop substantially. One of the main weaknesses of this project was that it was a one-step event and was not designed to correct the systemic problem. Mistakes also occurred in the assignment of the enterprises into the separate categories. The problem of creating long-term financial resources that would finance new feasible projects, especially those for the conversion of armament production, remained unresolved.

Another partial solution to the bad debt problem was the establishment of the Consolidation Bank. This bank was a special purpose bank, the main activity of which was to administer the indebtedness of the former military production-oriented enterprises that were being restructured under the program of conversion. This bank also dealt with bad loans associated with the "perpetuating stock and inventory". These loans were restructured and transferred to the Consolidation Bank. In return the banks received government bonds and/or loans for increasing their capital base. Additional amounts could be obtained for the writing off of these loans. However, this procedure only solved the problem of bad credits for inventories. The issue of bad loans remained unsolved.

The NBS, in close collaboration with the government, has been systematically dealing with the problem of bad debt. New regulations of the NBS on capital adequacy, liquidity, credit exposure and foreign exchange position were introduced, effective on January 31, 1994. In close collaboration with the Ministry of Finance and the Government, the NBS has continued to devise programs for the revitalization of the banking system within the context of enterprise restructuring and according to EU standards.

Restructuring Program

During the initial stages of restructuring, new rules were introduced for the classification of bank receivables and off-balance sheet liabilities by the risk involved and for the creation of resources for risk coverage (NBS Decree No. 3, March, 1995). The goal was to improve the existing conditions, create adequate resources for risk coverage, and improve the quality of risk analysis and risk management. The groupings of receivables and off-balance sheet liabilities included five categories: (1) standard, (2) special mention claims, (3) sub-standard, (4) doubtful, and (5) loss. Items are categorized based upon (1) an assessment of the client's financial position, including financial credibility, the level of liquidity, economic performance, reserves, profitability, and capital adequacy; and (2) the financial discipline according to the terms and conditions stipulated in the credit agreement (i.e., the application of the borrowed funds for a predetermined purpose and the repayment accounting to the agreed schedule).

After the categorization of receivables, provisions were created for loan loss coverage in the amount of 5%, 20%, 50%, 100% of the nominal value of the loan in groups No. 2, 3, 4 and 5 listed above. In the calculation, the value of collateral (guarantees, right of lien) were taken into account. The guarantee was excluded if the guarantor was in a bad financial situation, if the guarantee was doubtful, or if the collateral was illiquid. The assessment of the 'real' value of the collateral remains a problem. The process of creating resources for loss coverage and restructuring was spread over a period of three years. The burden of and the responsibility for the process of restructuring was concentrated in the banks concerned.

Table 11.4 Claims Classification

	Dec. 31, 1995		Dec. 31, 1996		June 30, 1997	
	SKK mil	%	SKK mil	%	SKK mil	%
a) standard	129.83	45.06	178.52	51.66	163.86	50.83
b)special mention	37.84	13.13	56.80	16.44	42.71	13.25
c) substandard	22.14	7.68	7.76	2.25	8.17	2.53
d) doubtful and litigious	12.57	4.36	10.37	3.00	10.21	3.17
e) loss	85.76	29.77	92.13	26.66	97.45	30.23
Total classified (c + d+ e)	120.47	41.81	110.26	31.91	115.82	35.93
Total (a + b + c + d + e)	288.14	100.0	345.57	100.0	322.39	100.0

Source: National Bank of Slovakia.

The banks that were affected by this NBS provision were obliged to submit an internal by-law to the banking supervision within three months from the day when the provision became effective (up to June 30, 1995). A newly-established bank had to submit such a by-law within three months from its establishment.

Although the creation of classified claims provisions did in fact begin in 1993, the substantial rise in its volume was observed in 1995, when NBS's Provision No. 3/1995 came into force. Until then the creation of provisions according to the SBCS was only recommended, not mandatory. Therefore, during that period banks did create reserves for covering losses, including loan losses. As for the taxation, these reserves were recognized as legitimate costs, while provisions were not tax-deductible yet.

Based upon (1) a loan portfolio analysis given the new rules of loan classification, (2) the actual level of loan loss provisions, and (3) the evaluation of the client's financial position and capital strength, banks may make proposals regarding projects that would enhance their own revitalization (e.g., cleaning up loan portfolios, recapitalization, etc.).

A significant aspect of the restructuring process in the banking sector is the relationship between banks and their clients (debtors). Eventually, the success of the whole process will depend upon the restructuring of the enterprise sector, that contains 'chronic' debtors, some of which are state-owned companies that were privatized within the small or large-scale privatization programs. The problem of insolvency is growing at a fast rate (estimated at Sk 180 billion). This problem remains unresolved and its effects include an increase in the banks' bad loan portfolios and a reduction of resources for the provision of new loans.

Since the process of the financial restructuring of the Slovak banking sector was initiated in 1994-1995, a relatively large package of measures have been introduced, including the rules of assessing bank receivables and off-balance sheet liabilities according to risk, the creation of resources for risk coverage, and an evaluation of restructuring projects. However, the process of financial restructuring has not been completed; it is stagnating, which may prolong not only the estimated time necessary for the recovery of banks but also delay the favorable consequences of financing promising future projects.

References

Annual Report of the NBS [1993-1995].
Bruni, F. [1995]. "Central Bank Independence in the European Union". Paper

presented at the Conference Toward More Effective Monetary Policy. Bank of Japan, October 26-27.

Kominkova, Z. [1996]. "Regulation of the Money Stock and Issues of Monetary Targeting in the Slovak Republic," *Biatec*, 4, No 8, pp. 29-36.

_____. [1997]. "Restructuring of the Slovak Banking Sector," The Vienna Institute for Comparative Economic Studies, *The Vienna Institute Monthly Report 1997/1*, pp. 16-23.

_____. and V. Muckova [1996]. "Slovakia: Restructuring of the Banking Sector." Background paper prepared for the joint OECD/WIIW seminar "The Progress of Bank Restructuring in Bulgaria, Romania, Slovakia and Slovenia," December 9-10, Vienna.

Legal Documents: Act on the National Bank of Slovakia, [1992]; Act on Protection of Banks Deposits, [1996]; Banking Act, [1996]; Foreign Exchange Act, 1995; Provision 1 - 5/1994 of the NBS; Provision N°.3/1995 of the NBS.

Muckova, V. and M. Nemec [1995]. "Bankensysteme in Ostmitteleuropa," Berlin Verlag Arno Spitz GmbH.

OECD Economic Surveys [1996].

Other Internal Sources of the NBS [1993-1996].

Programové vyhlásenie vlády SR [1995]. Pravda, January 16-17.

Research Studies of the Institute of Monetary and Financial Studies of the National Bank of Slovakia [1995-1996].

The Slovak Republic after One Year of Independence, [1994]. Study commissioned by Bank Austria AG, Vienna, July.

Slovakia: Restructuring For Recovery, A World Bank Country Study [1994]. The World Bank, Washington, D.C. September.

Statistical Office of the Slovak Republic Reports [1994-1996].

12 Economic Transition in the Former East Germany

ROBERT WAGNER

Introduction

The economic transition in eastern Germany is very different from the transition in the other eastern European countries. Eastern Germany had the distinct advantage to be integrated into a well-established economic system and legal system immediately after the economic, monetary and social reunification of the two Germanys. Due to the convertible currency and the membership in the European Union that they therefore enjoyed, the east-German companies had free access to the world market immediately after the reunification.

But there were also specific transitional problems. Due to the country's political history, there were and are uncertainties regarding ownership of both land and corporations in the "East" that hindered and still can hinder necessary investment decisions. Moreover, the breakdown of various industrial branches resulted in a widespread loss of jobs and a huge transfer of financial resources became necessary which could endanger stability of the currency.

Generally speaking, the integration of eastern Germany has been done well from an economic and financial viewpoint. However, it is still not clear whether there is enough economic potential in the "East" to even out the economic differences between east and west Germany in the long run.

Progress in the Transition Period

This section reports on the economic progress made in the former GDR with regard to economic growth, money supply changes, inflation, unemployment and government debt levels. It also discusses the issue of privatization, as well as foreign trade.

Though Germany today is again one nation, it still has two economies with very different characteristics. While western Germany is well recovered from the depression and even had an increase in exports, the situation in eastern Germany is not as positive.

The starting point of economic growth in eastern Germany in the early 1990s was relatively low. Productivity measured by the GDP per capita was only one quarter of the western German value and the stock of fixed capital was low. From such depressed levels, it was not surprising to find the weighted growth rate of eastern Germany's GDP in 1993/ 94 to be 9%. Growth has stabilized since albeit at a lower level of about 7%. Economic growth continues not only as a result of an improved economic situation but also due to many promotion activities and investment bonuses for companies that have invested in east Germany. However, the GDP per capita is on average still at only half the western German's value.

A main difference in the economic development in eastern and western Germany is connected to the completely different economic structures in these areas. The service sector and the industrial sector in eastern Germany have developed much too slowly while the agricultural sector and the building industry have already reached the level of western Germany. Since a big part of eastern Germany's demand can be satisfied by existing western German firms, new enterprises in eastern Germany have been slow to develop. Overall growth has been primarily a result of an increase of exports to western Germany and an increase in private home building activities in eastern Germany.

The exchange of the GDR's "Mark" (M) for the West Germany's "Deutschmark" (DM) had a decisive influence on the financial situation. The final agreement was an exchange rate of 2 M for 1 DM with one important exception. Private accounts between 2,000 M and 6,000 M were converted at a rate of 1:1. If the entire money exchange had been made at an exchange rate of 2:1, it would have been in agreement with the concept of the West German central bank, the "Deutsche Bundesbank." The idea was that the new money supply should be about 120 billion DM, or, in other words, 10% of the West German's money supply corresponding to the 10% difference between the production potentials. Due to the socially justified special exchange rate for private accounts, the DM money supply increased an additional 65 billion DM.

In addition to the financial supplies, the flow dimensions, pensions and wages, had to be converted as well and this was done at an exchange rate of 1:1. Such an exchange rate would have been justified if the prices published in the GDR had been true. Since published prices did not reflect true price changes, the result was an exchange rate that was a re-valuation of the "Mark" by 500%.

The new money supply in eastern Germany had a structure different from that of western Germany. In eastern Germany the money supply was almost identical with its gross monetary assets, but this changed in only one year. The so-called money supply, M3, decreased from 180 billion DM to 164 billion DM during the first six months after the monetary union, and at the same time 19 billion DM monetary assets were built up. In the long run this tendency could not be continued at the expected degree; thus the monetary targets for the most part were exceeded during 1991-1993.

Certainly it was very difficult for the "Deutsche Bundesbank" to adapt its monetary policy to the demands of the unified Germany. Structural differences made it extremely difficult to bring into line monetary and real variables. Moreover policymakers had to contend with different and sometimes even contradictory signals for monetary policy resulting from the various changes in economic and financial policy. Due to the consistent stability-oriented monetary policy of the "Deutsche Bundesbank," the DM is still one of the strongest and most stable currencies around the world, despite various national and international economic changes and a weak economic situation in eastern Germany.

The slowing of money supply growth that started in 1994 continued in 1995 due to the stabilization of long-term interest rates and the increase in the difference between long-term and short-term rates. Because of the stable monetary policy of the "Deutsche Bundesbank" which was consistently criticized for maintaining a relatively high interest rate level, the reunification could be carried out without the feared concomitant inflation phenomena. The 1995 price increase in west Germany at 1.7% was the lowest increase since 1988. The 1995 east German price increase of 2.1% can be called moderate as well, especially if one considers that an important part of the increase is simply the adjustment of flat rents. The entire unified Germany had a price increase in 1995 of only 1.8% (without flat rents, it was only 1%).

From the 10 million East Germans employed in 1989, there were still approximately 6 million left in 1992. About 1 million people moved to west Germany or became commuters. Another million are in early retirement or are receiving old-age pensions. An additional million people were in job-creation programs or re-training programs. The rise in unemployment was caused by (1) the sudden collapse of many industrial branches after re-unification due to lack of competitiveness, (2) the losses of east European trade partners, and (3) the slow economic recovery in east Germany. At the same time, the west German economy was in a recession, making the total labor market situation quite serious (see Table 12.1).

Even the improved cyclical situation could do very little immediately to change the generally bad situation of the German economy. In west Germany the overly high collective pay agreement prevented growth in employment and in east Germany the wages grew too quickly. Given the export-oriented economy like Germany, the high labor costs resulting from strong international competition became more and more important for the development of the labor market.

Figure 12.1   Labor Costs in East Europe in Comparison with Germany in 1994

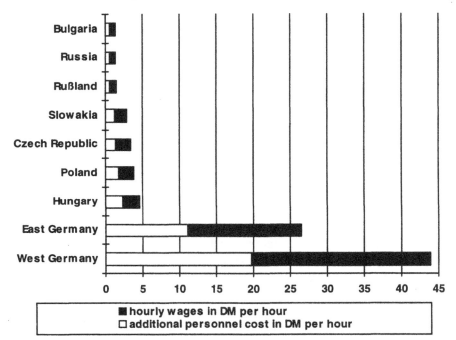

Source: OECD and Deutsche Bundesbank as well as IW-calculations, in: IWD (1996).

Labor costs are not the only reason for low employment growth. Other causes include a lack of flexibility in work organizations, high taxes and rates that hinder investment, and high social security and pension contributions. There was an increase in the number of wage earners in 1994, but this was only a short-term change due to increased building activities.   Since the middle of 1995 there has been an increase in unemployment even though industrial production has again started growing in eastern Germany.

For the labor market situation in eastern Germany, the numbers in Table 12.1 have only limited validity.   There are many job-creation programs and re-training programs that have significantly reduced the number of unemployed. One can expect long-term improvement of the labor market situation in eastern Germany and western Germany only if the economic and socio-political conditions foster an increase in economic growth based on increased competitiveness and higher flexibility of the labor market.

Table 12.1 Development of Unemployment in Eastern Germany and Western Germany

	1991	1992	1993	1994	1995	1996
Eastern Germany	11.2	15.5	15.6	15.3	14.0	15.5
Western Germany	6.1	6.5	7.3	8.2	8.3	8.7

Sources: Jahresgutachten des Sachverständigenrates 1994/95 and
        Jahreswirtschaftsbericht der Bundesregierung 1996 (annual expert
        opinion 1994/95 and annual economic report of the Federal Government
        in 1996).

Even if not in the foreground of public discussion, the government debt level has increased dramatically. Between the years 1990 and 1995, the total government debt level almost doubled to 2 trillion DM. In only four years, the east German per capita debt level reached 60% of the west German level that was produced in the past 45 years. From the available statistics, it is clear that the financial demand of the German unification was underestimated as seen in the figures from the fund, "Deutsche Einheit" ("German unification") in Table 12.2 below. A main component of financing the German unification was the increase in government debt. In the first all-German budget in 1991, the net new government indebtedness amounted to 61.5 billion DM, (4.4% of the GDP).

Government indebtedness in order to finance German unification has been criticized primarily for three reasons:
1. The money made available goes primarily into consumption and not investment.
2. The government debt level was increased during a time of recovery, which means the fiscal frame is very small in the current depression.
3. The increased government demand for credit leads to crowding-out effects.

The additional financing methods introduced later such as increases in taxation and the prolonged "Solidaritätszuschlag" (an additional "solidarity tax" as a percentage of income tax) could not remedy the difficult budget situation. From 1990 to 1994 receipts increased from 44% to 47% but during the same time expenditures increased from 46% to 50% of the nominal GDP. In the short run an improvement in the government debt situation is not expected because there are still very high expenses for subsidies, labor market policy, etc. However, an improvement is expected from the "Program for growth and employment" passed in 1994 by the German government.

Table 12.2 Financing of the Fund "Deutsche Einheit" (bill. DM)

	1990	1991	1992	1993	1994	sum
Volume						
-first approach	22.00	35.00	28.00	20.00	10.00	115.00
-increase in 1991	-	-	5.90	11.50	13.90	146.30
-increase in 1993	-	-	-	3.7	10.70	160.70
Kind of financing						
-borrowing	20.00	31.00	24.00	15.00	5.00	95.00
-subsidy from the Federal Govt.	2.00	4.00	9.90	14.23	19.45	49.58
-subsidy from west German federal states	-	-	-	5.97	10.15	16.12

Sources: Bundesminister der Finanzen (Federal Ministry of Finance), Deutsches Institut fur Wirtschaftsforschung (1995).

The "Program for Growth and Employment" consists of the following main components:
- to reduce the percentage of public expenditures to the (west German) level as it was before reunification by the year 2000
- to reduce government expenditures by cutbacks in various departments

Table 12.3 State of Privatization on December 31, 1994

I. Small privatization (June 30, 1991)	Amount	%
Total real estate amount	23,422	100.0
Privatized real estate:	15,250	65.1
Shops	10,740	45.9
Restaurants and Hotels	2,300	9.8
Drugstores	1,417	6.0
Book shops	475	2.0
Cinemas	318	1.4
Closed or not privatized for various reasons	8,172	34.9
II. Former state establishments and combines		
Total Portfolio	13,815	
Dissolved by merger / splitting up	328	
Property of mines (rights)	502	
Parts of the privatization agency's asset	484	
Shareholdings of the privatization agency		
(still to be checked)	1	
Other companies outside the gross stock	146	
Total (gross stock)	12,354	100.0
Totally or by the majority privatized:	6,546	53.0
Totally privatized	6,321	51.2
By the majority privatized	225	1.8
Reprivatization	1,588	12.9
Temporary transfer of the possession	45	0.4
Communalizations	265	2.1
Complete liquidation	157	1.3
Stock reductions (1991)	8,601	69.6
Stocks	3,753	30.4
among them: Liquidations / Bankruptcies	3,561	28.8
(still to be managed)		
Net stock	192	1.6
among them:Management Limited Partnerships	63	0.5
Investment promises (billion DM)	211.1	
Employment promises	1,508,000	

Sources: Bundesminister für Finanzen 1991, (Federal Ministry for Finance), Treuhandanstal, 1994 (Trust Company), and FAZ: Aus einer Treuhandanstalt werden vier Gesellschaften, No. 302, December 12, 1994.

- to have no wage increases in the public service sector
- to reduce and cut financing of work promotion measures
- to implement tax reform
- to deregulate and privatize the "Deutsche Bundespost" (Federal Post)
- to provide support for new businesses
- to provide support for the construction of new housing.

Because of the fact that some of the measures mentioned above will save money, the entire program is hailed as a "saving parcel".

Report on Privatization and Foreign Trade

Privatization was one of the most important and most difficult tasks that had to be done in East Germany. The main strategy of privatization in East Germany was to sell companies by private contracts. The state set up a privatization agency, the so-called "Treuhandanstalt" (trust agency), with the special duty to sell as many companies as possible. Its task was privatization, not redevelopment, a fact most east-Germans could not and did not like to accept. The task was as big as it was difficult and its success was as different as the structure of east-German companies. In a special campaign it was possible to sell 20,000 retail shops and restaurants within six months but there are some big companies that are still not completely privatized six years after reunification. As shown in the table below, the privatization of small real estate was already complete in 1991 and by the end of 1994, 53% of middle and big real estate was privatized. With the main part of privatization finished, the "Treuhandanstalt" was dissolved (there is only a follow-up organization to ensure the observance of the contracts made by the "Treuhandanstalt").

Reunification had a strong influence on foreign trade as evidenced by the relatively high current account surplus before the reunification and the current account deficit two years after. Contributing to the deficit was the spasmodic increase in demand for western industrial goods in east Germany, reflected in the increase in imports. The increased amount of East Germans traveling abroad can be seen in the higher deficit in the service balance.

At the same time, the foreign trade relations with the former CMEA (Council for Mutual Economic Assistance, better known as COMECON) members collapsed almost completely because these countries also had free access to western markets. Moreover, most of the export goods produced in eastern Germany were not competitive with western-produced goods. Governmental subsidies for some of the major firms producing for the East European market delayed this collapse but could not prevent it in the long run. Most of all, the steady revaluation of the DM since the reunification and the turbulence in the European Monetary System in 1992/93 had a bad influence on east German companies' export opportunities.

Table 12.4   Development of the Balance of Payments on Current Accounts (billions of DM)

Position	1989	1991	1993	1995
Foreign trade	134.6	21.9	60.3	91.2
Exports (fob)	641.0	665.8	632.2	732.3
Imports (cif)	506.5	643.9	571.9	641.1
Additions to the movements goods	-3.9	-4.5	-5.5	-5.8
Services	7.2	-16.4	-41.2	-50.3
Receipts	95.8	109.1	105.3	112.6
Expenditures	103.0	125.5	146.6	162.9
Earned and asset income	20.9	29.7	17.8	-2.0
Balance of current transfers	-36.9	-62.6	-58.3	-58.0
Balance on current accounts	107.5	-31.9	-26.9	-24.9

Source: Deutsche Bundesbank, Monatsbericht Mai, 1996 (German central bank, monthly report of May 1996).

However, foreign trade development overall could be called positive. The exports of German companies have increased, the exaggerated revaluation of the DM has decreased and there was a decrease in Germany's extra obligations to pay (e.g. for sending back the Russian army, for the Gulf War, etc.). Moreover, the economic recovery in the East European countries has had a positive effect leading to a strong increase in imports and exports.

Operations in the Banking and Financial Sectors

The former GDR's (German Democratic Republic, otherwise known as East Germany) banking and financial sectors, as all other fields, were regulated by the government. Important for the structure of these and other sectors in a centralized state-controlled economy is the role of money. Similar to the functions money has in market systems, money in the former GDR was a means to stimulate as well as to control the performance and rate of fulfillment of state-regulated economic plans. In establishing money as integral to the economic system, the following rules for the business cycle were created:[1]

1. Nearly all corporations were obliged to conduct their financial transactions using the governmental checking account net and its prescribed clearing systems. Such procedures included those for remittance, check processing, debit charge, and establishing letters of credit.
2. All combined collectives, state-owned corporations, production cooperatives and commissioners had to use a prescribed system of accounts.
3. There were to be no cash payments higher than 200 Marks between corporations. Cash was to be used only to pay private persons (pensions, wages, etc.).
4. Governmental banks had the monopoly for credit allocation.
5. Two different types of banks were created:
   (a) Universal banks with special, governmentally-selected customers, and (b) Special banks working in special fields of business, e.g. financing foreign trade.
6. All decisions about the rate of interest were centralized by the Council of Ministers of the GDR and the state bank of the GDR.

The main goal of these institutional regulations was to maintain the balance between purchasing power and (government-planned) goods production. For this reason, the banking system was subordinated to the Council of Ministers of the GDR.

The task of the state bank's commercial arm was to be both bank and creditor for industrial combined-collectives, to administer the exchange of foreign currencies and to set exchange rates. In its function as central bank, the state bank had to provide the economy with money and to execute all financial transactions of the governmental finance administration.

While this financial system was quite different from the system of West Germany official statistics showed no inflation whatsoever. However, there was inflation. The obvious signs of inflation were the queues, the

---

[1] See G.Gutmann (1987), p. 185.

black market and the high prices for used goods. East Germany was perhaps the only country in which a second-hand car was more expensive than a new one. People could not use their income to buy the things they needed, and they were forced to leave their money in the banks.

The main problem of the financial and banking sector was that money did not have the importance it should have in a long-term functional economy. Money did not function well as a unit of account, a general medium of exchange, a scarcity indicator or a store of value.

Prices were not determined by analyzing the current supply and demand conditions on the market but were controlled by the Council of Ministers or the price department. All prices of productive factors, labor, capital and soil, were directly or indirectly set so that the authorities defined the prices of the most important goods (food, flat rents, etc.). Administered prices were an important part of the plans of the GDR government. However, money in such a system can be neither a unit of account nor an indicator of scarcity and the economic results are misallocations of resources and a low level of goods supplied.

Due to the problems with inflation, money was actually of no value unless it could be converted to "hard" foreign exchange. Dollars or Deutschmarks (DM) could be used freely in special state-organized shops (the so-called "Intershops") but were especially used within the second "shadow" economy. Therefore, foreign exchange, even if scarce, functioned as a means of payment and a store of value in addition to the GDR "Mark." Foreign exchange should have been considered in the system of national accounts and for monetary management, but it was not.

Besides the GDR's own currency and foreign exchange (especially the "Deutschmark" due to the integration into the CMEA, a third monetary quantity, the "Transferable Rouble" (TR), was important for the financial system of the former GDR. The TR only existed as account money and was introduced mainly to make multilateral economic relations easier. It was, in fact, unable to reach this goal since it did not perform all of the necessary functions of a money, namely to be a general medium of exchange, store of value and unit of account. Most importantly, the TR had no uniform value. Due to the Moscow Procedure of Price Formation for the trade among CMEA members (which meant that prices were set based upon international market prices from the previous five years), the TR had different values in all bilateral trade relations. With ten members of CMEA, there were 45 different levels of value. The TR was neither scarce within the CMEA nor helpful for necessary quantity adjustments in foreign trade.

With a lack of convertibility and flexibility on the part of both the national currency and the TR, together with monetary and real isolation from the international market, the GDR economy was sensitive to destabilizing foreign trade impulses. Because the GDR was dependent on the West for high-tech capital goods due to the low innovative potential of its own economy, it needed a large stock of convertible foreign exchange. The GDR could not get this from its own export companies. Consequently, there was a permanent lack of foreign exchange and also a negative foreign trade balance with Western countries.

The financial situation was one of the essential forces that led to the political changes in 1989. From the financial point of view, two critical facts stand out:

1. The central bank lacked sufficient independence in policymaking. Due to its intertwining with the political leadership, it had to subordinate monetary policy to the political and economic aspirations of a state-controlled, centrally-administered economy.
2. The non-convertibility and non-flexibility of the currency resulted in a complete lack of orientation on the international market, a permanent deficiency of foreign exchange and decreasing competitiveness of the national economy.

As a result, the economy (the state) was not able to bring the stock of fixed capital to the production level necessary in order to compete in the world market. For example, in 1988 about 55% of industrial equipment (without buildings) was more than 10 years old and 21% was more than 20 years old; about 45% of industrial buildings was more than 20 years old and 20% was more than 50 years old. Production results naturally reflected this state of equipment.

For the private sector, the result was a poor supply of goods regardless of income levels. Governmental planning could never offer the supply of goods that would be possible under market economy conditions and this did not go unnoticed. The non-convertibility of the currency led to the establishment of a "shadow" economy based upon foreign exchange that performed the same functions as in a market economy. However, only the (politically) privileged class had access to this foreign exchange, resulting in a widening difference between poor and rich in the GDR, in blatant contradiction of the proclaimed equality of all. Thus, the demand for Western currency rather than the demand for privatization or contractual freedom played a key role in the introduction of a market economic system in East Germany. The importance of this currency issue in the initial transition period can clearly be seen in the famous East German slogan of the year 1990: "Wenn die DM nicht zu uns kommt, kommen wir zur DM!" ("If the Deutschmark does not come to us, we will come to the Deutschmark!").

The immediate goal after the revolution in 1989 was the reunification of the two German states in all fields of economy and policy. The German transition was different from those experienced in the other Central and Eastern European countries in that there was to be immediate integration of East Germany into the economic, monetary and legal system of West Germany and the European Community. In essence, East Germany was immediately part of a market economy.

On January 20, 1990 the "Sachverständigenrat" (advisory board of the government) published a special expert opinion paper on things to be done in the financial and banking sectors.[2] The following is a list of general areas to be considered:

(1) The reduction of surplus money, including the sale of asset values (shareholdings in companies, ownership of apartments and so on) to the people; price level effects of pricing reform; foreign exchange funds and the issuance of government loans; and the issue of public loans.

(2) Reform of the central bank, including the issue of its independence, its obligation to maintain economic stability, and the instruments for the control of money in circulation.

(3) The development of a two-tier banking system.

(4) Capital market/credit market concerns, including the development of the markets for shareholdings and bonds and the direct responsibility of commercial banks for credit allocation.

(5) Exchange rate (fixed exchange rate to the "Deutschmark").

(6) Convertibility, including immediate external convertibility, the free transfer for foreign investors and the temporary convertibility limits for private capital export. In regard to the exchange rate and convertibility, the politicians bowed to the pressure of the "people on the street" and introduced monetary union on July 1, 1990.

For the approaching monetary union of the former East Germany and West Germany, the Deutsche Bundesbank set up a "Vorläufige

---

[2] See Sachverstandigenrat (1990).

Table 12.5 Balance of the GDR's Banking System (bill. Mark (M) and bill. Deutschmarks (DM))

	Position	M	M:DM	DM
1	*Assets*			
2	Credits to corporations	242	2:1	121
3	+ housing credits	110	2:1	55
4	= credits to the economy	352	2:1	176
5	+ normal credits to the state	34	2:1	17
6	+ special credits to the state	36	-	-
7	of which: due to re-assessment of foreign debt in convertible currency	(30)	-	-
8	= credits to domestic non-banks	422	2.2:1	193
9	External claims			
10	+ to CMEA-states	18	2:1	9
11	+ in convertible currency	28	1:1	28
12	= credits altogether	468	2:1	230
13	+ other positions	21	-	13
14	= subtotal	489	2:1	243
15	+ equalization claims (net)	-	-	26
16	= sum of assets	489	1.8:1	269
17	*Liabilities*			
18	Deposits of private households			
19	+ exchange 1:1	65	1:1	65
20	+ exchange 2:1	100	2:1	50
21	+ monetary circulation	14	2:1	7
22	= monetary holdings of private households	179	1.5:1	122
23	+ deposits of corporations	102	2:1	51
24	+ deposits of the state	16	2:1	8
25	= monetary holdings altogether	297	1.6:1	181
26	+ investments in life insurance	14	2:1	7
27	External liabilities			
28	+ due to CMEA-states	1	2:1	0
29	+ in convertible currency	56	1:1	56
30	+ reserves for the "Richtungskoeffizienten" (reserves for repayment of external liabilities in convertible currency)	96	-	-
31	+ own capital	25	1:1	25
32	= sum of liabilities	489	1.8:1	269

Source: Deutsches Institut Fur Wirtschaftsforschung (1995), p. 389.

Verwaltungsstelle"[3] ("temporary administrative office") in Berlin and 15 additional branch offices on the former GDR's territory. Two hundred and sixty tons of coins and notes with a value of 28 billion Deutschmarks (DM) were transported to this area to make sure that enough money was available to exchange Marks (M) for Deutschmarks (DM). During the same time all people and institutions of the former GDR had to apply for the transition of their monetary assets and had to have their money in an account since a cash exchange was not possible. The balance sheet in Table 12.5 represents the GDR's banking system in July, 1990.

The first decisive step towards the transformation of the banking system into a two-level system had already been made on April 1, 1990, three months before the monetary union. The State Bank's scope of duties was limited to those of a central bank in a western model. The financial services for the state, corporations and housing rendered up until then by the state bank were taken over by the newly-founded "Kreditbank AG" ("credit bank"). The biggest part of the existing savings banks and state bank branches were taken over by West German commercial banks step by step during the following years. With the help of many West German bankers, the banks were adapted to the conditions of the market economy.

The Deutsche Bundesbank granted very high German Federal Bank assistance quotas to the banks on the territory of the former GDR. In contrast to West Germany, there were no first class bills of exchange with several acceptances. For this reason, the central bank bought and pledged simple bills of exchange as security for loans during a limited period of time even if these bills were drawn by the banks themselves. Thus the banks could get central bank money which they used for outpayments and to satisfy the minimum reserve requirements demanded by the Deutsche Bundesbank.

One of the biggest technical/organizational problems of the banking system's reorganization was to adapt the cashless payments system of the former GDR to the more modern western systems. During the first months of the reorganization there were many payment delays. However, now one will not find a difference between conducting financial transactions in a bank in Dresden (East Germany) or in Munich (West Germany).

Credit banks are mostly big banks like "Deutsche Bank," "Dresdner Bank," "Commerzbank" and other private banks. The savings banks are owned by local authorities. Credit cooperatives like "Volks- und

---

[3] It was still working until October 31, 1992.

Raiffeisenbanken" most often have cooperative goals while mortgage banks preferably make long-term loans secured by mortgages. Other banks are mainly post office savings banks, installment sales financing institutions and banks with special tasks.

On July 1, 1990, the day of the German monetary union, the first level of a three-level process towards the European economic and monetary union was realized also. This union will dominate Germany's monetary policy for the future. The end of this process (planned for 1999) is the transfer of the national central banks' monetary sovereignty to the newly-founded European System of Central Banks (ESCB) that consists of the European Central Bank (ECB) and the national central banks of the countries participating. If this is realized, there will be also a common European Currency with irreversibly fixed exchange rates between the national currencies.

Table 12.6 Laws for the Credit System

Laws with regard to the kind of institute	General legislation for the credit system	Laws with regard to the kind of business
-Savings Bank Law -Mortgage Bank Law -Cooperative Law -Bausparkassengesetz (Building and Loan Association Law) -Law for Investment Companies - Law for Holding Companies	-Credit System Law -Law for the "Deutsche Bundesbank"	-Consumer Credit Law -Deposit Law -Stock Exchange Operations Law -Cheque Law -Bill Law

Source: A. Mansfeld (1995), p 13.

Due to the fact that banks administer and control a big part of national wealth thus being responsible for the economic stability, the government defined general conditions to minimize the risks. The core of governmental regulations (see Table 12.6) is the "Kreditwesengesetz (KWG)" (Credit System Law). This law is not an interruption of bank autonomy but is made to limit the scope of bank activities and to reduce the economic risk of the credit business. The Credit System Law aims at establishing (1) operating standards (permission is necessary for doing bank business), (2) structural standards (there are minimum requirements for business operations), and (3) regular supervision.   The executive authorities are the "Bundesaufsichtsamt für das Kreditwesen (BAK)" (Federal Supervision Office for the Credit System) in Berlin and the Deutsche Bundesbank in Frankfurt am Main.

Although the same banks do business in East and West Germany, there are still some big differences in credit allocation between east and west German applicants.   One difference is the general consensus by banks that East German firm managers have a high technical knowledge but show a high deficit in commercial and management skills.   An additional complication is that it was and is very difficult for east German managers to provide enough collateral for long-term credits due to the bad conditions of their firms' capital accounts and the very small amount of equity capital.   The same problems arise with regard to the assessment of future market chances for East German corporations because former business relations have ceased and completely new products are being produced. Thus the banks' problems in eastern Germany are most of all due to the assessments of the East German corporations' creditworthiness.

The Central Bank of Germany

Due to its big influence on the businesses of the commercial banks, the Deutsche Bundesbank (DB) is called the "bank of banks". The main reason is that the liquidity of the banking system can only be maintained if the commercial banks can get enough central bank sight deposits (sight deposits that can be exchanged into cash) because the commercial bank's customers can order parts of their credits or deposits as central bank notes. Moreover commercial banks are obliged to deposit the non-interest-bearing part of their liabilities (the minimum reserve defined by the DB) at the Deutsche Bundesbank.   Because of this minimum reserve, the central bank can maintain its influence on commercial banks.

According to its legal order, the DB is also a service institution for handling cashless payments. After all, one third of all annual bank transfer and collection orders (subject to charge) are conducted using the giro network of the central bank.

Moreover, the DB supports the work of the BAK (Federal Supervision Office for the Credit System) in Berlin. The BAK makes fundamental decisions regarding Own Capital or Liquidity Principles and depends upon the agreement of the central bank. With the help of the Federal Central Banks, the Deutsche Bundesbank helps the BAK supervise the obligatory reports and the annual financial statements by collecting them and passing them on to the BAK with its comments.

Figure 12.2 Germany's Banking System

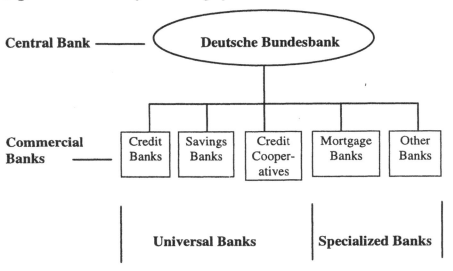

The main important authorities of the central bank are the Central Bank Council (supreme authority), the board of directors and the boards of the federal central banks.   The Central Bank Council and the board of directors have the same position as a supreme Federal authority, i.e. they are equivalent to federal ministers.

Members of the Central Bank Council are the chairman, the director of the DB (currently Prof. Dr. Dr. H. C. Hans Tietmeyer), the vice director of DB (currently Wilhelm Gaddum), the members of the board of directors and the directors of the federal central banks.

The board of directors of the DB has the same director and vice director as the Central Bank Council and up to 6 other members. They are suggested by the Federal Government according to their professional suitabilities.   After a hearing of the Central Bank Council, they are appointed by the President of the Federal Republic for at least 2 and at most 8 years. During this time they cannot be recalled except by their own request, by the insistence of the Central Bank Council, or under extraordinary circumstances.

The directors of the nine federal central banks are the chairmen of the board of directors of the federal central banks. They are suggested by the Federal Parliament and thus, as a rule, by the Länder (state) governments. Here one can recognize the federal character of the Deutsche Bundesbank Constitution which prevents a supremacy of the government from appointing members of the Central Bank Council.

The DB is a federal legal entity under public law in Frankfurt am Main and has a capital stock of 290 million DM with profits flowing to the Federal Government. Its business and economic effects on banks, the money supply, credit, foreign exchange and other areas are seen in Figure 12.3.

As a rule the Central Bank Council has meetings every two weeks and decides (by simple majority) the monetary policy of the Deutsche Bundesbank. After the monetary union on July 1, 1990, the Deutschmark became the only means of payment and the responsibility for monetary policy was taken over by the DB. The board of directors is responsible for the execution of the Central Bank Council's decisions. Other special tasks of the board of directors include:[4]

- Business with the Federal Government and its special assets
- Activites with banks having central tasks for the entrie Federal territory
- Foreign exchange transactions and activities involving trade with foreign countries
- Open market operations.

The federal central banks conduct business with public partners and administrative offices as well as with banks. The DB does not have any direct business with the private economy.

Generally, the Deutsche Bundesbank uses three different tools in conducting monetary policy: refinancing policy, minimum reserve policy and open markt policy.

Refinancing policy aims at influencing money in circulation and credit allocation. With the rediscount rate for buying bills of exchange and the Lombard rate for pledging securities, the DB defines the interest rates used for commercial banks when they borrow central bank money. (To obtain a scope for liquidity policy, the Central Bank Council also defines special

---

[4] See Deutsche Bundesbank (1993), p 8.

Figure 12.3 Business, Monetary and Political Authorizations of the Deutschen Bundesbank

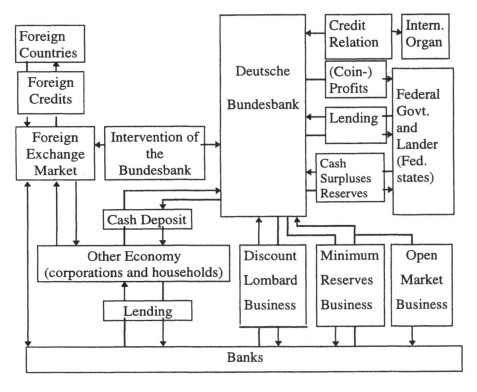

Source: Vertretung Der Europaischen Kommission in Der Brd [1993], 13.

rediscount quotas.) With the help of these two interest rates, the DB signals whether it supports or opposes an increasing demand for money.

In order to prevent commercial banks from using all of their deposits for credit allocation, the Deutsche Bundesbank defines within its minimum reserve policy the non-interest-bearing part of reserves that commercial banks are obliged to deposit at the DB. The lower (higher) this part is, the more (less) money the banks can lend. In other words, the DB controls the liquidity of banks with minimum reserve requirements.

Within its open-market policy, the DB directly affects the business cycle. For example, if the DB buys (sells) securities, it pays (receives) central bank money for it and thus increases (decreases) the money stock. Figure 12.4 describes the effect of the monetary policy instruments of the

Figure 12.4 Effect of the Instruments of the Deutschen Bundesbank

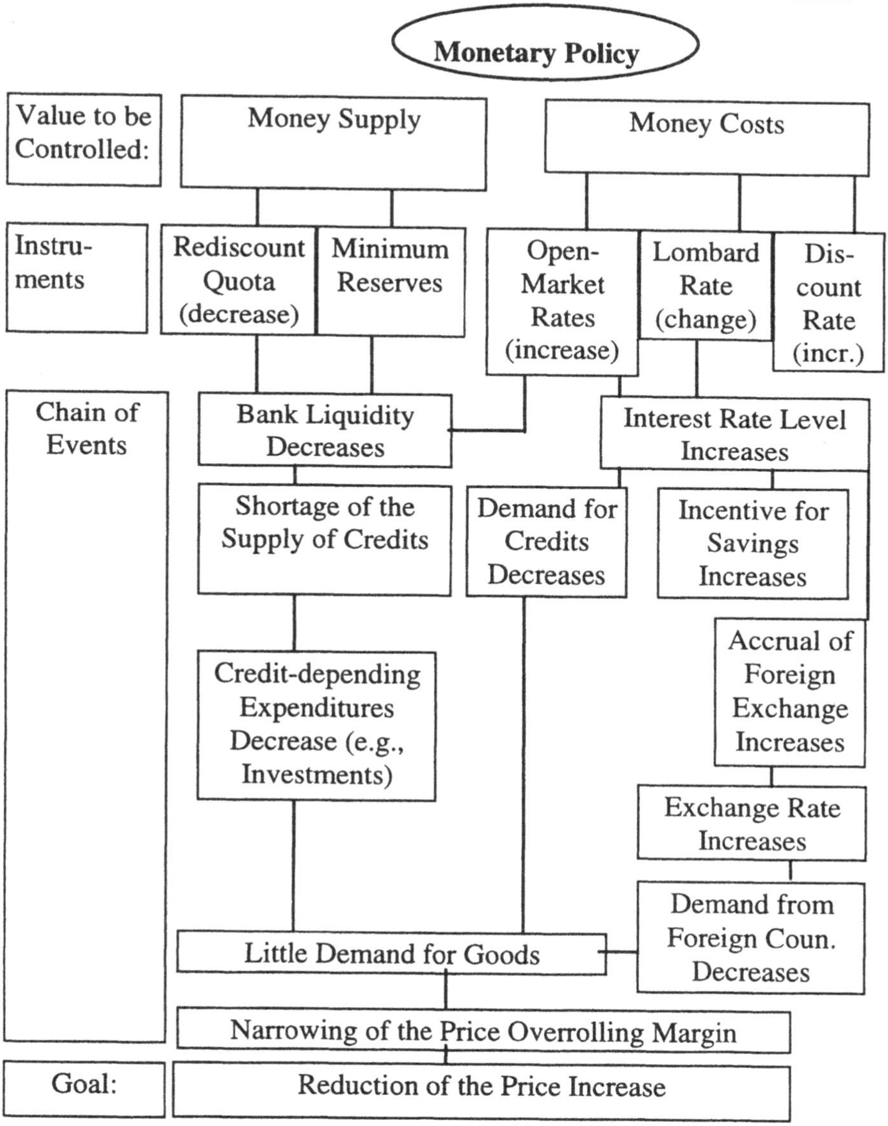

Monetary Policy

Value to be Controlled:	Money Supply		Money Costs		
Instruments	Rediscount Quota (decrease)	Minimum Reserves	Open-Market Rates (increase)	Lombard Rate (change)	Discount Rate (incr.)
Chain of Events	Bank Liquidity Decreases		Interest Rate Level Increases		
	Shortage of the Supply of Credits	Demand for Credits Decreases	Incentive for Savings Increases		
	Credit-depending Expenditures Decrease (e.g., Investments)		Accrual of Foreign Exchange Increases		
			Exchange Rate Increases		
			Demand from Foreign Coun. Decreases		
	Little Demand for Goods				
	Narrowing of the Price Overrolling Margin				
Goal:	Reduction of the Price Increase				

Source: Vertretung Der Europaischen Kommission in Der Brd [1993], p. 18

Deutschen Bundesbank.   According to section 3 of the Central Bank's Law, the central bank's task is to regulate the supply of money and credit in the economy and to aid the safety and efficiency of payment transactions. Within this framework, the maintenance of monetary stability is one of the most difficult tasks of the Deutsche Bundesbank. While the DB has to support the economic policy of the government in principle, it can do so as long as it has no negative influence on the (internal and external) stability of the currency.   Though the DB is also a house bank of the Federal Government, it can only grant limited short-term direct credits to the Federal Government (up to 6 billion DM) and the Länder (3.3 billion DM).   The DB helps the Federal Government by holding its current accounts and by working as a "fiscal agent" to get credits on the market through the issuance of debentures and Treasury bills.

To guarantee monetary stability, the independence of the federal central bank is of decisive importance.   Sections 12 and 13 of the Law for the Deutsche Bundesbank in its new edition (October 22, 1992) regulate the relationship between the state and the DB after the reunification. According to this law, the DB is obliged to support the general economic policy of the government, but it is independent of government instructions in executing its legal authorization.   Simultaneously, mutual participation of the decision-makers of the DB and the government is demanded, however without any voting rights.

Though the central bank's independence is assured by law, Germany also passed a law mandating that the DB support stability and growth of the economy.   Because the state as well as corporations and union associations can have a strong negative influence on monetary policy, these groups are obliged by law to support stability.   On the other hand external economic influence is more difficult to control.   For example, the Deutsche Bundesbank is obliged, within the European Monetary System (EMS), to intervene in favor of foreign currencies when necessary.   When inflation differentials exist, especially affecting the Dollar exchange rate, there may be exaggerated undervaluations and revaluations of the Deutschmark.

Due to the monetary union, eastern Germany immediately got the Deutschmark and thus an unlimited convertible currency.   In Germany the international money and capital transactions are completely liberalized. Possible capital movement limitations can be planned only within the framework of the "Law for Foreign Trade" but these limitations have to be coordinated with the DB.

The development of the money supply is a main indicator of the success of the Deutsche Bundesbank in Germany. The DB calculates three different money supply terms:

- M1: cash and sight deposits holdings of domestic non-banks
- M2 : M1 plus time deposits with maturities less than 4 years of domestic non-banks
- M3: M2 plus savings deposits at statutory notice of domestic non-banks.

The central dimension of orientation is the money supply, M3. When the monetary union occurred with East Germany, M3 immediately increased by 15%. The resulting excess liquidity was reduced very quickly and the DB decreased its accepted variation of M3 by 1% in 1991. During the following years, the DB accepted levels of the money supply that exceeded its goals due to increased foreign exchange inflows, cash hoards caused by taxes and strong activity in the capital market. Despite the higher money supply levels, the German reunification process was managed without significant inflation. The temporary high price increases in western Germany were due to collective wage agreements that were too high and not due to the monetary policy of the DB. The only reproach the Deutsche Bundesbank should accept is the too restrictive interest rate policy that prolonged the depression and delayed the reconstruction of eastern Germany's economy.

Summary and Conclusions

The transformation of the banking and financial sector deserves special attention because it has decisive importance for the economy's provision of capital and for expanding the existing economic potential of the system. From the financial point of view, the following criteria were the main causes of mismanagement in a centralized-state controlled economy:

- Money did not have the functions necessary for an efficient economy.
- Prices were not indicators of scarcity and thus not helpful for an optimal factor allocation.
- There was a lack of independence of the banking system.
- The currency was inflexible and inconvertible.

For these reasons the first steps in the transformation process should be the release of prices and the set-up of an independent banking system. The monetary policy of the central bank should aim toward monetary stability right from the beginning because even short-term concessions are difficult to reverse in the long run and, as a rule, the consequences are higher inflation rates. The valuation of the existing capital fund was difficult for both the monetary union and the adaptation of the own currency to a key currency (for example to the Dollar). Indeed it is very difficult to align monetary policy with the current and future potential of the economy if statistics are evaluated incorrectly.

The entire process of transformation in eastern Germany went very fast because the west German system offered both the economic and the institutional general conditions for taking over the monetary system with few adaptation problems. The transfer of know-how via a vital personnel exchange between east and west German banks was another important reason for the high speed of the transformation process.

The concessions that had to be made during the transformation process (for example the exchange rate 1:1) could only have been made because of the economic power of western Germany and the strong stability-oriented monetary policy of the Deutschen Bundesbank. This was accomplished without causing any significant inflation.

References

Apolte, T. [1992]. Politische Ökonomie der Systemtransformation, Hamburg: S+W Steuer und Wirtschaft.

Bundesminister der Finanzen [1991]. Bericht über ein Jahr Tätigkeit der Treuhandanstalt, in: Deutsches Institut fuer Wirtschaftsforschung [1995].

Bundesministerium der Finanzen [1993]. in: Deutsches Institut fuer Wirtschafts- forschung [1995].

Deutsches Institut fuer Wirtschaftsforschung [1995]. Fünf Jahre deutsche Einheit, Heft 3, 64. Jahrgang, Berlin: Duncker & Humblot.

Deutsche Bundesbank [1993]. Die Deutsche Bundesbank: Geldpolitische Aufgaben und Instrumente, Frankfurt am Main.

Deutsche Bundesbank [1996]. Monatsbericht Mai, Frankfurt am Main.

FAZ [1994]. Aus einer Treuhandanstalt werden vier Gesellschaften, No. 302, December 12.

Gutmann, G. [1990]. Das Ende der Planwirtschaft in der DDR, Tübingen: J. C. B. Mohr.

Gutmann, G. [1987]. Volkswirtschaftslehre: Eine ordnungstheoretische Einführung, Stuttgart; Berlin; Köln; Mainz: Kohlhammer.

Hamel, H. [1977]. BRD - DDR Die Wirtschaftssysteme, München: C. H. Beck.

Herr, H. et al. [1994]. Macroeconomic Problems of Transformation, Hants:

Edward Elgar.

Hitchens, D.M.W.N. et al. [1993]. East German Productivity and the Transition to the Market Economy, Hants: Avebury Ashgate.

IWD [1996]. Arbeitskosten in Osteuropa: Weiterhin attraktiv fürs Ausland, Informationsdienst des Instituts der deutschen Wirtschaft, Jahrgang 22, Nr. 6, 8. Februar, Köln.

Jahresgutachten des Sachverständigenrates 1994/95 [1994]. Jahresgutachten 1994/95 des Sachverständigenrates zur Begutachtung der gesamtwirtschaftlichen Entwicklung, Bonn: Bundesanzeiger.

Jahreswirtschaftsbericht der Bundesregierung '96 [1996]. Vorrang fuer Beschaeftigung, Bonn: BMWi.

Ludwig-Erhard-Stiftung [1992]. Vom Zentralplan zur sozialen Marktwirtschaft: Erfahrungen der Deutschen beim Systemwechsel, Stuttgart; Jena; New York: Fischer.

Mansfeld, A. [1995]. Möglichkeiten und Grenzen der Geschäftsbanken bei der Kreditgewährung für kleine und mittelständische Unternehmen in den neuen Bundesländern - Aufzeigen von alternativen Finanzierungsformen im Rahmen regionaler Entwicklungsziele, Zittau.

Merkel, W. and Wahl, S. [1991]. Das geplünderte Deutschland, Bonn : IWG.

Molitor, B. [1991], Der Übergang von einer zentralistischen Planwirtschaft zur Sozialen Marktwirtschaft, Tübingen : J. C. B. Mohr.

OECD [1995]. OECD-Wirtschaftsberichte, Deutschland 1995, Paris.

Pilz, F. and Ortwein, H. [1992]. Das vereinte Deutschland : wirtschaftliche, soziale und finanzielle Folgeprobleme und Konsequenzen für die Politik, Stuttgart; Jena: G. Fischer.

Propp, P. D. [1990]. Zur Transformation einer Zentralverwaltungswirtschaft sowjetischen Typs in eine Marktwirtschaft, Köln: Wissenschaft und Politik.

Sachverständigenrat [1990], Sondergutachten vom 20. Januar 1990, Bonn: Bundesanzeiger.

Schilling, G. [1975], Zur Einheit von materieller und finanzieller Planung, Berlin Ost.

Treuhandanstalt [1994]. THA-Unternehmensbestand, in: Deutsches Institut fuer Wirtschaftsforschung [1995].

Wagener, H.-J. [1990], Monetäre Steuerung und ihre Probleme in unterschiedlichen Wirtschaftssystemen, Berlin: Duncker & Humblot.

Weidenfeld, W. and Korte, K.-R. [1993], Handbuch zur deutschen Einheit, Frankfurt/Main; New York : Campus.

For Product Safety Concerns and Information please contact our EU
representative GPSR@taylorandfrancis.com Taylor & Francis Verlag GmbH,
Kaufingerstraße 24, 80331 München, Germany

Printed and bound by CPI Group (UK) Ltd, Croydon, CR0 4YY
08/05/2025
01864360-0004